International law, rights and politics

Recent political upheavals in Eastern Europe have led to a proliferation of new states on the world scene. This has, in many instances, led to deep, international concern about rising nationalism and these countries' relations with one another.

Rein Müllerson's book is concerned with the interplay of international law and politics in the changing international system. The author discusses, in the light of events in Eastern Europe and the former USSR, such issues as: the non-use of force, non-interference in internal affairs, the self-determination of peoples, the protection of minorities, the role of nationalism in inter-ethnic conflicts, and human rights in post-totalitarian societies. Controversial issues of continuity and succession of states and their recognition are analysed in the same context.

One of the main purposes of this book is to show how these developments influence the international system as a whole and how international law has to change in order to respond to new challenges.

Rein Müllerson is Visiting Centennial Professor at the London School of Economics. Between 1988 and 1992 he was a member of the UN Human Rights Committee and in 1991–2 he was Deputy Foreign Minister of Estonia.

Books published under the joint imprint of LSE/Routledge are works of high academic merit approved by the Publications Committee of the London School of Economics and Political Science. These publications are drawn from the wide range of academic studies in the social sciences for which the LSE has an international reputation.

The New International Relations
Edited by Barry Buzan, University of Warwick, and Gerald Segal, International Institute for Strategic Studies, London.

The field of international relations has changed dramatically in recent years. This new series will cover the major issues that have emerged and reflect the latest academic thinking in this particularly dynamic area.

International law, rights and politics

Developments in Eastern Europe and the CIS

Rein Müllerson

London and New York

First published 1994
by Routledge
11 New Fetter Lane, London EC4P 4EE

Simultaneously published in the USA and Canada
by Routledge
29 West 35th Street, New York, NY 10001

© 1994 Rein Müllerson

Typeset in Times by
Ponting–Green Publishing Services, Chesham, Bucks

Printed and bound in Great Britain by
T.J. Press (Padstow) Ltd, Cornwall

Printed on acid free paper

British Library Cataloguing in Publication Data

A catalogue record for this book is available from the
British Library.

*Library of Congress Cataloging in Publication Data has been
applied for*

ISBN 0–415–10687–7
ISBN 0–415–11134–x (pbk)

To the memory of Professor Grigorii Tunkin

Contents

Series editors' foreword

When we first conceived of a series on 'The New International Relations', we had in mind books that would take as their starting point the recent structural changes in international affairs. We also had in mind books that would be interdisciplinary, especially as concerned the chasm that so often divides theorists from empiricists. Therefore it is with the greatest pleasure that we introduce the first book of the series by Rein Müllerson. It is both auspicious and appropriate that our first author was a citizen of the former Soviet Union, for it was the collapse of his country that played such an important part in shaping the new international relations.

The purpose of this series is to assess the nature of change in international affairs. Some aspects of change, such as the collapse of the Soviet Union and the end of the Cold War, seem obvious and easy to assess. Detecting change in the underlying structure also requires an assessment of new technologies and perceptions. There can be no certainty about the shape of the new international relations as yet, if only because many changes have barely taken hold and others have faded before they had a chance to become entrenched. It even seems like ages since we began discussing a 'new world order', though in reality it has barely been three years. Early euphoria about that new order has given way to harsher cynicism about the limits of multi-lateralism and co-operation. In this era of rapid and often short-lived change, the pressure is increased on academics to develop a more sophisticated sense of what is new in international relations. It is still not clear either what the deeper structural changes are, or how much impact the ideological and power shifts of the last few years are going to have on the rest of the international system. The judgements of journalists got us through the first few years, but the pace of change seems to be slowing.

As we look back at what has changed in international affairs we are struck by the continuity in the categories of questions that can be asked about the international system, even though the details in the categories have changed a great deal. Thus one of the virtues of Rein Müllerson's analysis is the fact that his basic subject of analysis seems familiar. Self-determination, minority rights, human rights in general, as well as the debates about recognition of states and their rights and obligations of succession, are all topics familiar to observers of international relations well before the Cold War. If ever we needed a reminder that what is 'new' is often 'old', just wrapped differently, the reader might try replacing the Soviet Union with the Ottoman Empire and see how their judgement is affected.

Rein Müllerson's strength is based on a firm grounding in specific politics of the Soviet Union and the way in which its empire collapsed. This is a book about politics that uses insights from international legal analysis. It is equally a book about domestic politics that shape international affairs. If the reader takes away anything from this analysis it is the need to avoid narrow categories of thought. It is simply not possible to understand the implications of the collapse of the Soviet Union by remaining within traditionally narrow academic disciplines.

There are four clusters of issues that are used to illustrate the nature of post-Soviet international affairs. Rein Müllerson begins with aspects of self-determination because, after all, this was what brought the Soviet Union to its knees. But his analysis makes clear that the implications of self-determination in the modern world are far from simple. The Baltic states may have spun out of Russia's orbit, but there are important minorities in the new states that feel their rights to self-determination are now restricted. These vexed issues wrecked Bosnia-Hercegovina and are tearing their way through the Caucasus. Ethnicity has never been as actively debated this century, and the debates remain inconclusive because these are more questions of culture and politics than about law.

A related cluster of issues concerns minority and general human rights. Some may feel that these rights should be seen as universal and legally defined, but the reality is that politics and power are key factors in determining how these issues are handled. There is no obvious point at which minorities can seek self-determination as the events around Russia's rim and in southern Europe make plain. How small does a unit have to become before it accepts that its rights will have to be protected within a larger unit where it constitutes a miniority? So far we seem to be still slipping down the slope to micro-units, and thus it is especially useful to have Professor Müllerson take us back to basic principles. There seems to be no escape from considerations of ethnicity and culture, even in the realm of human rights. The United Nations review conference in Vienna in 1993 reminded us that these debates assume even greater vehemence in a post-Cold War world, in part because there is less to hold together the states of what was once referred to as the West.

The third cluster of issues discussed by Müllerson is that surrounding the recognition of new states. The essentially political nature of this process is obvious. States can be seen as increasingly artificial, as is evident in many of the former republics of the Soviet Union. The depth of the absurd was reached with the notorious Vance–Owen plan for Bosnia which envisaged a jigsaw-puzzle of a state. The Caucasus seems headed down a similar road where reality is best described as warlord-ism not deserving of international recognition. And yet we were all warned not to be hustled into recognizing Bosnia because the state was bound to collapse and for West European political reasons our governments ignored good advice. This is unlikely to be the last time we make that mistake.

The fourth cluster concerns the rights and obligations of new states as successors to old ones. Consider how Ukraine stands up to Russian pressure about defining their rights of succession to the Soviet Union, while many other members of the CIS clamber back into Russia's fold on Russia's terms. As Rein Müllerson makes plain, these matters are resolved in a realist fashion, with legal conventions barely providing categories of thought.

Professor Müllerson writes with the confidence of an international lawyer who recognizes that law can and will be manipulated where there is the political will to do so. Therefore he writes with the aspirations and ideals of an international lawyer, and the hard-headedness of a realist observer of politics. The result is analysis that manages to stay ahead of the changing reality and yet holds out hope for eventual control and manipulation of political instincts. Rein Müllerson challenges us to meet the new realities, and helps provide us with the tools to do so.

Barry Buzan and Gerald Segal
1994

Acknowledgements

The writing of this book would have been impossible were it not for the invitation by the London School of Economics and Political Science asking me to be Visiting Centennial Professor for two years. This is not only an immense honour for any scholar but, in addition, the work in this most renowned School, which next year will celebrate its centenary, is extremely stimulating and simply pushed me towards this inter-disciplinary research. Some of the chapters of the book are based on my lectures given at the LSE.

I am most grateful to my colleagues at the LSE who read the manuscript, or parts of it, and made valuable comments and suggestions: Daniel Bethlehem, Professor Leonard Leigh, Dr Margot Light and Professor James Mayall. Lectures given two years ago at the New York University on the legal problems of the dissolution of the USSR at the invitation of Professor Thomas Franck, and our resultant discussions, added great impetus to the research. I am also very grateful to Professor Asbjorn Eide with whom many issues raised in the book were discussed.

My special thanks go to Professor Rosalyn Higgins. Her help and guidance have always been invaluable. I am thankful to Cairo Robb who helped me to put the whole manuscript in order and to trace missing footnotes and quotations. My family – Irina, Jan and George – supported me in every possible way.

Finally, I thank the *International and Comparative Law Quarterly* and the *Modern Law Review* for their permission to use material from my two articles published in these journals.

Introduction

International law and politics are once more at a crossroads because at the end of the century the world is undergoing revolutionary changes. The sudden end of the Cold War overlaps with such fundamental but more incremental developments as the aggravation of the global problems and the emergence of new actors in the international system. These changes often point in different directions. So the latest dramatic events in the world have created not only serious dangers for individual countries as well as for the world community as a whole but also unique opportunities to face challenges for mankind.

There are probably more reasons than ever to assert that the current international system is today undergoing radical changes comparable with such historic milestones as, for example, 1648 and the emergence of the Westphalian international system, or 1789 and the French Revolution and the subsequent Napoleonic wars, or 1917 and the Socialist Revolution in Russia, or 1945 with the end of World War II, the creation of the UN and beginning of the Cold War. The liberation of colonies and the emergence of the Third World was, of course, a process of comparable significance but more extended in time.

It is not yet clear what date will become a short abbreviation for future historians to mark this radical transformation: 1985 with the start of the *perestroika* and *glasnost* era in the former USSR, which triggered off all following events; 1989 with its 'velvet revolutions' in Eastern Europe; or 1991 and the dissolution of the Soviet Union. It is likely that 1989 has the best chance because it comes exactly 200 years after 1789 and had its own Bastille – the Berlin Wall which came down in autumn 1989.

There are many angles from which to look at these revolutionary changes in the world. One of the most important of them is the perspective of the new international system and the role of international law and the institutions in it. How do these changes affect the structure of and the correlation of forces in the international system? What challenges do international institutions and norms face? Are these changes conducive to the effectiveness of international law and organizations? How did international law and its institutions respond to these drastic developments, and what changes – if any – are necessary for international law to correspond to new realities?

These are very broad questions and I will limit my research to those aspects of them which are closely related to or stem from the dissolution of the USSR and events in Eastern Europe (i.e. which directly result from the end of the Cold War).

Due primarily to the collapse of the USSR such problems as the self-determination of peoples and the protection of ethnic minorities, which both are closely linked to the question of the ascendence of nationalism in different countries of the world, have become once more crucial issues of world politics. The concentric circles engendered by the end of the Soviet empire are spreading far from the former USSR. The end of the Cold War has put forward, as well, the question of the prospects of democracy and human rights in post-totalitarian societies, which certainly is not an internal matter of these states. Not only are issues of democracy and human rights in individual countries legitimate concern for the world community as a whole but it is on the progress of domestic developments in former communist countries that the future of the international system will depend to a great extent. Therefore these important legal and political issues receive special attention in the book.

The dissolution of old states and emergence of new ones have always raised issues of recognition and succession, therefore political and legal implications of these problems are also analysed in respective chapters.

The book as a whole is concerned with the interplay of law and politics in the international system after the Cold War.

It has always been necessary to study international law in the context of an international system where the law is functioning and developing, and to analyse legal and political problems as inseparably intertwined (as in reality they are). But it is especially important to put international law into the proper context at times of revolutionary change in the international system. This means that inter-disciplinary research and a combination of different approaches to most issues, including international law, become absolutely necessary. As Rosalyn Higgins writes, 'there is no avoiding the essential relationship between law and policy'.[1] It is therefore desirable that

> the policy factors are dealt with systematically and openly. Dealing with them systematically means that all factors are properly con-

sidered and weighed, instead of the decision-maker unconsciously narrowing or selecting what he will take into account in order to reach a decision that he has instinctively predetermined as desirable.[2]

Therefore such important concrete issues as the self-determination of peoples and the protection of minorities (referred to above), where law and politics closely interact, can be properly analysed only if this analysis is put into an adequate wider context. This has necessitated the analysis of such general issues as the future of the international system, prospects of order and the role of international law and the institutions in it. This analysis forms the content of the chapter 1.

But before embarking on the analysis of these substantive issues, a few reflections of a methodological character – so far as they are relevant to the forthcoming analysis – seem to be necessary.

There is a phenomenon which is rather widespread, at least in writings on international law and politics. It is that some authors, including the most imaginative ones, often stick firmly to the favourite approach to their discipline and consider it to be if not the only possible one, then at least the only true one. Realists, behaviourists, structuralists and institutionalists in international relations theory have certainly all grasped many important aspects of the complex reality with which they are dealing. Similarly, legal positivism, the natural law approach, and especially policy-oriented jurisprudence have all contributed to the understanding and development of international law. But, on the other hand, they all put certain self-imposed limitations on themselves, thereby often making their analysis one-sided (of course, there are specialists on international law and relations who do not limit their research to one of the possible approaches to their discipline). The question of whether it is necessary to stick firmly to one of these or other approaches to the discipline in order to achieve positive results needs to be answered.

Perhaps it is important, for example, that an academic international lawyer, in order to penetrate deeply into the most difficult issues of international law, sees not only his or her discipline as the most important one but also his or her favourite approach as the only true one. Perhaps only by believing (usually erroneously) that his or her discipline is the most important one in the world, and that his or her approach is the only true one (usually also erroneously), does he or she find the necessary stimulus to embark on time-consuming research. Perhaps a social scientist, in order to achieve something noticeable, has to be an enthusiast – not only for his or her discipline but also for his or her approach. Quite possibly. But an enthusiastic structuralist, realist or normativist inevitably sees the reality in a one-sided way, at least, if not in a distorting mirror. The social reality is practically always too complicated to be approached by one particular method of analysis. But probably without such one-sided views (which are in many cases very deep indeed because only enthusiasts can go deep enough into a particular issue) it would be difficult to have a proper comprehensive analysis of the problem.

I am sceptical about the ability of any of these, or of any other approaches for that matter, individually to grasp the complexities of the most important issues of international law and politics. Moreover, although I am an international lawyer, I do not think that world peace can be achieved only through world law. Events in the former Yugoslavia, in Georgia, and in Somalia – as well as in some other parts of the world – witness that law without force, and the determination to use it in order to stop the most flagrant violations of international law and morality, is powerless. Legal positivism, certainly, is not a proper guide during revolutionary change, be it in a single country or in the international system.

But nor can I agree with those realists who see international law as a legal strait-jacket for international relations.[3] Moreover, sometimes an effective strait-jacket may be needed for some of these relations. I do not believe, either, that such broad values as respect, power, enlightenment, well-being, wealth, skill, affection, and rectitude, which are espoused by proponents of the policy-oriented approach to international law[4] (the content of which, moreover, is understood quite differently by different actors of the international system), can always serve as a proper or better guide than concrete rules, the observance of which may indeed sometimes make the realization of these values difficult or even impossible. As Richard Falk observes, these 'values are not currently specified in relation to any of the outstanding problems of mankind such as poverty, population pressure, violence, and ecological decay.'[5]

This does not, of course, mean that the creation, interpretation, and application of international law can be separated from international (or even domestic) politics, or that these or other societal values do not affect the decision-making in the international system. International law, though discernible in the fabric of international politics, cannot be extracted from it without damaging the fabric.

Certainly, the subject itself dictates analytical approaches. As John Lewis Gaddis writes,

good scientists, like good novelists and good historians, make use of all the tools at their disposal in trying to anticipate the future. That includes not just theory, observation, and rigorous calculation, but also narrative, analogy, paradox, irony, intuition, imagination, and – not least in importance – style.[6]

And even at the risk of being accused of eclecticism, I think that a methodological (e.g. either the normativist or policy-oriented approach) or disciplinary (e.g. either law or international relations theory) rigidity is a self-constraint which puts limits on the comprehensiveness of research.

This means that in the analysis of the different issues of contemporary international life presented in the forthcoming chapters, a purposeful effort to take into account both their legal and political aspects, and the use of a variety of approaches, is made.

1 The end of the Cold War
International law and politics at a crossroads

INTERNATIONAL LAW IN THE INTERNATIONAL SYSTEM

Every legal system is a part of a wider social system, where it performs its regulatory functions and which eventually determines the main characteristics of law, its role and its effectiveness. Though such wider systems determine the basic features of all legal systems, the latter do not passively reflect the nature of the former but play an important role therein. Without taking this into account it would be impossible to have a proper understanding of the functioning of law and of the very society of which the legal system constitutes a regulatory sub-system. Law, Henkin sums up,

> is a major force in international relations and a major determinant in national politics. Its influence is diluted, however, and sometimes outweighed, by other forces in a 'developing' international society. Failure to appreciate the strengths and weaknesses of the law underlies much misunderstanding about it and many of the controversies about its significance. 'Realists' who do not recognize the uses and force of law are not realistic. 'Idealists' who do not recognize the law's limitations are largely irrelevant to the world that is.[1]

Like all domestic legal systems which are rooted in different societies organized as states, international law also has its specific social environment where it performs its functions. It is a legal sub-system of the international system which, in essence, is considered by many as an inter-state system. Thus, Louis Henkin writes that 'international law is the normative expression of the international polity which has states as its basic constituent entities'.[2] Grigorii Tunkin even writes that international law functions in the inter-state system.[3]

But some specialists in international law, and others in international relations, are questioning such a state-centric view on their disciplines.[4]

I think that there are good reasons for this. From the point of view of an international lawyer, though states remain the most influential actors of the international arena and are the main subjects of international law, it is impossible to limit the social environment of the latter to the inter-state system because the functioning of international law quite obviously transcends inter-state relations (even in its largest sense, i.e. including relations where inter-governmental organizations and state-like entities participate). Different transnational relations,[5] the role of which is increasing in the contemporary world, are not outside the influence of international law. Issues concerning the protection of environment or the activities of transnational corporations, for example, if not always directly governed by international law, are nevertheless often affected by it.

This means that today, even from the point of view of an international lawyer (traditionally international law was considered to be inter-state law), it would be too narrow a comparison to equate the current social environment of contemporary international law with the inter-state system, though, of course, inter-state relations still constitute the core of the relations governed by international law. Therefore, a theoretical framework for studies of both international law and politics has to take account of 'increasing evidence of the importance and impact of so many factors excluded from the reigning model: individuals, corporations, nongovernmental organizations of every stripe, political and economic ideology, ideas, interests, identities and interdependence'.[6]

Consequently, international law has to be studied as a sub-system of the international system which encompasses all actors and relations and transcends state boundaries.

Moreover, international law often deeply penetrates into domestic relations. Robert Keohane rightly observes that in order to deal with issues concerning the compliance of states with their international commitments, '[w]e must look at the interaction between international politics and law and domestic politics,'[7] which he calls 'institutional enmeshment'. An international lawyer would have said that for its effective implementation international law should be steadily anchored in the domestic law and institutions.

Civil wars, and the plight of ethnic minorities and human rights in general, have become the object of legitimate concern for the international community. Such concerns as human rights or environmental protection have become what are sometimes called intermestic issues, which means that they are neither exclusively domestic nor international. This all means that international law's social environment has become much wider than inter-state relations.

It is not enough to study international law in the context of international politics simply because the international system itself emerges as a result of interaction between different domestic systems. As the international system is, in comparison with domestic systems, a loose system where actors are relatively autonomous *vis-à-vis* each other, its main actors – states and their internal characteristics – exercise crucial influence upon the nature of the international system. This means that impulses coming to the system from actors are decisive for the characteristics of the system.

Of course, the international system in its turn affects not only the foreign, but often even the internal politics, of all states.

States themselves should not, either for international relations theory or even for international law doctrines, be black boxes or snooker balls of different size. On the one hand, the internal characteristics of states determine the main features of the international system. On the other hand, international factors, including international law, penetrate deeply into domestic processes.

The influence of the internal characteristics of states on the international system is most strongly felt at times of drastic, revolutionary changes in the main actors of the latter. For example, the Cold War, being essentially an inter-state phenomenon, ended, as we will see below, thanks to revolutionary developments in the USSR and its communist satellites, though it is hardly possible to deny that external factors also played an important role in the collapse of the communist system and the Soviet Union.

It is difficult, therefore, to agree with Kenneth Waltz when he writes: 'We do not ask whether states are revolutionary or legitimate, authoritarian or democratic, ideological or pragmatic. We abstract from every attribute of states except their capabilities.'[8] And capability is defined by Waltz as power: 'States are differently placed by their power.'[9] Later Waltz wrote that 'we know that part of what happens internationally is shaped by the structure of international politics and part by the character of the acting units.'[10]

Nevertheless, it remains unclear how it is possible to have a comprehensive (or even not so comprehensive) theory of international relations which does not take into account all factors which shape 'what happens internationally'. The onesidedness of any theory which abstracts itself from the internal developments which occur in major actors of the international system becomes especially clear in times of revolutionary changes in the world (the word 'world' is used because such changes inevitably encompass domestic as well as international spheres).

Therefore there simply cannot be a viable international relations theory which completely abstracts itself from the internal characteristics of states. Of course, an author in his or her concrete study can concentrate only on the structure of the international system, but even in that case he or she has constantly to bear in mind that such a theory is only a partial theory of international relations and that even here there should not be complete abstraction from other issues and problems which includes the internal characteristics of states. The author in such a case simply uses results of the analyses of other researchers.

Burry Buzan writes of structural realism that it

> is only one theory among many, and we make no claim that it is the only valid way of conceptualizing the international system. It is simply one way that strikes us as being useful, not least because it can be made complementary to other perspectives, serving as a firm foundation on which to integrate many other elements of international relations theory.[11]

It is difficult not to agree with such an approach. However, any approach has its limitations and therefore should be used whilst taking into account other approaches and methods.

As international systems are not composed of abstract, similar or fungible entities which interact and thereby create bipolar, multipolar or other international systems endowed with certain characteristics, it is necessary for understanding crucial changes in this system to have a deep perception of domestic developments in at least the key actors of the system. Francis Fukuyama is right in criticizing extreme realists because

> in its purest form, realism tries to banish all considerations of internal politics, and to deduce the possibility of war from the structure of the state system alone . . . But this pure form of realism covertly introduces certain highly reductionist assumptions about the nature of the human societies that make up the system, mistakenly attributing them to the 'system' rather than to the units that make up the system.[12]

Like international relations studies, research in international law cannot abstract itself from the internal characteristics of states. The principal of sovereign equality of states no longer means that democratic and totalitarian states, peaceful countries and aggressors are to be treated equally. Moreover, the very role of the nation-state in the international system which until recently was beyond question, needs to be reviewed.

THE ROLE OF THE NATION-STATE IN THE INTERNATIONAL SYSTEM

One of the controversial issues of the changing international system is the question of the place and the role of nation states within it. The emergence of powerful transnational corporations, the activities of many non-governmental organizations (NGOs), the increasing role of the individual (who in some cases may challenge his or her own state before international bodies), and especially the development of international organizations with supranational characteristics (e.g. the EU), may lead one to the conclusion that the nation-state's role in the international arena is diminishing. Kenichi Ohmae even writes that 'the nation state has become an unnatural, even dysfunctional, unit for organizing human activity and managing economic endeavour in a borderless world'.[13]

The emergence of other actors in the international system means that the observer has to take these changes into account and may conclude that in certain domains (e.g. economic relations) other actors may often function more effectively than states. But the state is still, and in the foreseeable future will remain (notwithstanding the relative decline of its strength), the main and the most powerful actor. Paul Kennedy writes that the major argument of his book 'is that the nature of the new challenges makes it more difficult than previously for governments to control events. But they still provide the chief institution through which societies will try to respond to change.'[14]

This is certainly true. Even the considerable increase in the importance of multilateral diplomacy and, consequently, of international organizations, does not mean that they are going to replace the states as the major actors of the international system. Even in the EU, Brussels has not succeeded, and at least in the near future will not succeed, in replacing national authorities, though the European institutions perform many functions which traditionally belonged to the governments. International inter-governmental institutions have become an important tool, which not only increases states' capabilities but at the same time limits their behaviour. Nevertheless they are only instruments, though very important ones, of states and are not in themselves super-states.

In most important areas of global concern, such as environmental protection, issues of peace and war and even in the field of human rights protection, one may say that there is, thanks to modern means of communication, an emerging global 'constituency' represented mainly by different NGOs, which if not always directly participating in the decision-making process are at least exercising considerable influence on it. Often, though, it is only states which have sufficient means and powers to make decisions and to carry them out. States are far from perfect institutions for dealing with such global issues because their 'constituencies', and consequently their interests, are too narrow for the resolution of global problems and concerns. But, notwithstanding the important role of all green movements and national as well as inter-national NGOs on human rights, it was necessary to have inter-governmental decision-making world conferences on environmental protection in Rio in 1992 and on human rights in Vienna a year later. Therefore those writers on international law and relations, like ad-herents of critical legal studies[15] who leave the state out of their reckoning, sound rather detached from reality.

At the same time, of course, the relative influence of other actors (e.g., international organizations, NGOs, multinational corporations, or sub-structures of states) in international decision-making will increase. But, even more than from the rise of other competitors to the state in the international arena, the relative strength of states is being eroded by two tendencies which are often interrelated. Economic integration is a main propeller of the diminishing role of national frontiers. On the other hand, the fact that the processes of integration are accompanied by alienation and impersonalization of life in many societies, gives rise, *inter alia*, to nationalism and other forms of parochialism. Graham Fuller rightly observes that:

> In the end, even nationalism will prove insufficient to satisfy cravings for a more precise, more manageable sense of identity. It is not enough to be one of many tens of millions of Nigerians, Bengalis, or Indonesians. People revert to smaller communal groupings, the tribe or the region, the dialect or the local language.[16]

Separatism and secessionist claims may be confronted by increased centralization and repression (as was done, for example, in Sri Lanka in face of Tamil separatism, in China against Tibet's struggle for inde-pendence, in Georgia under Ghamsahurdia against South Ossetia and Abkhazia) and one may claim that such a policy results in the strengthening of state power. But secessionist claims may be confronted by more complicated and subtle arrangements such as autonomy and the diminishing importance of state boundaries. The movement for 'a Europe of regions' instead of a Europe of states may be far from achieving its aims, but, in Western Europe and North America, borders between states as well as the line between dependence and independ-ence have sometimes become rather blurred. The development of the EU and now probably the NAFTA may lead to a situation where objectively (not, yet, subjectively) it would be less important, for example, for Quebec to belong to Canada or not; or for Catalonia to be officially considered a part of Spain or to belong directly to the EU, or whether it should be called, as one of the advertisements before the Olympic games in Barcelona put it, 'a country in Spain with its own culture, language and identity'.[17]

Unfortunately, the second experience has been until now confined to Western Europe and North America. In other parts of the world separatism more often than not increases internal oppression and centralization of state powers, or leads to bloody wars of secession. Why it is so, and the essential relationship between democracy and the resolution of inter-ethnic problems, will be analysed in following chapters.

Such changes have considerably modified the international system. States are no longer the only actors of the system. Martin Shaw is right when he says that:

> We should stop seeing non-state actors as intruders into the system and society of states, and see them instead as actors within global society of which the state system is an institutional component, and whose intrusion is therefore entirely normal and inevitable.[18]

We may conclude by saying that though states remain the most influential actors of the international system, their relative role is diminishing for reasons other than simply the entrance of new actors into the system. The main reason is that states are often not the best resolvers of new issues, many of which are either too big or too small for the state. The emergence of global problems, and the democratization which is taking place in many societies as well as in the international arena, means that the importance of the two extreme participants of social relations – mankind as a whole and the individual – is increasing. Moreover, the interests of states and those of the societies which they represent or claim to represent do not always coincide. Societies themselves become more and more actively involved in world politics, often circumventing states as their representatives.[19] Michael Walzer predicts that the interest of political theorists over the next decades will lie above and below the level of the nation (and the nation-state). 'It will lie in the transnational formations of different sorts and in civil society.'[20] There are good reasons for such an assertion.

The process of the 'marketization' of economies in countries of planned economy also leads to the eventual decrease in the role of the state in international, especially international economic, relations.

All this means that international law should be studied as a part of the wider international system, the political core or the most important sub-system of which is the state system. And to understand the functioning of and changes in the international system, including international law, it is necessary to follow closely what is going on inside the major actors of this system.

THE COLD WAR INTERNATIONAL SYSTEM

Main characteristics

To perceive current developments and their influence on the future of the international system and international law it is necessary to dwell briefly upon the main characteristics of the Cold War international system.

Morton Kaplan distinguished six different international systems: the balance of power system, the loose bipolar system, the tight bipolar system, the universal system, the hierarchical system in its directive and non-directive forms, and the unit veto system.[21] Only two of them – the balance of power system and the loose bipolar system – have had concrete historical analogues. Other systems are hypothetical, possible only under certain conditions.

The international system of the Cold War era was, according to Kaplan's theory, a loose bipolar system which had replaced the previous balance of power systems existing in the nineteenth century and at the beginning of the twentieth century. The loose bipolar system is characterized by the presence of two major bloc actors, a leading national actor within each bloc, non-member national actors, and universal actors, all of whom have a unique and distinctive role within the system.[22] Indeed, the main political – military actors were two opposite blocs – NATO and the Warsaw Pact – both of which had their indisputable leaders, the USA and the USSR. Then there were non-aligned countries, whose territories were the objects of competition between the major actors, and there was a universal actor – the United Nations and its related international bodies – which was often paralysed because of the conflicting interests of the superpowers and their allies.

These were significant, but formal, characteristics of the international system of the Cold War era. Even more important were the substantive ones. The Cold War was a rivalry between two different ideologies – the liberal democratic system of the free-market economy was confronted by the one-party totalitarian system of the command economy. As John Mueller observes:

> The Cold War had much more to do with ideology than with armaments. Although it is frequently argued that it was the bomb that

dominated and principally shaped the contest, it seems rather that the Cold War essentially sprang from the oft-proclaimed expansionary goals of communism: when these changed, everything changed, even though the bombs remained very much in place.[23]

Here we see once more that the internal characteristics of the major actors of the system determine the structure and other basic features of the international system. Without these two competing socio-economic systems and superpowers representing and personifying them, not only would there never have been such characteristics of the Cold War bipolar system as nuclear deterrence, ideological competition in the Third World, etc., but the very bipolar structure of the world would have been non-existent, or at least it would have been a completely different one.

The Cold War distorted relations, not only between actors belonging to the different blocs but also relations inside both blocs and those of superpowers with 'neutral' actors were affected as well. While the USSR supported Castro in Cuba, Mengistu in Ethiopia, and even at one time Bokassa in the Central African Empire (or Republic), the United States had its own clients who matched the Soviet ones. Robert Jervis observes that 'for Reagan the promotion of democracy meant support-ing any non-communist forces'.[24] President Kennedy said after the assassination of Trujillo of the Dominican Republic:

There are three possibilities in descending order of preference; a decent democratic regime, a continuation of the Trujillo regime, or a Castro regime. We ought to aim at the first, but we really can't renounce the second until we are sure that we can afford the third.[25]

States, as well as the majority of academics, looked at most, if not all, international problems in the light of the East–West confrontation. This inevitably distorted many of them and made their solution difficult or even impossible. Fuller writes that

the ideology of anticommunism as a guiding principle of foreign policy came to overshadow an emphasis on democracy and freedom. While democracy and anticommunism are hardly mutually exclusive, they are also not the same, and at times tactically conflict.[26]

The influence of the Cold War was certainly not confined only to inter-state relations. Domestic issues were equally affected. The Cold War in the international arena was an impediment for democracy and human rights and freedoms even in democratic countries. Walter LaFeber writes:

It is now a truism to note that US officials could not have con-
ducted their global military and economic policies without solving
the central problem that Locke, Madison, and Tocqueville, among
others, anticipated more than 150 years ago: the problem of turning
an individualistic, open, commercial, and domestic-oriented society
into a consensual, secret, militaristic, international force.[27]

The Cold War was used also by the Soviet leadership to mobilize the
population for carrying out the tasks put forward by the Communist
Party and to further restrict rights and freedoms of the Soviet citizens.
Therefore President Kennedy was right in noting in 1963, that 'the hard-
liners in the Soviet Union and the United States feed on one another'.[28]
Consequently, the Cold War, being first and foremost an inter-state
phenomenon, had a decisive influence on domestic issues in many
countries. McCarthyism in the United States, certainly, would not have
been possible without favourable international conditions.

The end of the Cold War bipolar international system, which in itself
did not show any signs of destabilization let alone imminent collapse
before the *perestroika* and *glasnost* era in the former USSR, was caused
by internal changes in one of the major actors of the system.

The Cold War bipolar system was relatively stable, and without
drastic changes in the domestic realm of one of the major actors it may
have persisted for years. Robert Gilpin observes:

> Although the decades following World War II frequently have been
> called an age of political turbulence, the international system in that
> period has actually been characterized by remarkable resilience. It has
> accommodated a number of major developments: an unprecedented
> process of decolonization, rapid technological changes, the emergence
> of new powers (India, Brazil, China), socio-political revolutions in
> developing countries, massive shocks to the world economy, and the
> resurgence of non-Western civilizations. Yet the basic framework of
> an international system composed of two central blocs and a large non-
> aligned periphery has remained essentially intact.[29]

Waltz also considered that bipolar systems were inherently more stable
than their multipolar counterparts, because the existence of only two
major adversaries minimized the possibilities of misperception and
increased predictability.[30]

But this was a stability, and I would add, rigidity, fraught with the
potential for a major explosion, like the stability of a powder keg. And
the cause for such an explosion may not have been only the possibility
of a nuclear war, had deterrence failed. The collapse of one of the

superpowers and of one of the competing ideologies also inevitably resulted in the blowing up of the entire system.

Limits on international law in the Cold War international system

The bipolar system imposed a discipline, which approximated sometimes to military discipline, on all participants. The behaviour of states, especially at the highest political level, was governed not so much by international law as by the rules of the game. Each superpower had spheres of interest or influence where the other did not usually interfere.

International law existed and even governed many issues in this international system. Henkin's famous words that 'it is probably the case that almost all nations observe almost all principles of international law and almost all their obligations almost all of the time'[31] were probably true even in the Cold War era. But the higher the political and military strategic interests of states, the more readily they sacrificed legal principles if the latter seemed to limit their behaviour. And Hans Morgenthau was not so wrong when he wrote in the Cold War era that the iron law of international politics was 'that legal obligations must yield to the national interest'.[32] And the national interest in its turn was usually interpreted rather narrowly in terms of the 'zero sum' game. Upholding of international law was rarely seen by superpowers as being in their national interests.

In balance of power international systems the most important interstate relations were also not governed by norms of international law, let alone by international organizations, but by the rules of the balance of power. Kaplan described six rules essential for this system,[33] the most important of which was that every shift of power in the system threatening the equilibrium had to be counterbalanced by some change of alliances or even by a war against an actor seeking or seeming to achieve predominance. Similarly, in the Cold War bipolar system the rules of the game and the spheres of influence of the superpowers and their blocs were often much more important than what was written in the UN Charter or decided upon by the International Court of Justice. In some cases (for example, during the Cuban missile crisis of 1962) it was not article 2(4) of the Charter, but nuclear deterrence which averted the use of military force. This example also shows that political 'rules of the game' and norms of international law may support each other. Norms of international law reflect, support, and are in their turn supported (as well as undermined) by, different values, interests, and power-structures. Nuclear deterrence was supportive of the principle of non-use of force, at least between the superpowers and other bloc members. But this phenomenon did not prevent, and to a certain extent even facilitated, use of force by the superpowers or their clients in their respective spheres of interest (e.g., so-called proxy wars), never formally agreed upon, but nevertheless well understood by states. The balance of power system as such may also be supportive of the requirements of international law, if, for example, the maintenance of the equilibrium demands the use of force against an aggressor. But what if, on the contrary, the maintenance of the balance requires the first use of force?[34] Therefore, other guarantees of the implementation of norms of international law are necessary.

The veto in the UN Security Council, used and abused mainly by the Soviet Union, often blocked the system of collective security provided for in the Charter. The content, and especially the functioning, of international law were negatively affected by such important characteristics of the international system as the deep distrust between opposing blocs and the use of the same legal language or terminology often with completely different meanings. One of the crucial failures of international law in the Cold War international system consisted in the paralysis of the UN Security Council in dealing with threats to peace, breaches of the peace, and acts of aggression. Use of third-party settlement of international disputes (e.g. the International Court of Justice, or arbitration) was also rather limited. States preferred to remain judges in their own cases. Agreeing on rules of behaviour, states were reluctant to accept monitoring procedures let alone mechanisms of enforcement, and therefore in the Cold War environment the implementation of the norms of international law suffered even more than their content.

Because of the failure of the UN system of collective security it was not surprising that the unilateral use of force re-emerged or did not even disappear. Michael Reisman observes that 'because the Charter's constitutive solution of the collective security problem did not work, operational norms emerged which, not surprisingly, diverged in many details from how the collective security system was supposed to work'.[35]

In the Cold War international system the role of international law was limited because two competing political, military and ideological systems could not often agree on the content of norms of international law, and even when they agreed they preferred to remain judges in their own case. Further, in the Cold War international system, which was sharply divided into two practically equal blocs (in terms of power), both blocs, and especially their leaders, enjoyed the power of enforcement of their understanding and interpretation of international law, particularly if by doing so they did not interfere in the sphere of interest of the other bloc.

Such a duality of power is the most unfavourable environment for law and order. In domestic systems it usually leads to revolutions, *coup d'états* or civil wars. The end of the Cold War may be indeed considered as a revolution in the international system which *inter alia* resolved the problem of duality of power. It remains to be seen what impact this has on international law.

PROSPECTS FOR THE FUTURE: THREATS AND OPPORTUNITIES?

Rigidity, chaos and order

As we have seen, the roots of the Cold War did not lie in the structure or in other characteristics of the international system. The ideology, policy and economic system of communism were major factors which gave birth to the bipolar international system of the Cold War. I am not arguing by this that other states were blameless, or that they did not contribute at all to the birth and maintenance of the negative characteristics of this system, or that without the communist revolution in Russia in 1917 we would now have something like paradise on the Earth. Not at all; but the Cold War as we knew it certainly could not have taken place without the Bolshevik revolution in Russia.

The end of the system came about as a result of internal changes in the USSR and the extinction of one of the blocs of the bipolar system. This systemic change is affecting all the actors of the international system. Ken Jowitt is absolutely right that 'the Leninist extinction is not an historical surgical strike that will leave liberal and "Third World" "friendlies" unaffected. Everyone's horizons, including the West's, will be dramatically affected'.[36]

It is not by chance that in the 1990s multiparty elections have taken place for the first time in various countries of Africa and some of them have adopted new constitutions and legalized opposition parties (Burkina Faso, the Central African Republic, Guineau-Bissau, Kenya, etc.) and that the People's Republic of the Congo and Zimbabwe have abandoned Marxism-Leninism.[37] The positive developments in the Arab–Israeli relations in autumn 1993 would have been impossible in the Cold War environment. But neither it is by chance that civil wars have broken out in some African countries – the end of the great power rivalry has left power vacuums which need to be filled.

In Eastern Europe and in the new states which have emerged in place of the former USSR, promising economic reforms and significant increase in civil and political rights go hand in hand with economic hardships, civil wars, ethnic cleansing and heightened nationalism.

To put it succinctly, there is great instability not only in many new and even not so new states, but also in the international system as a whole. Could it have been otherwise?

Of course, many negative things could have been avoided and more progress may have been made in certain areas. Many mistakes were made and even crimes were committed. But generally it would be naïve to expect that, for example, a country such as Russia could become democratic overnight or that one international order would replace another one without a transitional period characterized by, among other things, instability and chaos.

In autumn 1989 Lawrence Eagleburger, then Deputy Secretary of State, asserting that for all its risks and uncertainties the Cold War was characterized by a remarkably stable and predictable set of relationships among the great powers, predicted that a sudden end to the East-West standoff could bring disorder, leading to government crackdowns, the re-establishment of dictatorships, and war.[38]

But chaos, like order, is never absolute. There is always some order in chaos as well as some elements of chaos in any order, at least in human relations. System transformations are always characterized more by chaos than order, because one structure and order is being replaced by another structure and order. Such a situation is inevitable because order can emerge only from chaos, not from frigidity, which may be stable but which is not amenable to changes.

In a society, be it domestic or international, order does not usually come out of chaos automatically, without purposeful efforts of different social forces. On the direction of these efforts depends the character of a new order. I agree with those who assert that 'the modern international system is increasingly being reproduced on an intentional basis'.[39] This is well understood by different social forces in many countries. Secessionist movements, different religious groups, extreme political forces – all believe (and quite rightly believe) that this is the right moment to achieve their goals. 'Now or never' – this is a slogan of many destructive forces (and also, of course, of some non-destructive forces).

Armenians and Azeris in Nagorno-Karabakh, Abkhazians in Georgia, and warring tribes in Tadjikistan understand well that if they do not achieve their specific goals – which they sometimes have nourished for years – in this disorder, then they will not have the same chance again, at least in the near future. Therefore 'ethnic cleansing' intensified in some areas of Bosnia Herzegovina when the UN in the spring of 1993 showed signs that the 'Vance-Owen' plan would be implemented by the use of military pressure if necessary. All sides immediately tried to grab as much territory as possible before some kind of order would be imposed on them. The same happened in the autumn of the same year when Owen and Stoltenberg seemed to be close to imposing an agreement which would lead eventually to the division of Bosnia-Herzegovina along ethnic lines.

The collapse of one of the pillars of the bipolar international system could not fail to create chaos, not only inside this pillar but also in the system itself. What analysts really failed to predict was the rapid collapse of the communist regimes and the USSR. Therefore, neither they nor politicians were always ready to react adequately to events.

But the current disorder, and even the possibility of the aggravation of situations in different countries or regions, does not mean that future world order is impossible, unforeseeable or that it does not have a good chance to be more just than the previous one.

The efforts of all constructive forces are needed, therefore, to create a relatively stable future world order which will be lasting and more just and democratic than the previous one and with as little loss as possible. This is really the time not only of fundamental threats, but also of enormous opportunities. The task of political leaders is to minimize, or where possible to avoid, risks and not to miss opportunities.

Trends and by-products

I think that it is necessary to distinguish between trends which are essential for the transition from one international system to another and the by-products which sometimes may be inevitable and even dangerous, but which will not determine the eventual outcome of the development of the international system. It is also necessary to make a distinction between short- or medium-term developments and long-term tendencies.

Two recent books predict rather different outcomes for the world order. Ken Jowitt writes that:

> The Leninist legacy in Eastern Europe consists largely – not exclusively – of fragmented, mutually suspicious, societies with little religio-cultural support for tolerant and individually self-reliant behaviour; and of a fragmented region made up of countries that view each other with animosity . . .[40]

The analysis of the likely consequences of the Leninist extinction leads him to conclude that 'we face a period of global, regional and national turmoil over boundaries and identities'.[41]

It is difficult to refute this analysis. These developments are already here. But they are, as Jowitt rightly puts it, consequences of the Leninist extinction. The main event or process is the Leninist extinction itself. This process in itself is positive, but it has, as we see, some negative consequences.

Francis Fukuyama takes the different view, writing that as

mankind approaches the end of the millennium, the twin crises of authoritarianism and socialist central planning have left only one competitor standing in the ring as an ideology of potentially universal validity: liberal democracy, the doctrine of individual freedom and popular sovereignty.[42]

The result of such developments for the international system will be that peace will arise out of the specific nature of democratic legitimacy, with its ability to satisfy the human longing for recognition.[43]

These two visions of the future seem to be irreconcilable. Without attempting to reconcile them, I think that they both reflect the same reality, though they put emphases not only on different aspects and trends of this reality, but, more importantly, they choose different historical perspectives. While Jowitt analyses the Leninist phenomenon and its legacy after its extinction, Fukuyama's research comprises a much longer historical period extending deeper into the history of mankind as well as trying to forecast not so much the immediate results of the collapse of the existing international order but trends extending into the more distant future.

Valerie Bunce, speaking of the Gorbachev reforms in the erstwhile Soviet Union, is right to conclude that 'the real issue is not what is going on today or yesterday, since these are best understood as the inevitable costs of changing domestic and international orders at the same time'.[44] From her point of view the Gorbachev reforms are best understood as investments, albeit risky, in the future of Russia, Europe, and the international system.[45]

The roots of my cautious optimism lie in the directions of ongoing changes in many countries. 'Marketization' and democratization, which do not always, of course, go hand in hand, are now processes common to different regions of the world.

If one strives not for an ideal, which means a utopian, world, but for a relatively orderly, gradually improving international system, capable of resolving major challenges to mankind (both natural and man-made), then an orderly international system is not an impossible idea. At least some of the tendencies leading to it are already discernible.

Though in the emerging international system liberal democratic states may still be in the numerical minority, their relative weight will be considerably enhanced in comparison with the previous international system. Not only has the main political, military and economic adversary of the liberal democracies disappeared, but practically all the Eastern European countries and many republics of the former USSR are at least striving to introduce liberal democratic values into their societies. Even if some of these newly born countries fail to become relatively democratic in the near future, the most plausible option for them would not be communism or some other form of totalitarianism, but rather what Jowitt calls 'liberal authoritarianism'.[46]

The end of the Cold War means that in the emerging new international system there will numerically be more democratic (or at least non-authoritarian) states, and more importantly their relative weight will be considerably increased. As some authors have noted, democracies have never fought wars against each other.[47] This in itself is a rather positive tendency and provides hope that in the future there will be less place for violence and the use of military force. The democratization of domestic societies has changed and certainly will continue to change the characteristics of international relations also.

Although there are many reasons not to be satisfied with the observance of the principle of non-use of force in international relations, which will be discussed in some detail later in the chapter, here I would like nevertheless to remind the reader that the attitude in the world towards international violence has considerably changed over time. There were poems written to glorify the conquests of Alexander the Great, Peter the Great, Genghis Khan, Napoleon, and many other empire builders. Now Milosevic and Karadzic are international outcasts for their attempts to create a Greater Serbia. Every aggressor nowadays has to justify his actions and, as a justification, can accuse others of doing what hundreds of years ago was not only lawful but honourable for a statesman and a warrior. So, over 2,000 years ago during the Peloponnesian war the Athenian delegation did not try to conceal its understanding of international justice, explaining to the Council of the Melians that 'since you know as well as we do that right, as the world goes, is only in question between equals in power, while the strong do what they can and weak suffer what they must'.[48] There are, of course, still politicians who even today think like the Athenians did more than 2,000 years ago but they prefer to keep their thoughts to themselves. This, though hypocritical, is at the same time also certainly a sign of significant progress in the development of civilization.

Disillusionment with current developments in the world may be to a certain extent due to too high expectations at the end of the 1980s.

Immediately after the changes in the Soviet Union gained momentum and Gorbachev renounced and denounced some foreign policy actions of the previous Soviet leadership (such as Afghanistan, Czechoslovakia, etc.), there was a certain euphoria amongst many politicians and experts on international relations. This was, of course, untimely euphoria. But equally untimely, from my point of view, are lamentations about the future of the world order based on disappointments caused by the current disorder.

Sometimes what is feasible is put in doubt because the unfeasible is expected. So Denise Artaud writes that the Gulf crisis, the danger of nuclear proliferation, and other developments raise doubts about a New World Order of everlasting peace, and also about the real unthinkability of a return to East-West tensions.[49] But there are many other reasons besides these to conclude that everlasting peace is not yet, if ever, foreseeable. Certainly, civil wars and even local international conflicts are not excluded, and international terrorism, drug trafficking and economic 'wars' will not only continue but sometimes, probably, become even more widespread. Mueller is right that '[w]hat seems to happen is that when big evils vanish, lesser ones are quickly promoted to have their place'.[50] Utopians, maximalists or idealists would always be disappointed by the reality.

Challenges and threats

But what has been said above does not mean that the foreseeable future will be without conflicts, even military ones, or that human rights will flourish everywhere or that all societies will become even relatively well-off. I probably lack Fukuyama's ability to foresee a distant future, but in the future which I can envisage by no means all states will be liberal democracies. Though the tendency in the world as a whole testifies that in the 1960s there were more liberal democracies than in 1919, and in the 1990s more than in the 1960s, and that a number of countries have reverted to democracy after a period of authoritarian or even totalitarian rule,[51] this does not necessarily mean that all countries will inevitably become liberal democracies. Religious, especially Muslim, fundamentalism,[52] and historical traditions (like economic and social underdevelopment in many countries and regions of the world), as well as deep cultural differences, are not short-term phenomena. There is not only a huge gap in wealth between the North and the South but differences of cultural and even civilizational nature. Samuel Huntington even predicts that '[t]he next world war, if there is one, will be a war between civilizations'.[53] One of the threats to the international system comes from the revival of nationalism in different parts of the world – especially in Eastern Europe and in the former Soviet Union. Nationalism deserves a special attention in the framework of this book and therefore will be analysed in some detail in the following chapters.

All of these factors may constitute not only an obstacle for the development of liberal democracy in many societies, but also a potential threat for the world order in the foreseeable future. But not all of these challenges for liberal democracy are necessarily detrimental to the future international system.

The end of history, had it been possible even in the philosophical sense, as described by Fukuyama, would not be only boring.[54] This would have led to a kind of decadence and stagnation of mankind. Hegel saw in wars between states a remedy against decadence and the means to keep up the spirit of a nation: 'Just as the movement of the ocean prevents the corruption which would be the result of perpetual calm, so by war people escape the corruption which would be occasioned by continuous or eternal peace.'[55]

Certainly, this remedy has become too strong and destructive not only for individual states but for the international system as well. But there are other challenges. Environmental crisis, overpopulation, under-development and other global threats will not allow mankind to feel bored. And there will certainly be different, even radically different, ideas on how mankind should react to these and other challenges. Graham Fuller writes:

> Fukuyama's intriguing propositions notwithstanding, history is not over in any sense, because history is not linear, even as the Hegelian dialectic evolves. In fact, if we must assign geometric similes, it is circular. Fukuyama is fundamentally wrong. Ideas, including the grand hoary concept of political collectivism, never die. They simply are recycled, and come around again and again, in ever new cultural garb and particular vocabularies to feed on the failures of democratic and individualistic government. Leninist communism may be dead, but collectivism in some form will surely be back again with us, challenging our failures, sooner than we think – maybe not as an ideology controlling half the world in an armed camp, but nonetheless waiting in the wings to redress our fundamental democratic failings. It is the permanent counterweight to libertarianism, the indispensable foil against which our own concepts of democracy are measured, the collectivist Yin to the libertarian Yang. No victory is permanent. History won't go away.[56]

Disagreeing with Fukuyama as to the end of history, I nevertheless do not think that Fukuyama is more fundamentally wrong than many other specialists. He has put forward some brilliant ideas concerning the future of the world. But even if we cannot define the major challenges to liberal democracy today, this certainly does not mean that there will not be any. The presence of the communist challenge may have not only overshadowed, but may even have completely suppressed some other challenges. It is quite natural that when one ideological clash, which suppressed other ideological rivalries, has ended, other competitions of ideas, perceptions or cultures will replace the previous struggle of ideas.

But the emergence of such new ideological challenges to liberal democracies will not necessarily mean that the world will have a kind of new cold war between two or more mortal competitors. Challenges, and mankind's reactions to them, are a natural form of development of all societies and the world as a whole. It may even be that just as domestic societies need opposition parties in order not to become authoritarian or too corrupt, the international system also needs competing ideas and visions of the future. And there will certainly be many of them.

But these challenges can hardly, at least in the foreseeable future, lead to a schism comparable to the one that existed in the Cold War international system. Chris Brown writes:

> Where systematic alternatives to liberalism do exist – for example in 'Islamic Republics' such as Iran – they assume forms which have little attraction for the inhabitants of industrial societies, and indeed may actually be incompatible with such societies in the long run. Clearly not all states are or will be 'liberal' in the foreseeable future, but it does seem likely that most of the major centres of power in the world will, one way or another, fit this description, while those that do not will be illiberal in an unsystematic way rather than offering a conscious alternative to the prevailing political form. It does make some kind of sense to talk of the triumph of Western liberalism.[57]

One of threats to the international system comes from Islamic fundamentalism.[58] Paul Kennedy is right in observing that:

> Far from preparing for the twenty first century, much of the Arab and Muslim world appears to have difficulty in coming to terms with the nineteenth century, with its composite legacy of secularization, democracy, laissez-faire economics, transnational industrial and commercial linkages, social change, and intellectual questioning. If one needed an example of the importance of cultural attitudes in explaining a society's response to change, contemporary Islam provides it.[59]

Islamic fundamentalism, though continuing to create serious troubles not only to many individual countries but also to the world community as well, can hardly become a global threat which would lead to the new split of the international system. The reasons for this are that not all Muslim countries are fundamentalist and that most countries of the world are non-Muslim. The most important reason which argues against Islamic fundamentalism becoming a global threat and replacing the Soviet Union in its capacity of the 'evil empire', lies in the fact that fundamentalist Islam like, for example, fundamentalist Catholicism in the Middle Ages, is a brake on the economic and social progress of any society which, at the end of the day, is the basis of the technological or military competitiveness. Islamic fundamentalism, like any other religious or ideological fundamentalism, will inevitably lead to a social cul-de-sac.

Another profound reason why Muslim fundamentalism will not be able to compete with liberal democracies lies in its confusion regarding the domains which belong respectively to Caesar and God. The matter is not that priests or mullahs are not always the best politicians or administrators. This would be a relatively minor problem. Simply, an idealogue, a philosopher or a cleric would loose holiness and immunity from criticism if they started to deal with mundane issues. It is not difficult to imagine what would have happened to the Papacy had the Pope also been the Prime Minister of Italy in 1993.

And Islam is not only divided into the moderate regimes and fundamentalists, Shiites and Sunnis, but also into countries which all have different geopolitical and national interests.

But all this does not mean that fundamentalist Islam does not constitute any danger at all. Terrorism and gross human rights violations are almost inevitable concomitants of any religious or ideological fundamentalism, especially when it becomes clear that the fundamentalism is leading into a dead end. Therefore, Islamic fundamentalism will remain a serious threat to regional and even world stability.

The collapse of the Soviet bloc has raised fears that the end of the rivalry between the East and the West would exacerbate existing contradictions between the North and the South. Certainly, many of these contradictions may become more prominent, especially if the North does not pay necessary attention to the specific problems of Third World countries. The poverty and economic underdevelopment of most of them, and the huge discrepancy in wealth between the North and the South, is one of the global problems which affects all states. Often additional sensitivity in resolving issues concerning Third World countries is necessary. Therefore, the North should not display a lack of sensitivity (or even sensibility) that would lead to the situation where contradictions and rivalry between the East and the West would be replaced by rivalry and animosity between the North and the South.[60] A new policy of what was previously considered to be the First and the Second Worlds towards the Third World has to elaborated to replace the current non-policy. The character of North-South relations in the emerging international system will to a great extent determine the character of the international system as a whole.

Chinese communism, if it can properly be called communism at all, will hardly replace the 'real socialism' led by the Soviet Union as a counter-balance to the Western countries; but its uncertain future presents a big challenge, if not a threat, to the rest of the world. What will happen in China after the ideological lacquer vanishes is rather unclear. Whether it will be a relatively prosperous and powerful country pursuing pragmatic national interests in the world, or whether it will become a kind of super-state with a complex of the Middle Empire, or something else, is hardly foreseeable. In any case, China will be the most crucial actor in any future international system.

One of the threats to the stability of the emerging international system stems from the instability of the internal orders of many states. Barry Buzan is right in concluding that 'so long as weak states constitute a significant proportion of the international community, high levels of insecurity in much of the system will be unavoidable'.[61] Jervis sees the greatest danger to the peace and stability of Western Europe, and by extension to the United States, in 'large scale violence – either international or civil – in Eastern Europe and the Soviet Union'.[62]

Indeed, the stability of the international system, and especially of its European component, depends on the characteristics and stability of the new states which have emerged in territories of the former Soviet Union.

The Cold War ended with the collapse of one of the adversaries. This former adversary most probably will remain one of the major actors of the international system, but is now in a state of disarray which affects the whole world. Therefore, it is opportune to pay special attention to the prospects of the country which continues the existence of the erstwhile USSR – Russia.

RUSSIA – A PROBLEM OR SOLUTION?

One of the conundrums which no doubt will considerably influence the fate of the international system is the future of Russia. Usually the dilemma is formulated in the following way: will Russia become a democratic country which cooperates with other democracies in the resolution of complicated world issues or will it return to some kind of totalitarianism, be it of communist, nationalist, or of some other colour.

Lawrence Freedman writes that 'Russia is more likely to be part of the problem than the solution'.[63] Is it really so or will Russia perhaps be both?

The world is not only watching the developments in Russia with anxiety, but is trying to influence them in a positive direction. As President Clinton put it during the Vancouver summit: 'It is the self-interest and high duty of the world's democracies to stand by Russia's democratic reformers in their new hour of challenge.'[64]

Of course, it is very difficult to foresee what direction events in Russia will take at the end of the day. But without going into great detail, it is highly improbable that any of the two extreme options referred to above will materialize. On the one hand, reforms in Russia, notwithstanding all the difficulties and even backlashes, have gone far enough to allow us to conclude that the threat of the return to communism is practically impossible. But Russia is and, at least in the near future, will remain, rather unstable. The competition between the various political forces in Russia as well as between the federal authorities and its different regions is not yet over and it will certainly create enormous problems, not only for the country itself but for many other states as well.

Because of its huge problems and its historical traditions one would hardly expect that Russia will quickly become a stable democratic country like, say, the West European democracies.

One of the tenets of Marxism-Leninism asserted that not all countries had to go through all the stages of historic development from slave-owning societies up to socialism and communism. Some 'lucky' ones could transform 'from feudalism to socialism directly by-passing the capitalist stage of development'. The Soviet Central Asian republics and Mongolia were usually given as examples. One of the conditions of such a transformation was considered to be the vicinity and assistance of 'brotherly socialist countries', which in practice meant that 'Big Brother' served the role of the 'dictatorship of the proletariat' in the absence of any proletariat in a given country.

Applying this formula to current developments in the former Soviet Union and Eastern Europe, it is possible to predict that some smaller former totalitarian countries or parts of them will relatively quickly create market economies and become more or less democratic and human-rights-friendly states. The vicinity and assistance of Western countries and their organizations, and the inclusion of new or renewed countries in these organizations, can play a decisive role in this process. But even in the cases of such lucky states it will take time and effort, and nationalism and inter-ethnic problems will be serious obstacles to hinder the achievement of their goals. Russia's case is much more complicated.

It seems to me that Russia, because of the dimensions of its problems, shows much more clearly than other countries in a comparable situation that the transition from totalitarianism to democracy can hardly be a direct and easy one. The dismantling of totalitarian structures did not, and one may now conclude, could not, lead directly and quickly to democracy. Though there have been, of course, many positive achievements (and the dismantling of the totalitarian empire is certainly the most important among them), the collapse of the totalitarian system has also led to disorder in the country.[65] Such an environment is hardly conducive to the creation and development of democracy and democratic institutions. The current economic, political and social situation contributes to the difficulties as well.

In order to cope with the situation a strong executive power is needed in Russia. This in itself does not, of course, automatically exclude democracy, but under the circumstances there are some arguments for the view that 'an (enlightened) authoritarian regime is more or less foreordained'.[66] The consolidation of the federal executive power at the expense of the legislative branch and regional authorities after the suppression of the October 1993 revolt and the adoption of the new Constitution may be beneficial for economic reforms, the success of which, at the end of the day is also the best guarantee of democracy in the country. At the same time it puts strains on the very process of democratization. But even this does not necessarily mean, as Hyland writes, that in Russia 'the eventual revival of an autocratic state, probably well armed and potentially hostile toward its neighbours'[67] is more likely.

There is a rather strong democratic and intellectual potential in Russia and, it seems to me, the Western mass media is not always right in portraying those who do not unreservedly agree with recipes prescribed by the IMF as non-democrats. President Yeltsin made the same mistake, for example, at the end of 1992 – beginning of 1993, in the power-struggle with the Congress of People's Deputies. Migranjan seems to be right in observing that Yeltsin's advisers and ministers succeeded in persuading him that there was no substantial difference between the political programmes of the 'Civic Union' and the 'Front of National Salvation'.[68] Lenin's famous formula that 'those who are not with us are against us', applied in this case by President Yeltsin, proved once more to be wrong. Such an approach only enhanced the position of hard-liners in the Russian Parliament.

One of the factors making any prediction of Russia's future even more difficult is the relationship between the political regime of the country and its federal structure. On the one hand, the presence of numerous sub-units claiming more powers and desirous to be called 'sovereign states' and 'subjects of international law' creates dangers of secessionism, which may result, if not in civil wars, then at least in ineffective governance, further disruption of economic relations and slow down of economic reforms. But on the other hand, the inevitability of the federal structure for Russia speaks in favour of democratization rather than some kind of strong authoritarian rule. The USSR, notwithstanding the fact that it was nominally called a federation, was in reality a very centralized unitary state. And it could not have been otherwise. Totalitarianism and genuine federalism are incompatible. Now Russia's future as a state seems to lie in her genuine federal structure.

During the period of struggle between the President and the Supreme Soviet, which lasted until the dissolution of the latter in autumn 1993, both central bodies were vying for the support of the regions and republics of Russia and therefore made significant concessions to them. But the reverse trend, which began to show immediately after the tragic events in Moscow in October 1993 and which found its reflection in the new Constitution, does not mean that Russia will return to the unitarism of the Soviet period. Certain balances of power between the central authorities and regional authorities, which may change from time to time, will probably be a continuous feature of the Russian Federation.

Attempts to rule with a strong hand from Moscow over all regions may be even fraught with a threat of the dissolution of Russia. It seems that President Yeltsin understands this well. Therefore, federalism in Russia, though sometimes making the adoption and implementation of reforms more difficult, could at the same time be one of the remedies against the emergence of authoritarian rule from the centre.

On 21 September 1993 Yeltsin did indeed act in an authoritarian way by dissolving Parliament and fixing new elections for December. In his TV address to the Russian people the President stated that the security of Russia and its peoples is more precious than a formal obedience to contrary norms created by legislature which has finally discredited itself.[69]

The Russian Constitutional Court found this act unconstitutional under the Russian (Soviet) 1978 Constitution (1993 edition). According to this document the President did not have the authority to dissolve either the Congress of People's Deputies or the Supreme Soviet.

I would not be so categorical in assessing the constitutionality of the act of President Yeltsin. The Constitution which had been amended many times by the Congress of People's Deputies had become a document full of internal contradictions and had led the country into a dead end. Also, the Parliament which was elected when Russia was still part of the Soviet Union had lost its credibility and had become the major obstacle in the way of economic reforms. In the April 1993 referendum the majority of Russians expressed their support for Yeltsin and his reforms and 63 per cent of those who voted said 'Yes' to the question 'Do you think it necessary to have early parliamentary elections?'[70]

Though Yeltsin took more than a small risk not only for himself but for the country as well, and clearly circumvented the black letter of the Constitution, I think that it would be an extreme normativism to declare his behaviour illegal.

Jurists in Ancient Rome used to say: *fiat justicia, pereat mundus*. In the case of Russia this would have sounded something like: long life to the 1978 Constitution (1993 edition) even if Russia perishes. But it would really be a distortion of the very idea of law to find something justifiable from the point of politics and morality or to say, like *The Economist* did, that 'Mr Yeltsin's gamble this week is the least risky – perhaps the only – way of stopping the slide into chaos',[71] and at the same time find these very acts illegal. This would mean, on the one hand, that law is something rather remote from reality and, on the other, that a text of a legal act, whatever its content, is law.

Different forces in Russia are trying to foresee its future and to propose different ways and directions for its development. No doubt this is normal. What seems worrying is that many influential forces are still trying to find a special way of development for Russia, which should be quite different from the way in which other countries have developed. What they mean is that Russia cannot automatically copy the experience of other states, these being different, and that it has to take into account its geographic and geo-political position, traditions and many other factors. This would be quite natural. But there is also a search for a grand national idea, for a certain Russian messianism. Russia has to have a certain predestination which is usually formulated in rather irrational terms. As a famous Russian poet of the second half of the nineteenth century, Fiodor Tjutchev wrote: one cannot understand Russia by one's mind, or gauge it by a common yardstick, she has a special stance – one can only believe in Russia.[72] Lev Kopelev – a Russian writer and dissident who spent years in Soviet labour camps and had to leave the USSR – wrote that:

The Russian idea at the turn of the millennium is not simply a national or a nation-state idea, but it is at the same time a global idea of the salvation of mankind and salvation of life on earth.[73]

Vladislavlev, one of leaders of the influential 'Civic Union', and Karaganov, one of Yeltsin's advisers, assert that 'the Russian idea or, better, the idea of Russia is a powerful idea but it has not yet been properly formulated'.[74]

Sergei Stankevich, a policy adviser to Yeltsin, writes that Russia's mission in the world is to initiate and support a multilateral dialogue of cultures and civilizations, and states: 'Russia the conciliator, Russia connecting, Russia combining.'[75]

Eldis Pozdniakov, who has published many articles on the future of Russia from the point of view of a Russian nationalist, writes that there would be few in Russia for whom the words 'Russia is a great power' would not be natural and even commonplace, on which it is not even necessary to deliberate. He continues: 'There were times which were even worse than the time Russia faces now, but it has always overcome difficulties and remained a great power'. Most importantly, he writes, such confidence in Russia is in the genes of the Russians, it is imbibed with their mother's milk. 'No proofs are needed to confirm this. Such proofs can even destroy everything'.[76]

Certainly, it is difficult to have a comprehensive understanding of a country, especially one as large as Russia. But how can one believe in it without first understanding it? Notwithstanding all its historical vicissitudes (and what country does not have its vicissitudes) and its seventy years of the communist experiment, I think that Russia remains comprehensible, though, naturally, great intellectual efforts are necessary in order to understand it.

What democratic politicians in Russia are trying to do is to make a normal country of Russia – naturally, a big country, and also a powerful one, even a superpower, but most importantly a normal one without messianic irrational and hardly comprehensible predestinations.

The new Constitution of Russia adopted by the referendum in December 1993 states that the Russian Federation (or Russia) is a democratic rule of law country with a republican form of government; that the individual, his or her rights and freedoms are the supreme value of the Russian Federation; and that the recognition, observance and protection of inalienable rights and freedoms is a duty of the state. Of course this cannot be taken as a statement of fact, but even as an aspiration and a constitutional principle it sounds quite promising.

A document called 'On the concept of the foreign policy doctrine of

Russia', elaborated by the Council of Foreign Policy headed by Foreign Minister Kozyrev and published in January 1993 in Moscow,[77] asserts, *inter alia*, that the foreign policy of Russia must conform to its national interests, guarantee sovereignty, independence, and the territorial integrity of the state, enhance its security in all aspects and contribute to the resurgence of Russia as a democratic country. Priority should be given to the interests of every human being, the rights of individuals and minorities. Russia leaves behind for good the previous global division of the world and establishes its relations with other countries on the basis of global cooperation governed by international law. Relations of partnership and alliance should be developed with Western countries on the basis of shared democratic values.

However, the basic guidelines of the foreign policy of the Russian Federation approved in April 1993 by the Russian Security Council chaired by Yeltsin, are less idealistic and contain more elements of *realpolitik*.[78] They state that Russia, notwithstanding the crisis, remains a great power because of her potential influence as well as responsibilities. Russia is responsible not only for the new world order, but especially she has to be seen as a guarantor of stability in the territories of the former USSR.[79]

The interests of Russia, according to the document, lie in the closest possible integration, on a voluntary basis, of the former Soviet republics in all respects. Russia is also interested in the strengthening of the external borders of the Commonwealth of Independent States.[80]

There is probably nothing surprising in these pretensions of Russia, taking into account her history and potential. At the same time the former Soviet republics, which once were parts of the Russian, and then the Soviet, Empire can hardly be expected to wholeheartedly welcome Russia's role as a guarantor of their stability.

Therefore, even if Russia continues her market reforms and democratic processes this will not mean that she will always be a solution and not a problem for other countries. Russia will remain a problem first of all for her neighbours. Its solution depends equally on Russia as well as on these neighbours. On the one hand, the foreign policy of Russia is not always sensitive enough towards the newly independent states which were part of the Russian and Soviet empire. And for many Russians, for politicians as well as for men in the street, it is difficult to come to grips with the new reality that, for example, Ukraine or Belorussia are foreign countries, or that Crimea does not belong to Russia. And Russia has to understand that its behaviour, at least in the near future, will be looked at by them with suspicion even if there are no real grounds for it.

Russia's initiatives on peace-keeping in the territories of the former

Soviet Union are sometimes regarded by the newly independent states as an unwillingness to leave behind Soviet imperial ambitions, though this may not be the case and Russia may be genuinely concerned with peace near its borders. But the behaviour of Russian troops, in Moldova and Abkhazia for example, has exacerbated suspicions about Russia's real intentions.

In February 1993 Yeltsin, in his address to a Civic Union forum for example, said that 'the time has come for distinguished international organizations, including the UN, to grant Russia special powers, as a guarantor of peace and stability in the former regions of the USSR'.[81] The reaction from the former Soviet republics was, from my point of view, quite predictable. The Ukrainian Foreign Ministry, for example, issued a statement warning that practical implementation of Yeltsin's concept 'is likely to produce blatant violations of all the existing norms of international law'.[82]

Even Russia's activism in keeping together and making more effective the Commonwealth of Independent States (CIS) is seen by smaller partners as an effort to preserve something from the erstwhile USSR. (On the Russian policy towards so-called 'near abroad', see Chapter 3, pp. 113–4). Shirinovsky's phenomenon is even more worrying.

On the other hand, 'the great danger is that the republics that seceded might prove increasingly recalcitrant in their nationalist intoxication, unwilling to accommodate Russian legitimate interests'.[83] It will be very difficult for both sides to learn how to build good-neighbourly relations between them. And one of the reasons for concern lies in the fact that, besides the existence of the democratic potential, there is another quite powerful tendency in Russia.

Many of those who think that Russia's predestination is to be completely different from other countries, especially from Western ones, have a strong nostalgia for the glorious past. And if a return to the communist past is hardly a realistic perspective, various messianistic (which often is tantamount to imperialistic) notes are still evident in the foreign policy of Russia.

Pozdniakov, whose views are typical and are expressed rather vigorously in most respectable Russian journals, writes that 'one of the major reasons [for all the calamities in Russia] in 1917 as well as in the current period seems to be the militant striving of some forces in Russia to squeeze Russia into the Procrustean bed of Western schemes'.[84] But according to him, 'Russia does not belong to Europe as to its spirit, culture, religion, morals, and mentality.'[85]

He even tries to glorify not only the Russian Empire which, from his point of view, was quite different from other empires in the sense that it was not an artificial but a natural or organic one. It created an order in which all internecine wars were absolutely eliminated. And he concludes: 'an empire is . . . a reality which is much more serious and fundamental than democracy'.[86]

Russian nationalists with imperial ambitions are dangerous indeed, not only for the fledgling democratic developments of Russia; they constitute a threat for other countries as well.

Russia is certainly a European country, if not so much by reason of its geography, then much more because of its culture and mentality. And the Russian Empire was not so different from other empires. And, hopefully, democracy, notwithstanding the scarcity of democratic traditions in Russia, is not a complete *terra incognita* for the Russian mentality.

Although agreeing with Samuel Huntington that the disappearance of an ideological division has caused the re-emergence of a cultural or civilizational division I do not think that the fault-line in Europe lies 'between Western Christianity, on the one hand, and Orthodox Christianity and Islam, on the other'.[87] The main difference between Russia and other European states is not cultural or civilizational. Western Christianity's division into Catholics and Protestants is of the same significance as the division into Western and Orthodox Christianity. It is difficult to see why the cultural differences, say, between the Swedes and Italians are smaller than those between, for instance, the Russians and the French. What makes Russia really different is, of course, its size and geography, not culture or mentality.

Certainly, Russia contains rather significant Turkic and Muslim components (e.g. the Tartars, Bashkirs). But at the same time, and this may even be surprising taking into account that there are many ethnically based sub-units in Russia which claim their sovereignty, Russia is ethnically one of the most homogeneous Soviet successor states – 81.5 per cent of its population are ethnic Russians.[88] The exaggeration of Russia's cultural or even civilizational differences from those of other European countries, which, most importantly, is simply untrue, well serves those Russian nationalists who yearn for the lost empire. I think that Jeane Kirkpatrick is much closer to the truth when she writes:

> And what is Russia if not 'Western'? The East/West designation of the Cold War made sense in a European context, but in a global context Slavic/Orthodox people are Europeans who share in Western culture. Orthodox theology and liturgy, Leninism and Tolstoy are expressions of Western culture.[89]

The struggle between these two main tendencies in the internal development of Russia – one towards democracy and normalcy, on the one hand, and the search for a special mission (and missions are always carried out not at home but abroad), on the other – will eventually determine her place in the new world and, to a significant extent, also important characteristics of this world.

But it seems that neither of these tendencies will prevail in a clear-cut or absolute way. They are deeply rooted, both in the history of Russia (e.g. the perennial dispute between Westernizers and Slavophiles) and also in her geographic, geo-political and strategic position and interests. These tendencies will inevitably influence Russia's domestic and foreign policy in the future, with the foreign policy most probably being a combination of or a compromise between the European (Western) and Eurasian visions of the role of Russia in the world.

In his speech in London on 27 October 1993, the Foreign Minister of Russia, Andrei Kozyrev, declared that 'the historic, national and state interests [note that national and state interests are not considered as one and the same thing] of the Russians' lie in a United Europe.[90] At the same time he opined that 'this brings into sharper positive contrast the fact that Russia is a great Eurasian power with wide-reaching global interests'.[91]

However, there is not only a sharp contrast, but an obvious and significant contradiction in such a vision of the role of Russia. This, of course, is not only a contradiction in mentality but, more importantly, also a contradiction in reality, which will inevitably put strains on Russia's foreign policy. I think that Russia's 'Europeanness' is, at least to a certain extent, similar to the Europeanness of Great Britain in the seventeenth and eighteenth centuries, and especially to that of the United States today. In other words, Russia has one leg in Europe and one leg beyond it.

The fact that Russia supported some controversial foreign policy actions of the USA without reservations (e.g. the bombardment of Baghdad in June 1993) is hardly due just to temporary weakness. A more important contributing factor is that she is probably preparing herself, initially, for the role of a Eurasian superpower, with that of a global superpower to follow in due course. If we wish to find comparisons for the future foreign policy of Russia in the foreign policies of other states, I think that some similarities with the foreign policy of the United States are probably the closest.

Russia will most likely continue to consider the so-called 'near abroad' (i.e. former Soviet republics), as her backyard – just as the US has done in respect of Latin America. A kind of Monroe Doctrine for the 'near abroad' is in the process of formation. Rather strong messianism is also common for both of these countries. If many Americans have the conviction that 'America has a particular obligation, almost a moral mandate, to set the world straight'[92] many – even among democrats in Russia, as we saw above – consider the mission of their country to be, if not the salvation of mankind, a bridge between or conciliator of different civilizations.

For Western countries, to the extent that they can influence developments in Russia, it is necessary that they help to bring Russia closer to Europe rather than alienate her. It is preferable and less costly to try to integrate Russia into European structures than to prepare for defence against her.

TOWARDS A LOOSE UNIVERSAL INTERNATIONAL SYSTEM?

The end of the Cold War has created a situation where different options are open for the development of the international system. Among these options the emerging international system has a good chance of approximating, if purposeful efforts are made by individual states, international organizations and interested transnational forces, to what Kaplan called 'the universal international system,[93] though I doubt very much that in the foreseeable future such a system will be the integrated system based on solidarity described by him.[94]

Why is a universal system, and not some kind of multipolar, hierarchical or even anarchical international system of the unit veto (all described by Kaplan as hypothetically possible), the probable international system of the future?

Some kind of hierarchical international system may seem quite plausible as the United States is now the only superpower in the world and undoubtedly the most powerful member of universal as well as of some regional organizations. But the USA or even the West as a whole can hardly establish an hierarchical international system. Joseph Nye, Jr writes:

Today, however, the definition of power is losing its emphasis on military force and conquest that marked earlier eras. The factors of technology, education, and economic growth are becoming more significant in international power, while geography, population, and raw materials are becoming somewhat less important.[95]

And 'the problem for the United States will be less the rising challenge of another major power than a general diffusion of power', and

although the United States still has leverage over particular countries, it has far less leverage over the system as a whole. It is less well-placed to attain its ends unilaterally, but it is not alone in this situation. All major states will have to confront the changing nature of power in world politics.[96]

Jervis writes that the configuration of the new world is so odd that we cannot easily determine the systems polarity:

> Is it unipolar because the United States is so much stronger than the nearest competitor, bipolar because of the distribution of military resources, tripolar because of an emerging united Europe, or multipolar because of the general dispersion of power? Thus even if polarity were a major determinant of world politics, it would be hard to tell what we should expect.[97]

The world had become quite different even before the collapse of communism. The emergence of global problems and the rising interdependence of all countries had already called for effective multilateral actions for many years. But political, ideological and military confrontation between the East and the West was considered by states as the most imminent threat for their survival, overshadowing all environmental, demographic, health, economic and other concerns. What the end of the Cold War has brought about is that now these and many other concerns (terrorism, narcotics, etc.) as well as new problems, created or exacerbated by the current chaotic situation in some countries and in the international system, can have their proper place in the agenda of the world community, which means a place not distorted by the 'main contradiction of the contemporary historical period'.

At the end of the twentieth century the world is undergoing at least two or maybe even three equally dramatic overlapping changes. One is the abrupt end of the Cold War era with its bipolar world, which is in the focus of this study, and the other is the more incremental but nevertheless rather pressing phenomenon of the emergence and aggravation of so called global problems. There may be a third equally dramatic, though less clear, development under way. This is the changing role of a nation-state in the international system, which was considered above. It may be, indeed, that the heyday of the so-called Westphalian model of the international system, which has been marked by the incontestable power of territorial states, is approaching its end – at least in some parts of the world.

On the one hand, the coincidence in time of these processes seems to further increase the complexity of the challenges mankind is facing. The demographic explosion in many Third World countries, the deterioration of their economic situation and environmental crises, were serious enough problems for the world community to tackle even before new difficulties were created by the collapse of the USSR and the following dramatic changes in Eastern Europe. But, on the other hand, is the end of the Cold War not a response by mankind to global challenges, such as environmental, economic or demographic crises? Does not the disappearance of the threat of the nuclear conflict between two rival military-political blocs bring mankind closer to the resolution of other challenges which until recently were overshadowed by the global confrontation between the East and the West and which therefore seemed, if not secondary from the point of view of 'high' politics, at least more remote from the point of view national security. Kennedy writes of global threats to mankind, saying that

> human beings are usually unwilling to make short-term sacrifices to achieve a distant (and uncertain) improvement in general good – and most politicians' perspectives are shorter still. Unlike traditional threats to national security, these dangers are less obvious and therefore less likely to induce a unified, determined response.[98]

This means that those in charge of national security issues in different states can perceive and have to learn to perceive these dangers as dangers for national security and react adequately.

Though the international community of states is now paying more attention and applying more resources to the immediate challenges stemming from the collapse of communism than to global problems, the end of the Cold War has removed one of the biggest obstacles for the resolution of these problems – ideological, political and military confrontation between the East and the West. The world simply could not afford to remain divided into two hostile political-military camps facing global challenges and threats.

The continuous proliferation of nuclear weapons, and the existence of authoritarian and anti-democratic regimes, means that there will be a threat of the emergence of what Kaplan called 'the unit veto international system', where many actors are capable of destroying each other. To prevent any possibility of the emergence of such an Hobbesian international system it is necessary for the world community not only to strengthen the regime of non-proliferation of nuclear weapons but actively to oppose existing or emerging dictatorships through multilateral efforts.

Neither the United States alone, nor even the Western countries together can cope with these problems without the support and co-operation of other states. Attempts to impose solutions, even if seen as beneficial for those upon whom they are imposed and undertaken with noble aims, usually engender counter-reaction and even resistance. Therefore cooperation among all the regions of the world is necessary, and this calls for more effective functioning of universal international organizations and international law.

The universality of the emerging international system does not mean that all states will cooperate equally and support the maintenance and development of such a system. There will inevitably be leaders and enthusiasts for it, as well as reluctant followers and even outcasts or opponents. There will be the centre and the periphery of the system, and such a situation will certainly constitute a threat to its stability. In certain domains (e.g. the world economy) the system will be multi-polar. Lawrence Freedman writes that 'the West is now composed of three distinct poles – North America, the European Community and Japan' and that 'each of these poles acts as a regional magnet – the United States for the countries of Latin America and the Caribbean, Japan for East Asia, and the EC for central and eastern Europe and, to some extent, North Africa'.[99] But the emergence of certain regions where the pull of some Western countries and their special interests are especially felt does not necessarily lead to fragmentation of the world. The actions of the world community of states, often under the aegis of the UN or other international organizations, in the former Yugoslavia and the USSR, Somalia, Cambodia or other parts of the world which, it is true, are not always effective and satisfactory, nevertheless show that the world has become too small to be frag-mented. Regional approaches and organizations do not run counter to, but will, on the contrary, be essential for the functioning of a universal international system.

The universality of the international system is by no means tanta-mount to its centralization. The principle of 'subsidiarity' in the universal system should be much stronger than that provided for in the Maastricht treaty. What would be best accomplished at the regional, sub-regional or domestic levels should be dealt with at these levels. From my point of view, ideas of a world government are not only utopian but also rather dangerous. As Hedley Bull noted:

> The system of plurality of sovereign states gives rise to classic dangers, but these have to be reckoned against the dangers inherent in the attempt to contain disparate communities within the framework of a single government. It may be argued that world order at the present time is best served by living with the former dangers rather than by attempting to face the latter.[100]

I doubt very much whether there will ever be something like a world government. The world is simply too complicated to be governed from one centre. But the idea of the international system comprising states, inter-governmental bodies, non governmental organizations, individuals, private corporations and other different groups participating in international relations which will have more effective international law and order seems to be a feasible reality.

The new international system, contours of which seem to be emerging out of the current chaotic state of the transitional period, may be called a universal international system because its multipolarity in some areas will probably not be a ubiquitous or dominant feature of the system. Buzan, Jones and Little write that this time 'multipolarity is occurring on a truly planetary scale, and there are strong signs that the substantial ideological harmony among the major powers will serve as the foundation for something like a global concert.'[101] But the lack of solidarity between all parts of the system, the presence of the centre and the periphery (even the zones of peace and zones of turmoil), and the low degree of integration of the system as a whole, all seem to indicate that, at least in the near future, this system will be a loose universal system.

Having quoted Bull, it is impossible for an international lawyer writing also about international relations to by-pass his ideas concerning international society. Not only because Bull was one of those rare specialists on international relations theory who extended his hand to international law, but mainly because his ideas concerning the international society have a better chance of being realized after the Cold War than before or during it. The international society, as described by Bull, not only presupposes international law, but is a proper environment for it.

If a system of states is formed simply by the interactions of states

[a] society of states (or international society) exists when a group of states, conscious of certain common interests and common values, form a society in the sense that they conceive themselves to be bound by a common set of rules in their relations with one another, and share in the working of common institutions.[102]

Bull writes that 'the element of international society has always been present in the modern international system'.[103]

Of course, in the Cold War international system there were common interests and even certain shared values. But the interests were usually weak and controversial, while the values were often shared only at the most abstract level. The end of the sharp division of the world, which was first of all a division concerning different basic societal values, means that the international system will quite realistically have stronger 'societal' elements.

This does not, of course, mean that all states will share all values equally, let alone actively support them. But in the pluralist but universal international system there will hopefully be more room for shared values and common interests than in the sharply divided bipolar world. This will be conducive to the development of international law and especially to its implementation, as neither a balance of fear nor even a balance of interests can form, without a certain minimum of shared values, an adequate basis for an effective legal system. As Nguyen Quoc Dinh, Patrick Daillier and Allan Pellet correctly wrote 'un état de tension caractériserait fondamentalement la vie en societé basée uniquement sur l'intérêt.'[104]

CHALLENGES AND OPPORTUNITIES FOR INTERNATIONAL LAW

What will be the fate of international law in the new situation? Is it ready to respond to new challenges? What can be done to make it more effective?

Some of these questions will be dealt with in detail in the following chapters where concrete international law issues will be analysed. Here I would like only to make some general observations concerning the possible role of international law and organizations in the current transitional period and in the emerging international system.

Certain characteristics of the emerging international system which were outlined above are directly relevant to the functioning of international law. Such developments as the expansion of democratic countries and the relative increase of their influence; an ideologically and culturally different, but not sharply divided, international system which, at the same time, is less disciplined and more volatile and unstable; the absence of one single dominant security threat and the presence of lesser but multiple security concerns (nationalism, civil wars, terrorism, threat of the proliferation of nuclear weapons, environmental and demographic crises, etc.) inevitably influence the content and especially the functioning of international law.

International law: a strait-jacket or guide for international relations?

The fact that the emerging world will not be so sharply divided into equally powerful and irreconcilable political, economic and ideological systems means that in the future the majority (not all, of course) of actors in the international system will hopefully be able to reach a consensus on what values such as peace, democracy, human dignity, etc. really mean. And there will be less room for situations in which one person's terrorist is another person's freedom-fighter.

In these circumstances, more contextual and innovative approaches to the interpretation and application of international law become possible and often inevitable. I wrote above that no single intellectual approach to international law, and indeed to international relations, can satisfactorily and comprehensively explain this complex phenomenon and that therefore interdisciplinary research and a multiplicity of intellectual approaches become necessary, especially at times of revolutionary changes in the international system. How does this general assumption apply to international law in the current circumstances?

Notwithstanding a multiplicity of doctrines of international law, I think that there are two major trends: the positivist or normativist approach, and the contextual approach, which sees international law as a kind of social engineering. Among the latter, the most prominent is the policy-oriented approach or the New Haven school of international law. This approach makes purposeful efforts to take account of all relevant factors and have as comprehensive as possible an analysis of international law. The major shortcoming of the policy-oriented approach consists, probably, in its consideration of itself as the only true and comprehensive approach, which is completely different from other approaches.

While the normative approach considers international law to be 'a dense, intricate body of rules and practices'[105] the policy oriented approach conceives international law

> not merely in terms of the rules that officials and others use in explaining and justifying decision, but rather as decision itself, combining both authority and control, and constituting a continuous flow of decision of transnational origin and impact. Authority would be conceived in terms of community expectations about future decision, and control in terms of actual participation in decision.[106]

A very important place in the policy-oriented approach belongs to the 'comprehensive set of goal values which should have decisive influence in decision-making.

Though it seems to me that the majority of contemporary international lawyers who may be considered as normativists, because they conceive international law mainly as a body of norms, hardly ever abstract their research from social reality. Kelsen's 'pure theory of law' has few adherents nowadays. On the other hand, clear policy-oriented international lawyers in their research of concrete issues of international law often pay due respect to rules of law and legal texts. Of course, emphasis is usually different and this is not without importance. The policy oriented approach makes comprehensive, systematic, and conscious efforts to take into account all relevant factors in decision-making in the international arena.

In many cases this difference in approach plays, from my point of view, an insignificant role in resolving concrete issues. But in politically the most sensitive areas, where different principles and norms usually govern the same matter and often indicate different outcomes, where 'grey legal areas' are common, this difference in approach becomes rather relevant. And it seems that in the universal (which is by no means uniform) international system, characterized not only by the absence of the old sharp ideological and political division of the world but also by volatility and rapid changes, the policy-oriented approach which in the dichotomized world often led to situations where everybody had their own international law, will be quite adequate – especially if we take into account that adherents of this approach have in practice usually paid much more respect to formal sources of international law than they have done in their theoretical works. Thus, Professor Reisman, who is undoubtedly one of the most prominent representatives of the policy-oriented approach to international law, has often shown great respect for international treaties and customary norms. For example, in his article concerning the refusal by the American authorities to grant a visa to Yasser Arafat, Reisman quotes different articles of the Agreement between the UN and the US regarding the Headquarters of the UN of 1947, as well as respective US statutes, and concludes that 'the visa refusal had neither a treaty nor a statutory basis'[107] and that '[t]he U.S. action in the Arafat visa affair violated the nation's conventional and customary obligations'.[108] Professor Reisman did not refer to the higher values which, probably, may have justified, at least from the point of view of many people, the refusal to grant a visa to a man who at that time was considered by the American authorities as a terrorist. Such an example shows that there are no insurmountable differences between the policy-oriented approach and other, more traditional, approaches to international law.

As the Cold War international system was split into two hostile camps, with different, often irreconcilable, systems of values, orientation to these values in the foreign policy behaviour of states meant, for example, that while the Soviet Union intervened in Czechoslovakia in 1968 to uphold socialism against popular revolt, easily sacrificing the

'abstract bourgeois principles of non-interference and self determination',[109] the USA, as we saw, put anti-communism higher than
democracy when intervening in Latin American countries.

It is hardly surprising that one of the most important principles of
international law, which suffered heavily in the divided world, was the
prohibition on the use of force in international relations.

The Soviet violations of the principle of non-use of force in 1956
against Hungary, and especially in 1968 (together with four other
socialist countries) against Czechoslovakia, led to the emergence of the
so-called 'Brezhnev doctrine' under which the USSR and other socialist
states claimed their right to intervene, if necessary by force, in the case
of threats to socialism in fellow-socialist countries. The interests of
socialism were to have unconditional priority over norms of international law, such as respect for sovereignty which was dubbed then 'an
abstract bourgeois rule'.[110]

The Soviet aggression against Afghanistan in 1979 was justified by
the Soviet authorities as collective self-defence and intervention by
invitation. Though the term was not used by the Soviets at that time,
repeated invitations by the Afghan authorities were referred to as one of
the reasons for the intervention.[111]

All these acts, like the United States interventions in the Dominican
Republic in 1965, Grenada in 1983 or Nicaragua in the 1980s,
undermined the principle of non-use of force. Interestingly, the invitations by the Czechs or Afghans to justify the Soviet interventions, and
the invitation from Grenada extended to the Americans, were very
similar in the sense that they did not proceed from competent authorities
and were received *ex post facto*.[112] The Johnson and Reagan doctrines,
like the Brezhnev doctrine, had primacy over and distorted international
law. For instance, President Reagan declared that '[s]upport for freedom
fighters is self-defense and totally consistent with the OAS and UN
Charters'.[113]

This reminds me very much of the approach of Evgenii Korovin, one
of the first Soviet international lawyers, who in the 1920s wrote:

The sharply negative attitude of working people of Russia towards
any type of interventionist intentions of the Entente is not a rejection
of intervention as a method of class struggle, but a rejection and
condemnation of that particular intervention. Under certain conditions intervention might become a powerful instrument of progress,
a surgical interference facilitating the pangs of childbirth of a new
world, but in the hands of the Entente it was a synonym of the most
flagrant retrogradation.[114]

Though the Soviet Union later never openly espoused such an approach to intervention, in practice this double standard was used very often. I am not thereby trying to say that intervention cannot ever lead to positive results or even be necessary. But in the dichotomized world, with sharply different values and visions of the future, unilateral interventions more often than not were contrary even to values espoused by intervening states themselves.

Therefore, Jean Kirkpatrick and Allan Gerson were not so wrong when they wrote:

> Like most American 'doctrines', the Reagan Doctrine emerged in response to circumstances: it was developed in response to the Soviets' objective of a global empire and in response to Soviet claims of legitimacy in their imperial venture embodied in the Brezhnev Doctrine and the doctrine of 'national liberation wars'.[115]

It is interesting to note that closed totalitarian states, like the Soviet Union, and open societies, for example, the USA, differed in their approach to international law even when they both tried to use its norms for their own narrow and often messianic ends. Soviet diplomacy as well as its legal doctrine gave, for example, quite a restrictive and strict interpretation of the right to use force in international relations. According to the Soviet approach, use of military force was permitted only in two types of situations: by decision of the UN Security Council under article 42 of the UN Charter, or as an act of individual or collective self-defence against armed attack under article 51 of the Charter (and an armed attack was construed in the narrowest sense).[116]

Nevertheless the Soviet Union used military force in flagrant violation of international law as it stood, and even more as it was interpreted by Soviet diplomacy and doctrine: in 1956 against Hungary, in 1968 against Czechoslovakia and in 1979 in Afghanistan. Legal norms were not stretched to make them conform to the facts, but the very facts were denied or distorted. In a closed society this was possible. The public opinion of these societies, at least, did not question the lawfulness of Soviet actions.

The same was not possible in an open society. The use of force by the United States in the Dominican Republic in 1965, against Nicaragua in 1980s, Grenada in 1983 or Panama in 1989 could not be denied or justified in the light of the strict interpretation of international law prohibiting the use of force. International law had to be stretched to cover the actions undertaken by the USA. The doctrines of intervention by invitation, humanitarian intervention or intervention to protect the lives and property of American citizens became not only widely accepted but also abused by American diplomacy and were supported by some prominent international lawyers.[117]

Was it possible in such an international system, where force was used not only in the furtherance of different, conflicting values but where values themselves were subordinated to the struggle with world communism or with capitalist imperialism, to use a policy – or value-oriented approach to international law?

Rosalyn Higgins writes:

> Where there is ambiguity or uncertainty, the policy directed choice can properly be made. Some will say that, in a decentralized legal order, to allow one party to interpret the law to achieve desirable outcomes merely will allow another, less scrupulous party to claim to do the same. I am not greatly impressed with that argument. There is no escaping the duty that each and every one of us have to test the validity of legal claims. We will each know which are intellectually supportable and which are not, and it is a chimera to suppose that, if only international law is perceived as the application of neutral rules, it will then only be invoked in an unbiased manner.[118]

It was, of course, perfectly possible that even in an ideologically divided world lawyers, politicians or statesmen could test for themselves the validity of the legal claims of parties to a dispute and also to find which of them were intellectually supportable and which were not. But it was also quite probable, and in practice happened often, that such a test could lead to completely different results. And it was not only ideological opponents who tested the validity of such claims differently. Following, for instance, the ICJ judgment on the Nicaragua case, American international lawyers were divided almost evenly into those who thought that the US Government had violated international law *vis-à-vis* Nicaragua and generally agreed with the judgment of the ICJ, and those who found no violation on the part of the USA.[119]

There is nothing wrong or even surprising in the fact that academics differ among themselves. But states, and not only those who belonged to the opposite political-military blocs, also had different legal evaluations of politically important and sensitive acts.[120] In the Cold War international system this often meant that not only academic international lawyers but also states had their own international law.

I am not suggesting that a rule – oriented approach to international law, especially to its norms purported to regulate the use of force, would have been a proper solution. First of all there were no clear, concrete and non-controversial rules governing the use of force. And there could not have been. States having different values could hardly be expected to agree on concrete rules concerning the attainment of these values. And even more importantly, though it is desirable and now probably possible to have some lacunae in the principle of non-use of force eliminated and some controversial points clarified, such principles of international law can never be put into the Procrustean bed of detailed rules. Therefore, I can only partly agree with Joseph Weiler who writes:

> The clearer the system's rules for evaluating the legality of use of force and the more sophisticated the legal techniques for applying these rules, the more difficult it will become to maintain this Kantian-like cleavage between action as it really is, and as it is claimed to be. If it were possible to ascertain in every instance precisely and unequivocally the legality or otherwise of action taken, it would not be possible to play the double game.[121]

Though it is desirable and now probably possible to have clearer and less controversial norms in some domains of international law, the application of norms governing the use of force and other similar politically sensitive issues always necessitates a serious contextual analysis of all issues concerned. In these domains we cannot have rules like those governing, for example, diplomatic immunities and privileges.

The end of the Cold War has at least significantly narrowed, if not eliminated, the reasons for such unilateral interventions and justificatory doctrines, and through multilateral decision-making it is also possible to narrow the gaps in the interpretation of the principle of the non-use of force.

But the norms of international law, especially in areas of high political importance, will hardly become as detailed and as 'normative' as the norms of domestic legal systems because in the international system there are considerably fewer participants in legal relations and their conduct is more individualized than that of the subjects of domestic legal systems. The behaviour of the former is often characterized by uniqueness and is less normative.

There are already some new developments discernible in the legal regulation of use of force in international relations.

Though it is not yet clear whether the current increase in civil wars will be a temporary phenomenon caused by the end of the Cold War, or whether this tendency will continue, it seems clear that the line between civil and international wars and consequently between internal and international use of force has become rather blurred.

The domestic use of force may have constituted a grave violation of human rights such as genocide, or may have threatened international security and peace, and therefore could have become a legitimate concern for the world community of states. But events in the former Yugoslavia, in the Caucasus and in the former Soviet Central Asia have shown that it is not always easy to make a distinction between internal and international armed conflicts. So the former US Secretary of State James Baker, even before the dissolution of Yugoslavia, spoke of 'aggression within Yugoslavia'.[122] Though from the point of view of existing norms of international law the term seems controversial, I think that international law should develop in order to cover internal use of force from many points of view, not only from that of international humanitarian law. For example, use of force against minorities (or under certain conditions by them) may be one of the cases governed by international law. The sharp distinction between the use of force across international borders and often much more brutal military operations within state boundaries is, it seems, a hangover from the times when states were the only subjects of international law and when what happened within a state constituted its internal affairs. Nowadays such a distinction looks too statist.

International law has to respond effectively to terrorism, especially to state-sponsored terrorism. The Cold War era international law could not find adequate responses. In this context, was the US bombing of Baghdad with Cruise missiles in June 1993 in response to the failed assassination attempt on the former President of the United States an adequate response to international terrorism? Does it correspond, if not to existing norms of international law, then at least to how these norms should develop in the emerging international system?

The US referred to their right to individual and collective self-defence under article 51 of the UN Charter.[123] Some states supported this action without reservations (Great Britain, Germany, Italy, Russia). The Russian Foreign Ministry, for example, stated: 'In the opinion of the Russian leadership, the US actions were justified as they stem from the right of any state to individual and collective self-defence in accordance with article 51 of the UN Charter'.[124]

The Russian characterization of the US raid as an act of self defence is even more interesting as the USSR, the predecessor of Russia, held, as we saw, a completely different view on self defence (in theory, not in practice). For example, in 1986 after the American attack on Libya in response to that country's involvement in international terrorism, Gorbachev accused the Reagan administration of poisoning the inter-national atmosphere.[125] Does Russia's radical change of attitude to-wards self-defence mean that Russia is simply following the United States as the latter is the only remaining superpower? Or does it mean that Russia is ready to use force, especially in neighbouring countries in order to respond to possible attacks against its citizens or other un-friendly acts against Russia?[126] I think that both scenarios are equally damaging for the emerging international order. Many countries con-demned the American raid. For example, the Arab League 'condemned the use of force without the sanction of the Security Council'.[127]

Of course, a terrorist attack may constitute an armed attack which justifies self-defence under article 51.[128] Though the Iraqi regime had recently committed an act of aggression, is guilty of gross human rights violations and often defies the UN sanctions, it seems that the assassin-ation attempt, if it was what it seemed to be, did not form 'a consistent pattern of violent terrorist action'[129] against the US and was not even presented by the United States as such. That kind of act would call for 'retaliatory' or 'punitive' self-defence doctrines which are unknown to international law.

The problem with such a response is also that it can be applied only by some states (e.g., the USA, Russia) against mainly, if not exclusively, Third World countries. Are the latter going to accept such a uni-directional (from the North to the South) use of force? Is this conducive for the promotion of the emerging world order?

Another principle of international law undergoing radical change (not without resistance, it is true) is non-interference in the internal affairs of states. Should we allow civil wars to devastate cities, villages and their populations; dictators to engage in genocide or mass killings of their subjects and thereby to comply with the principle of non-interference; or should we interfere in order to stop atrocities? When India intervened in Eastern Pakistan (Bangladesh) in 1971, Vietnam in Cambodia in 1978, and Tanzania in Uganda in 1979 these unilateral interventions were seen by many as illegal interventions in the internal affairs of other countries, even though humanitarian considerations played a role in all of them.[130] But it is true that in reality their role was only secondary. Gary Klintworth writes that:

> Vietnam, of course, did not undertake its long and costly occupation of Kampuchea for altruistic humanitarian motives. And nor did India, or Tanzania, undertake their respective actions just to rescue fellow human beings . . . While saving human beings from being killed was an inevitable consequence of intervention by Vietnam, and earlier by Tanzania and India, it was always a secondary consideration to the overriding priority imposed by concern for vital security interests.[131]

Unilateral interference for humanitarian purposes indeed often had motives far removed from humanitarian ones. But interference by or on the authorization of competent international bodies, which has become possible after the end of the Cold War (in the former Yugoslavia and Somalia, for example), may become one of the means of enforcement of international law. David Scheffer writes that

> a modern doctrine of humanitarian intervention should establish the legitimacy of certain types of non-forcible and forcible intervention undertaken without the express consent of the target country's government, but with collective authorization or, in some limited circumstances, unilaterally or multinationally for the purpose of defending or alleviating the mass suffering of people for whom no other alternative realistically exists.[132]

Of course, such a sharp surgical instrument as humanitarian intervention should be used with the utmost caution even if decisions are not taken unilaterally but through universal international organizations and in accordance with relevant procedural rules. The reason for such caution is not only that it is practically impossible for the world community to intervene in all internal conflicts which call for intervention (and inevitable selectiveness may raise the question of double standards), but even a perfectly lawful intervention with legitimate and noble aims may be counter-productive if all extralegal factors such as the reaction of the population on whose behalf the intervention is undertaken, the cost of the intervention in human lives, etc. are not taken into account.

The principle of non-intervention remains, and in the foreseeable future will remain, one of the fundamental principles of international law. But this principle, like other principles, is not absolute. This means that it does not prohibit intervention under every circumstance. This has hardly ever been the case. In the light of the development of international human rights law, and especially taking into account the fact that massive violation of rights and liberties in any country not only shock the conscience of mankind but encroach upon quite practical interests of other, especially neighbouring, states (problems of refugees, border issues, the necessity for a non-democratic country to have external enemies in order to suppress discontent at home, etc.), humanitarian intervention is not contrary to the non-intervention principle. The legality of a concrete intervention depends on the different modalities of the intervention (in what circumstances, on whose authorization, the effects of the intervention in the light of international law, etc.). Political considerations are intertwined in the legal assessment of a given intervention.

One of the lessons of a perfectly lawful intervention which was undertaken on morally irreproachable grounds – that of the intervention in Somalia – is that if political and even psychological factors are not properly taken account of, even a genuine international intervention may be seen by many of those on whose behalf an intervention is undertaken as an intervention of alien forces, and may even lead to the consolidation of powers of repressive regimes or warlords. Though these factors concern not so much the legality of an intervention but rather its political expediency, they should be taken no less seriously than legal considerations in the process of decision-making on issues of intervention. As these factors influence the outcome of an intervention to a considerable extent they also become legally relevant. Adam Roberts is right in saying that '[o]nly in rare circumstances can civil wars be ended by outside intervention, or democracy successfully imposed on a society with little experience of it'.[133]

Therefore, one may conclude that though intervention on humanitarian grounds in many circumstances would not be illegal *per se*, it will be nevertheless rather an exception than a rule in the future world.

Many states still put non-interference in internal affairs above even genuine humanitarian intervention. The Security Council Resolution No. 794 on Somalia, authorizing the UN interference in that country on humanitarian grounds, stresses 'the unique character of the present situation in Somalia',[134] which means that intervention on humanitarian grounds even on the authorization of the Security Council is not considered, at least by some members of the Security Council, as a normal remedy. As the uniqueness of the situation consisted in the absence of a government in Somalia at that time, one may conclude that for the world of governments it was simply a shock that there was no government in the country and therefore the world community of states agreed to intervene. Does this mean that had General Aideed been not a war-lord, but president or prime-minister, he could have killed and starved the population to death without any interference?

Interventions of member states of the Security Council during the special meeting of the Council in January 1991 also showed that countries such as China and India still emphasize sovereignty and non-interference more than human rights.[135] Joseph Nye, Jr is right when he says that 'among the staunchest defenders of the old system are the poorly integrated post-colonial states whose elites fear that new doctrines of multilateral intervention by the United Nations will infringe their sovereignty'.[136]

But there has been a clear tendency away from absolute non-interference, and the scope of matters which are essentially within domestic jurisdiction is constantly narrowing. The end of the Cold War will accelerate this process, though various dictators are still waging fierce rearguard battles for their 'right' to rule without interference.

'Clever' norms and legal procedures

Some of the features of the new international system will probably be greater flexibility, volatility, and even unpredictability. Lawrence Freedman is probably right asserting that

> attempts to make stability the central strategic value of the new age are doomed to continual disappointment. Any relevant framework must reflect the creative opportunities as well as the dangers inherent in perpetual instability. Policies and institutions are already coming to be judged by metaphors of adaptation and movement: flexibility, versatility, agility, resistance and pressure, pushes and drives.[137]

The new international system will therefore probably be more complex than the bipolar system, and there will not only be more actors but the roles of the actors will become more diverse.

Such a situation presents great challenges to international law, which like any legal system is better adapted to be an agent of stability and order rather that of change and flexibility. One of the very functions of law is to make social life more predictable.

Richard Falk observes that

> to the extent that change rather than stability is of prime concern, law tends to function in a regressive fashion, insulating and rigidifying existing domains of control, obscuring and rejecting demands for change, sustaining privileged positions, exonerating and insulating structures of inequality and domination from formal change.[138]

Of course, existing law sometimes may be an obstacle for necessary changes, especially when changes are profound and occur practically across the board.

To face these challenges there should be more room for 'clever' or 'sophist' norms in international law and their role in international decision-making should increase as more important decisions are taken not unilaterally, but in and by international organizations or according to procedures set up by international law. Thomas Franck has most convincingly explained the difference between, what he calls, 'idiot' norms, which lack fine-tuning and do not ask, for example, why or under what circumstances the behaviour is prohibited, and which give simple, single-minded solutions to all questions, regardless of their complexities, and 'sophist' rules, setting out standards of compliance which are measured in complex qualitative terms, or which are hedged by why and to whom exculpations. While the first category of norms lack the fine-tuning and are thus likely to be perceived – at their margins – as unreasonable and illegitimate in their demands, the second category of norms may be difficult to apply in practice.[139] The application of 'clever' norms always necessitates their contextual interpretation. As Franck himself rightly points out, '[w]ere it not for the lack of global agreement on the content of sophisticated rules incorporating *why* and *to whom* factors, and even more, the absence of credible institutional processes for applying such inevitably complex, textually indeterminate standards',[140] most international lawyers would probably reject 'idiot' norms and opt for 'sophist' or 'clever' norms wherever possible.

As we will see in the Chapter 4 of this book, the interpretation of the principle of non-interference in internal affairs as an 'idiot' rule in the case of the former Yugoslavia in the second half of 1991 and at the beginning of 1992 led, first to the inactivity of the world community of states, and then to the recognition of new entities as states in order to transform the internal conflict into an international one. Both approaches turned out to be wrong.

Principles of international law, such as non-use of force, non-interference in internal affairs, and self-determination can never be transformed into such 'idiot' rules like the requirement that nobody should cross the street when the red light shows.

Of course, the complex quality of most important norms of international law opens the way to manipulations, and Michel Virally is right in observing that:

> Cela pose un problem grave: celui de son [international law's] aptitude à resister à telles manipulation, car une elasticité excessive lui fairait perdre tout utilité pour ordonner les relations internationales par d'autres voies que celles des purs rapports de forces, qu'il reproduirait fidèlement (accusation qui lui est souvent adressée).[141]

My answer to this problem is the following. First, as we have seen, it has been possible to manipulate international law where there has been the political will to do so, even in cases when its norms were, in principle, interpreted rather strictly or normatively. Second, norms of international law which are too rigid or detailed and purport to govern international relations 'simple-mindedly' without taking all relevant extralegal factors into account, will be doomed to lag behind the changing reality and therefore would not be applied. Third, international law is in any case a part of international politics, being a normative and procedural expression of the latter. It is a model for international relations and it has to correspond to the basic characteristics and tendencies of development of these relations. It has to be 'better' than the international reality, but not idealistic nor out of touch with the reality it purports to govern.

One of the remedies against possible excessive manipulation of international law can be multilateral decision-making and the presence of international procedures through which decisions are taken. Therefore, the relative weight of procedural rules of international law will probably have to increase because, in situations where it will often be impossible to foresee in detail what to do and how to react to concrete new challenges, it will become more important to have procedures through which it is possible to make adequate decisions than to have ready rules of behaviour. As Higgins writes:

> We must expect in the international system an endless kaleidoscope of problems. Major changes in the international system – such as those we have witnessed in the last ten years – will change the pattern of the problems, but not eliminate the phenomenon. *International law is a process for resolving problems.* [Emphasis added.][142]

In the new emerging international system this aspect of international law will certainly become more and more prominent.

The universal international system necessarily has to rely much more upon international organizations, mechanisms and procedures. Power vacuums and the resulting disorder emerging after the collapse of the bipolar international system, which had a disciplining effect on international and even domestic relations, have to be filled by effective functioning of international organizations. Some institutional reforms may be necessary, but generally the ineffectiveness of international institutions does not lie in their normative or structural faults. The lack of political will[143] and opposite, often mutually excluding, visions of the world and its future are to be blamed.[144]

One of most important reforms required concerns the UN Security Council. Its composition no longer reflects the changed correlation of forces in the world. The report prepared by the Netherlands Advisory Council on Peace and Security notes, *inter alia*, that '[t]he disadvantages of the growing dominance of three Western permanent members of the Security Council (the United States, the United Kingdom and France) should also be recognized'.[145] The report of the UN Secretary General, *Agenda for Peace* stresses that 'agreement among permanent members must have the deeper support of the other members of the Council, and the membership more widely, if the Council's decisions are to be effective and endure'.[146]

There are different proposals to reform the Security Council. In February 1992 Boutrous-Ghali suggested increasing the number of permanent members by five in 1995 and referred to Japan, Germany and India, Brazil and Nigeria as possible candidates.[147] In July 1993 the United States formally supported the admission of Germany and Japan to permanent membership of the Security Council.[148]

The necessity to reform the Security Council partly lies in the fact that there are now more UN member-states than in the 1960s, when the Council's membership was increased from 11 to 15, and that Germany and Japan – two former enemies of the United Nations – are now among the most powerful states in the world. However, I feel that the main concern should be to avoid the situation where unanimous decisions or consensus of the permanent members of the Security Council are met with disapproval by the majority of Third World countries.

The post-Cold war effectiveness of the Security Council in decision-making may become counter-productive in the long run, if these decisions are met with disapproval by developing countries or even by a substantial number of them. The East–West confrontation, among its many negative aspects, had one positive side: both the East as well as the West saw to it that acts of neither the East, nor the West in the developing world which were contrary to international law, remained without reaction in the UN. In the new situation it is necessary to avoid a situation where the Security Council may be seen as an instrument of the North where the South does not have any real say.

This means that without jeopardizing the effectiveness of decision-making in the Security Council it will be necessary at the same time to make the Council an instrument of the world community as a whole.

An interesting and, it seems to me, quite practical idea was put forward by Reisman who asked the US to initiate a proposal for the formation of a 'Chapter VII Consultation Committee' of the General Assembly – a 21-member body which would have a consultative role in all Chapter VII issues before the Security Council.[149]

In the new international system much more attention should be paid to cooperation and coordination between universal and regional organizations, especially in matters of international peace and security. In many instances the latter should become regional arms of the UN.

Though law usually develops more slowly than the social relations governed by it and therefore often lags behind developments in that area, legal norms, institutions and procedures are able to react rather quickly to social changes. The UN measures against Iraqi aggression; its operations in Angola and especially in Cambodia; humanitarian intervention in Somalia; its involvement in the former Yugoslavia and the creation of the International Criminal Tribunal to try war crimes and crimes against humanity committed in that country, are all acts which would have been impossible before the end of the Cold War. Some of these operations may be more of a failure than a success; some may raise questions about the double standards of the UN and especially of Western countries. But I think that they all outline the general direction of changes in the world community's reaction to different challenges in the emerging international system. The failures are due, at least partially, to the fact that neither individual states nor the world community as a whole was ready to face such challenges.

International law has an important role to play in the changing international system. It can perform its functions not in the form of ready prescriptions simply waiting to be revealed and applied in concrete circumstances. It is not an inflexible strait-jacket, but rather a guide which takes account of past experience, current realities and future perspectives, and which has to be approached creatively as a constantly developing and changing instrument contributing to the stability and development of positive trends, and to the change and suppression of negative ones.

2 Self-determination
Right to secession or entitlement to democracy?

The developments in the former USSR and Eastern Europe unfolded to a great extent under the banners of the right to self-determination and gave an additional impetus to similar processes in other parts of the world. Dependent on the way these issues will be resolved is the future of many peoples and states as well as that of the international order.

SOME HISTORICAL REMARKS

The principle of the self-determination of peoples is rightly considered to be a successor to the political principle of nationality, which became widely recognized in nineteenth century Europe and related to the emergence of nation-states.[1] Since then, hardly any political or legal principles have been a highly praised and supported by some and a strongly denied by others as has that of self-determination.

After World War I the principle received a new boost. In 1917, in the famous Decree of Peace, Lenin wrote:

> If any nation whatsoever is retained within the boundaries of a given state by coercion, and despite its expressed desire it is not granted the right by a free vote, . . . with the complete withdrawal of the forces of the annexing or generally more powerful nation, to decide without the slightest coercion the question of the form of state existence of this nation, then it is an annexation. . .[2]

President Wilson was an ardent proponent of the principle. In his 'Fourteen Points' he enunciated that 'peoples and provinces must not be bartered about from sovereignty to sovereignty as if they were chattels or pawns in a game', and that territorial questions should be decided 'in the interest of the population concerned'.[3]

But at the same time Secretary of State Lansing wrote in a note of 30 December 1918:

The more I think about the President's declaration as to the right of 'self-determination', the more convinced I am of the danger of putting such ideas into the minds of certain races. It is bound to be the basis of impossible demands on the Peace Congress and create trouble in many lands . . . The phrase is simply loaded with dynamite. It will raise hopes which can never be realized. It will, I fear, cost thousand of lives.[4]

Senator Moynihan quotes Frank P. Walsh to whom President Wilson himself had acknowledged that when he had uttered the words on the right to self-determination he had done so without any knowledge that nationalities existed which were coming to them day after day.[5]

Already at that time proponents of the principle interpreted it not only differently, they also interpreted it as being not simply an end in itself but as a means of achieving different ends. For Lenin this principle was subordinated to interests of socialism and was considered as a stage and condition of the final merger of all nations into one socialist society.[6] Hurst Hannum is quite right that it 'should be underscored that self-determination in 1919 had little to do with the demands of the peoples concerned, unless those demands were consistent with the geopolitical and strategic interests of the Great Powers'.[7]

By the turn of the millennium the principle of the self-determination of peoples has travelled the long road from its origin political slogan to being one of the fundamental principles of international law. But as Hannum writes:'Yet the meaning of and the content of that principle remain as vague and imprecise as when they were enunciated by President Woodrow Wilson and others in Versailles.'[8]

In the 1990s the self-determination of peoples is once more not only a topical subject for dissertations, but has become a slogan of political struggle in different parts of the world. If after World War I the principle was applied only to Eastern European nations which had hitherto been parts of the Ottoman and Austro-Hungarian empires, and in the 1960s determined outcomes of the anti-colonial struggle in Africa and Asia, at the end of the 1980s came the turn of the Russian (Soviet) Empire.

All Soviet republics, while seeking independence from the USSR or demanding more autonomy from the centre, vigorously claimed the right to self-determination. But even before these republics could achieve their independence, different ethnicities living in their territories where they constituted minorities (for example, Tartars and Chechens in Russia; Crimeans in Ukraine; Crimean Tartars in their turn in the Crimean peninsula, which was their historical motherland; and

Ossetians and Abkhazians in Georgia) started to use the same slogan in the furtherance of their claims.

It seems that the chain of fission is a law not only of the physical world but of the social world as well. When a society breaks up not only are other societies affected by way of example, but newly born states themselves often start a new round of disintegration.

The birth and existence of the Soviet Union had a twofold effect on world society. On the one hand, it was a source of expansion of communist ideas and a resource for different left wing organizations all over the world. On the other hand, the Soviet experience served as a warning for different peoples, averting them from repeating this social experiment.

In the same vein, recent and even some current events in the former Soviet Union as well as in the former Yugoslavia, though certainly providing a source of inspiration for many secessionist movements in other countries should, at the same time, sound as a warning.

Generalizations, of course, should always be made cautiously because seemingly identical events may have their roots in different reasons and lead to different results. But there may have been something symbolic in the picture I observed in Geneva in autumn 1992 at the time when Georgians and Abkhazians were killing each other in the Caucasus, when ethnic cleansing was in progress in the territories of the former Yugoslavia, and the UN Human Rights Committee, of which I was a member, considered emergency reports of Bosnia-Herzegovina, Croatia, and Yugoslavia (Serbia and Montenegro) on their implementation of such basic human rights as the right to life and freedom from torture and other inhuman forms of treatment. Looking out of the windows of the Palais des Nations one could see the 179 flags of the UN member states flutting in the cold autumn wind. At that moment I did not feel especially proud of seeing so many new member-states' flags, but thought more of the cost of every flag in human lives and suffering. And this notwithstanding the fact that in 1991–92 I was myself actively involved in the process of the dissolution of the Soviet Union as Deputy Foreign Minister of Estonia.

This does not mean that all sacrifices for the liberty and independence of many peoples have been in vain. Social progress has often been, unfortunately, accompanied by violence, and liberty has rarely been achieved without human sacrifice. And violence has been used not only by tyrants, but against them as well. But as I have already written in the first chapter, one of the indicators of the progressive development of mankind is, if not actual reduction of violence, then at least the change of attitude of most people to it.

Therefore, I think that a sober or even a sobering analysis (legal, political, economic and, most importantly, humanitarian) of the right of peoples to self-determination in the light of events in the former Soviet Union and in Eastern Europe is necessary.

Because of the political explosiveness of the principle and the presence of conflicting claims in any self-determination case, I think that here one would indeed need something like Rawls's 'veil of ignorance' in order impartially to explore the content and implications of the principle. It is necessary to know everything that is possible to know concerning the principle, its application and impact on different values, while remaining at the same time ignorant of one's own personal position: whether one belongs to a people or a minority, what kind of minority and where, etc. This is not an easy task, but it seems to be necessary in order to avoid taking sides in analysing this principle.

SELF-DETERMINATION, TERRITORIAL INTEGRITY AND HUMAN RIGHTS

No one doubts any more that the principle of the self-determination of peoples is a legal principle and many declare it to be a *jus cogens* norm of international law.[9] What is much less clear is the content of the principle and its relation to other principles of international law having the same legal force. This last aspect is especially important because such grandiose events like those which have taken place in the erstwhile USSR and in Eastern Europe are never governed only by one principle or norm of international law. Different principles and norms, all being expressions of different real values and interests, if taken in isolation, may often indicate opposite outcomes. Therefore the task of an international lawyer is to apply these principles and norms creatively to concrete events, taking into account not only these legal principles but also important extra-legal factors and possible outcomes as well.

The right of peoples to self-determination is not only one of fundamental principles of international law governing inter-state relations. It is at the same time a very important human rights norm and therefore rightly belongs to both Covenants on human rights. The Vienna Declaration and Programme of Action adopted by the World Conference on Human Rights in June 1993 emphasizes that the Conference considers the denial of the right of self determination as a violation of human rights and underlines the importance of the effective realization of this right.[10]

This is so because, first, its so-called internal aspect, that is the right of all peoples freely (there are some limitations of even this freedom as I will show later) to determine their political status and to pursue their economic, social and cultural development is the entitlement of all peoples to democracy. Second, even its external aspect, that is the right of peoples freely (so far as this freedom does not infringe upon the freedom of other peoples) to determine their place in the international community of states, is becoming more and more influenced by other human rights norms.

When the principle of self-determination as a legal norm started its development in the context of the process of decolonization this link between self-determination and human rights meant that individuals could not be free if the peoples to which they belonged were under an alien yoke.[11]

But the process of development of the principle of respect for human rights – one of the most rapidly and radically evolving principles of international law – has influenced many international law principles and norms and the principle of the self-determination of peoples has not remained unaffected either because, as was said in the 1970 Friendly Relations Declaration, all principles of international law are interrelated and each principle should be construed in the context of other principles.[12] Though in the Friendly Relations Declaration the principle of respect for human rights was still absent, there is no doubt that the following developments in international law have confirmed the place of this principle amongst the fundamental principles of international law. The Final Act of the Conference on Security and Cooperation in Europe contains the principle of respect for human rights and fundamental freedoms and also stresses that all principles should be interpreted whilst taking the others into account.[13]

The principle of respect for human rights has been particularly dramatically developed in the framework of the Helsinki process. The Document of the Copenhagen Conference on the Human Dimension of 1990 not only speaks of concrete rights and freedom and elaborates respective monitoring mechanisms, but for the first time gives the parameters of a society conducive to the protection of individual rights.[14] And for the first time an international document states *expressis verbis* that freedom of choice by peoples of their political, social, economic and cultural systems is not absolute. Peoples are free to establish their respective political, social and economic systems so far as these systems guarantee respect for international standards of human rights. The states' parties to the Conference on the Human Dimension of the CSCE confirmed that they will respect each other's right freely to choose and develop, *in accordance with international human rights standards* [emphasis added], their political, social, economic and cultural systems. In exercising this right, they will ensure that their laws, regulations, practices and policies conform with their obligations under international law and are brought into harmony with the provisions of the Declaration on Principles and other CSCE commitments.[15]

One may at first assume that such a clause limits the freedom of choice of peoples with regard to the formulation of their respective economic, social and political systems. In reality, however, it does not curb peoples' right to self-determination but, on the contrary, strengthens the principle by placing limits on rulers or other antidemocratic forces in a society.

This link between principles of the self-determination of peoples and respect for human rights – or maybe it would be better to say the filling of the principle of self-determination with humanitarian content – found further development in the processes of the dissolution of the USSR and Yugoslavia and especially in the reaction of the world community of states to these processes.

On 16 December 1991 the Council of the European Communities adopted a Declaration on 'Guidelines on the recognition of new states in Eastern Europe and in the Soviet Union'.[16] This document establishes the criteria and conditions for the recognition of new states which, following the historic changes in the region, have constituted themselves on a democratic basis, have accepted the appropriate international obligations and have committed themselves in good faith to a peaceful process and to negotiations. The Declaration refers specifically to the principle of self-determination as a basis for recognition.

As I will deal with issues concerning the recognition of new states in Eastern Europe in detail (and rather critically) in Chapter 4, here I would like only to emphasize that, according to the EC Declaration, new states, in order to be accepted as members of the international community, must be democratic countries where human rights are respected.

Application of the principle of the self-determination of peoples is strongly influenced (or one may say, balanced) also by the principles of the inviolability of frontiers and the territorial integrity of states. 'The sovereignty, territorial integrity and independence of states within the established international system, and the principle of self-determination of peoples, both of great value and importance, must not be permitted to work against each other in the period ahead', states a report prepared by the Secretary-General of the UN Boutros-Ghali.[17] The principles of the self-determination of peoples, the inviolability of frontiers and the territorial integrity of states are inseparable and support each other, which means that they should be balanced in the same way as justice and order need to be balanced in any society. One cannot have justice without order, while order without justice is not only inhuman but it also does not last long. Max Kampelman rightly observes that '[t]he inviolability of existing boundaries is an integral part of this process [self-determination], not because the boundaries are necessarily sound or just, but because respect for them is necessary for peace and stability'.[18]

The principle of the self-determination of peoples developed in the UN mainly in the context of the process of decolonization. Though no document confines the principle to the decolonization of colonies of overseas parent states (so called 'salt-water' colonialism), it was natural that at that time this aspect of the principle became the most prominent and for some states even the only one.[19] Therefore Hector Gross Espiell wrote:

> The United Nations established the right of self-determination as a right of peoples under colonial and alien domination. The right does not apply to peoples already organized in the form of a State which are not under colonial and alien domination, since resolution 1514 (XV) and other United Nations instruments condemn any attempt aimed at partial or total disruption of the national unity and the territorial integrity of the country.[20]

It seems to me that, there are two flaws in this approach. First, that the principle applies only to peoples under colonial or alien domination and, second, the assumption that application of this principle to a sovereign (even multi-ethnic) state would inevitably be fraught with the disruption of its national unity or territorial integrity.

In the colonial context the principle meant the independence of colonies from their parent state.[21] However, the attitude of states[22] as well as that of international bodies[23] clearly shows that the principle of the self-determination of peoples has a universal application and is an ongoing right of all peoples. Outside the colonial context, however, the meaning of the principle becomes less clear and more controversial.

THE DISSOLUTION OF THE USSR AND THE DECOLONIZATION PROCESS

Though this may sound paradoxical, the self-determination claims of peoples in the Europe of the 1990s should not be considered as having nothing in common with the decolonization process. Events in the

Soviet Union in the 1990s were, inter alia, accomplishing what should have occurred much earlier.

The Soviet Union was a continuation of the Russian Empire and even Yugoslavia and Czechoslovakia retained some legacies of the Austro-Hungarian Empire. There were strong elements of artificiality in the creation of the Soviet Union, though artificiality in the creation of a state does not in itself mean that such a state should necessarily have a fate similar to that of the Soviet Union.

The USSR, of course, was not a traditional empire where a metro-politan nation exploited underdeveloped peoples overseas. The Russians suffered no less than other ethnicities and some of the latter were even better off than representatives of the titular nation of the Soviet Union. But nevertheless it was an empire – that is, an involuntary union of different peoples – in which the people themselves did not have and had never had their say in determining either their present or future. After the 1917 Bolshevik revolution in the Russian Empire, the metropolitan nation was replaced by the metropolitan regime. And this regime not only exploited the Soviet people as a whole but also oppressed every ethnicity as such, enduring that their national feelings and expressions of national identity were suppressed. The theoretical reason for it was that according to Marxism-Leninism all nations would eventually merge into one.

Lenin proclaimed the principle of the self-determination of nations to be one of the pillars of the Bolshevik's approach to inter-ethnic relations,[24] and he himself called the Czarist Russia 'the prison of peoples'. The right of secession was provided for in different Soviet constitutions. But in reality no nation was ever asked whether it wanted to be part of the Soviet Union. On the contrary, any hint of a desire for secession from the USSR was labelled as a manifestation of bourgeois nationalism and considered a crime. Many Ukrainians, Estonians, Latvians and representatives of other nations were sentenced when not even claiming, but merely speaking of independence. Therefore not only those nations, which were incorporated into the Soviet Union involuntarily and in violation of the even then existing norms of international law (Estonia, Latvia, Lithuania), but also those nations which became part of the Russian Empire long before international law prohibited forceful conquest of other nations, were never able to express their opinion on questions directly concerning their fate. That is also why when the regime loosened its grip the Empire started to fall apart.

Therefore it is possible to consider the process of the dissolution of the USSR as, in some ways, a continuation of the process of decolon-ization. And this ought to be taken into account when, in the light of events in the former Soviet Union and Yugoslavia, one tries to approach such questions as whether the right to self-determination includes the right to secession and whether and to what extent events in Eastern Europe and the former Soviet Union have contributed to the clarification of this controversial point.

The disintegration of the Soviet Union has, of course, created and will create in the future enormous problems, and it seemed to many that it would have been easier to deal with one state which had already started to change its totalitarian nature than to have at least fifteen mostly unstable separate countries. So, Brent Scowcroft, the national security adviser to President Bush, stated at the beginning of 1991: 'Our policy has to be based on our own national interest, and we have an interest in the stability of the Soviet Union.'[25]

It may indeed have been preferable to democratize the Soviet Union without its disintegration, had it been possible. But the process of dissolution of this doubly artificial creature (both ideologically and by its composition) was not only an objective but seems also to have been inevitable.

The situation was different in Yugoslavia and Czechoslovakia. It is difficult to agree that the demise of these countries – and especially Czechoslovakia – was also inevitable. As Branka Magas writes: 'Yugoslavia thus did not die a natural death; it was destroyed for the cause of a Greater Serbia.'[26] There were also, of course, other reasons for the dissolution of Yugoslavia, but interestingly, even there, the fact that the federal authorities, controlled by Serbian leaders, started to play a kind of imperial role and rejected the proposals of some republics for a looser federation was really one of the causes which finally led to the destruction of the country and civil war.

It seems to me that the fact that events in the former Soviet Union, and to a certain extent even in Yugoslavia, had the character of the decolonization process explains why the aspect of the principle of self-determination which, using the words of the relevant paragraph of the Friendly Relations Declaration, emphasizes that 'nothing in the foregoing paragraphs shall be construed as authorizing or encouraging any action which would dismember or impair, totally or in part, the territorial integrity or political unity of sovereign and independent States',[27] did not work.

It is well-known that the same Declaration in the same paragraph states in terms very carefully chosen by the representatives of states, that the territorial integrity or political unity of those sovereign and independent states which conduct themselves in compliance with the principle of equal rights and the self-determination of peoples should be respected, and each should be allowed a government which represents the whole population belonging to the territory without distinction as to race, creed or colour.[28]

The principle also prohibits the use of 'force to deprive peoples of their national identity'.

As I have already indicated, the Soviet regime tried to deprive different peoples of their national identities. Moreover, the USSR was not a voluntary union and the regime did not represent the whole population belonging to the territory without distinction as to race, creed or colour. Of course the regime did not distinguish much between different races, creeds or colours, but it was non-representative and totalitarian and suppressed not only any ideological or political dissent but also all national feelings, thereby putting in danger the national identities of all ethnic groups within the USSR.

Though we find some of the reasons for the collapse of the Soviet Union within the imperial character of the USSR the world community did not recognize this easily. (There were, of course, other reasons, one of them being the ineffective economic system, but this had more to do with the collapse of the command economy, and efforts to replace it with a market oriented one, than with the decomposition of the country.) Even in the context of this specific decolonization process the majority of states were very cautious lest they should encourage secession, aware that any fragmentation of the world political map usually creates more problems than it resolves. Only when it became obvious that all attempts to maintain the territorial *status quo* would in fact create more problems than solutions and would lead (or had already led) to violence, did the majority of states start to recognize the inevitable. I have no doubts that the acceptance of the dissolution of the USSR and Yugoslavia and the recognition of new states was influenced, first, by the character of these predecessor states and, second, by promises concerning democracy and human rights within the newly born entities.

But even here secession was recognized only as a last resort, when maintenance of the *status quo* seemed to be not simply unjust but would have been seen to be dangerous by other states – if not for the world, then at least for regional stability.

SELF-DETERMINATION IN DEMOCRACIES AND IN AUTHORITARIAN (TOTALITARIAN) STATES

The situation, though often far from ideal, is not the same in democratic countries. There, different ethnic groups participate on an equal basis with the rest of the citizens in governing the affairs of the society as a whole and accordingly are able to express their wills on matters concerning the specific problems of these ethnic groups. For example, the Welsh or the Scots in the UK or the Quebecois in Canada have not only been able to express their views but in reality have repeatedly expressed their wills in matters of the governance of their respective states (this, of course, does not mean that they are always content with how these matters are governed – but who is?), thereby creating legitimate expectations for other parts of society. By so doing, they have become integral parts of their societies. Even if historically such multi-ethnic states were not voluntary unions (most of them were historically involuntary) democratic participation has legitimized them. Therefore, there are no moral or legal grounds under international law for claims of secession from democratic states, though constitutions may provide for such a right and *de facto* secession may, of course, be possible even without any moral or legal right. But the case is different when we have peoples who have never had an opportunity to express their will either in matters of general concern or in questions relating directly to their own fate.

Thomas Franck writes that 'it might be argued that when an entire population – as opposed to a targeted minority – is the object of maltreatment, then the appropriate remedy is revolution, not an act of self-determination by one segment of the society'.[28]

Generally speaking I think that this argument of Professor Franck's sounds quite reasonable. But self-determination and revolution are not entirely different options. Every popular revolution is also an act of self-determination. It usually happens when constitutional means of self-determination are non-existent or totally ineffective. Therefore, revolution and self determination are not mutually exclusive. On the contrary, the former may be an extreme form of the latter. And it seems to me that not only revolution but secession similarly is an extreme form of self-determination and that they both should have equal status under international law.

In multi-ethnic countries, however, it often happens that a totalitarian or authoritarian regime, by oppressing the whole population, at the same time suppresses the national aspirations of ethnically distinct communities in particular. In such a case, even if members of these communities sit in state bodies (which, of course, are devoid of representative character), they do not represent their communities, and the aspirations of the latter never find expression in the policy of the state. This means that such communities have never had their say, not only in matters concerning the society as a whole but also in matters concerning their specific problems, one of these being the resolution of their position in relation to the rest of the society.

Professor Franck, attempting to formulate a coherent new principle of self-determination capable of distinguishing, for example, between the Algerian and Biafrian cases, writes that

> self-determination is a right applicable to any distinct region in which the inhabitants do not enjoy rights equal to those accorded all people in other parts of the same state. Conversely, the right is not applicable to regions of an existing state if its inhabitants enjoy the same rights as inhabitants of any other part of the country.[29]

It seems to me that Franck's conclusion corresponds with the trends of development of the principle. I have only two observations or clarifications. My first remark would be that Franck is speaking here not so much of the principle of self-determination as of secession, because later he writes that 'the Welsh would not be entitled to independence, because they do enjoy the same rights and status as all other British nationals'.[30] My second observation is of a substantive nature. I seriously doubt whether Franck's thesis is similarly applicable to those states where all existing ethnic groups are equal in the sense that they are equally deprived of all rights. The norm that the territorial integrity of those states which possess governments representing the whole population without distinction as to race, creed or colour, should be respected, does not mean that the territorial integrity of those states which do not possess representative governments at all and in that sense do not distinguish on the basis of race or ethnicity, should always be respected in the same way or to the same extent.

As I have already mentioned, in the Soviet Union there was generally no discrimination against minorities, except, of course, during certain periods against Crimean Tartars, Chechens, Volga Germans, who were deported by Stalin, and Jews and some other selected ethnicities at certain periods of the history of the USSR. Minorities were generally equal with the majority in their lack of rights and freedoms. But in a non-democratic state, ethnic and religious minorities usually find themselves doubly oppressed. They are deprived not only of their civil, political, economic and social rights as human beings and citizens, but also of their minority rights. Therefore, the discontent of such minorities is directed not only against general oppression, but often also against the suppression of their specific minority rights in particular.[31] This means that in such countries revolution and secession may coincide and constitute in substance two sides of the same coin.

Taking into consideration previous practice, relevant international documents and also the latest events in the former Soviet Union and Eastern Europe, one may conclude that secessionist movements may gain international support and recognition in the situation where seces-sion by ethnically distinguishable groups is sought from totalitarian and unrepresentative regimes, and where breakaway communities are com-mitted (or at least they themselves claim to be committed) to democratic values and human rights, including the rights of minorities.

Of course ethnically distinct groups may seek secession from demo-cratic states and may even succeed, though I cannot recall any ex-amples, which is in itself rather significant.[32] The very sophisticated constitutional arrangements in Belgium aimed at resolving problems and tensions arising from the co-existence of three ethnically different communities is a striking contrast to methods used to resolve inter-ethnic problems in the former Yugoslavia. Protracted negotiations in Canada, whatever their final outcome, also show that in democratic countries inter-ethnic problems, however difficult they are, may be resolved without recourse to violence.

But there is certainly no right of secession for ethnically distinct groups in democratic societies. As a rule ethnically distinct groups, though often demanding more autonomy, rarely seek secession from democratic states; and secessionist movements existing in such coun-tries, especially of those extremist stock, do not represent the majority of the ethnic groups to which they belong. For example, a 1982 sur-vey indicated that 38 per cent of the Basque population considered members of ETA, a Basque terrorist organization, to be patriots and idealists, while 31 per cent thought they were fools or criminals. But only 8 per cent of Basques said that they supported ETA, while 77 per cent were opposed to its activities.[33] It is interesting to note that Patrick Brogan writes that ETA leadership was particularly concerned to defeat the government's plan for Basque autonomy: they wanted the Basques oppressed, so that they would rise in revolt and usher in the new order.[34] Similarly, the Corsican separatists led the vio-lent struggle against the French authorities despite obvious lack of public support.[35]

On the other hand, democratic governments which naturally repre-sent different ethnic minorities can usually find solutions to inter-ethnic problems which satisfy at least the majority, if not all, of those who belong to their minorities. One can say that in democratic countries different ethnic groups have more opportunities to gain independence but that they have less incentive to do so.

This does not mean that ethnically distinct and relatively large groups in non-democratic countries have an unconditional right to secession under international law. Contemporary international law simply does not contain such a right. This is the conclusion of states and of most experts. Nguyen Quoc Dinh, Patrick Daillier and Allain Pellet, for example, write that 'it is useless to try to find in positive international law texts or practice anything which would permit us to conclude that the right to the self-determination of peoples means the right to secession'.[36] The UK Foreign Minister in 1983, in his written reply to the parliamentary question about the problem of self determination for the Somalis in Ethiopia, stated:

> It is widely accepted in the United Nations that the right of self-determination does not give every distinct group or territorial sub-division within a state the right to secede from it and thereby dismember the territorial integrity or political unity of sovereign independent states.[37]

The right of nations (*sic*, not peoples[38]) to self-determination up to secession was the Bolsheviks' and especially Lenin's formulation before and immediately after the 1917 Revolution in Russia.[39]

The distinction made here between democratic and non-democratic countries means that in countries of non-representative character oppressed ethnic minorities may gain support of the world community in their claims to independence. Though even in the case of the clearly oppressive Iraqi government we see that other states, while taking coercive measures against the regime of Saddam Hussein, nevertheless unequivocally supported the territorial integrity of Iraq in the face of the claims of the Kurds to independence.[40]

Had international law contained the unconditional right to secession, we would have had an incentive to, and therefore an even bigger threat of, the endless 'tribalization' of the world. The larger the ethnic groups in independent states, the larger also the probability that they themselves contain other ethnically distinct groups.

SELF-DETERMINATION AS A PRINCIPLE OF INCLUSION, NOT EXCLUSION

In the light of the above discussion, my answer to the question as to whether the principle of self-determination contains a right to secession, must be in the negative, with some qualifications.

Analysis of relevant international documents and practice (including the process of the dismemberment of the USSR) leads to the conclusion that there is no right of secession in international law. The right of peoples freely to determine their political status and freely to pursue their economic, social and cultural development (article 1 of the Covenants on human rights[41]) should be construed in the context of the right of those states which conduct themselves in compliance with the principle of equal rights and the self-determination of peoples, and thus possess a government representing the whole population belonging to the territory without distinction as to race, creed or colour, to have their territorial integrity and political unity respected (1970 Friendly Relations Declaration).

The implementation of the right to independence by colonial peoples was not, strictly speaking, secession. Paragraph VI of the Friendly Relations Declaration provides that 'the territory of a colony or other Non Self-Governing Territory has, under the Charter, a status separate and distinct from the territory of the State administering it'.[42] Therefore, when, for example, Nigeria or Ghana became independent the territorial integrity of the United Kingdom was not violated by this act. Populations and territories of parent states and their colonies did not constitute either *de facto* or even *de jure* the population and the territory of one and the same state. A parent state and a colony were united only by one element of the statehood – authority, which could have had its source of legitimacy only in the population of the parent state. Populations of overseas colonies were not represented in the legislative or other bodies of parent states.

Application of the principle of the self-determination of peoples, which is, as we have seen, one of the most important human rights norms, should not lead to the limitation of existing human rights – especially the rights of minorities. On the contrary, its implementation must result in greater protection of the rights and freedoms of individuals as well as of minorities.

Therefore I think that emerging from the balance of the three interrelated principles of international law, i.e. the self-determination of peoples, respect for human rights and respect for the territorial integrity of states, is a guideline which establishes that secession is tolerated or at certain stages even supported by the world community of states when it leads, or there are reasonable grounds to believe that it may lead, to considerably greater protection of human rights and fundamental freedoms without constituting unreasonable risk for regional or even for world stability.

But the main trend in the development of the principle of self-determination is that it is becoming employed more and more in support of an entitlement to democracy than as an encouragement to fragment the political map of the world. Professor Franck is absolutely right that the principle of the self-determination of peoples has 'stopped being a principle of exclusion (secession) and became one of inclusion: the right to participate. The right now entitles peoples in all states to free, fair and open participation in the democratic process of governance freely chosen by each state.'[43]

Here the sixteen-year practice of the Human Rights Committee supervising the implementation of the International Covenant on Civil and Political Rights is rather significant. While at the beginning of the functioning of the Committee more attention was paid to the attitude of state-parties to problems of non-self governing territories and to the self-determination of the Palestinians or the Namibians, now the Committee, dealing with issues under article 1 of the Covenant, concentrates mainly on the implementation of the right to self-determination by the peoples of the reporting states themselves. When representatives of some not-so-democratic regimes start to explain at length how they support the right of other peoples to self-determination, the Committee always tries to delicately push the delegation into the discussion of affairs concerning their own people. And the Committee invariably links the implementation of article 1 with issues under article 25 which provides for the right of every citizen to take part in the conduct of public affairs, to vote and to be elected at genuine periodic elections which shall be by universal and equal suffrage and shall be held by secret ballot, guaranteeing the free expression of the will of the electors. The attitude of most state-parties has also changed. For example, the second periodic report of Tanzania, considered by the Human Rights Committee in 1992, regarding article 1 of the Covenant states that:

> In Tanzania's understanding, the principle [of self-determination] affirms the right of citizens to freely choose their government and its leaders without internal or external interference and to freely pursue economic, social and cultural development on the basis of equality without discrimination on grounds of race, colour, class, caste, creed or political conviction.[44]

PEOPLES AND/OR MINORITIES?

The International Covenant on Civil and Political Rights makes a clear distinction between the right of peoples to self determination (article 1) and the rights of ethnic, religious or linguistic minorities to enjoy their own culture, to profess and practise their own religion, or to use their own language (article 27). It would not be correct to say, as it is sometimes asserted, that there is no right of self-determination for minorities. It would be more accurate to say that they can exercise the right of self-determination together with the rest of the population of a given state, as a part of this population.

Of course, one may say that while there is more or less a clear distinction between the rights of peoples and the rights of minorities, it is impossible to make such a distinction between peoples and minorities themselves. The UNESCO meeting of experts on the further study of the rights of peoples (Paris, 1990), to which a reference was made in the Report of the Saskatoon 1993 Symposium on the right to self-determination, identified the following criteria as being commonly taken into account in deciding that a group of individuals is a 'people': common historical tradition, racial or ethnic identity, cultural homogeneity, linguistic unity, religious or ideological affinity, territorial connection and common economic life.[45]

But the more I think of this problem, the more I become convinced that it is impossible to find an international law criterion or criteria which would help us to divide ethnicities into peoples, minorities, tribes, nations, etc. Why do, for example, the Russians constitute a people, while the Tartars should be dealt with as a minority? Or why is the population of Bosnia-Herzegovina more of a people than are the ethnic Serbs who live in Bosnia-Herzegovina? The criteria proposed above are applicable to hundreds of ethnicities which do not form their own individual nation-states, and many apply also to populations which belong to different states.

J. Brossard affirms, for example, that Quebec has the right to self-determination as the Quebecois constitute a people because they meet all necessary criteria for that: 'political dimension', territory and power structures; a viable future; acceptance of principles of the UN Charter and international law; a will to independence.[46]

The first criterion simply means that Canada has taken measures to protect the rights and interests of the Quebecois as a distinctive minority (I am not thereby prejudging, of course, whether these measures have been sufficient or adequate), and therefore Quebec has a 'political dimension', territory and proper structures. As I will try to argue below, this speaks rather strongly against secession. Had they been deprived of that, they may have had a small point in favour of their claims.

One may go even further, using the arguments of J. Brossard, and assert like W. Shaw and L. Albert that 'if Quebec can opt out of Canada, then obviously sections of Quebec that preferred to remain part of Canada could opt out of Quebec'.[47] They may, of course, if they can, but neither case would have any support in international law.

Therefore, I think that contemporary international practice tends to lead towards the conclusion that in the post-colonial era peoples, for the purposes of self-determination under international law, can be defined as populations of independent states, while minorities constitute a part of peoples, having distinctive ethnic, religious or linguistic characteristics.[48]

MINORITIES VERSUS MAJORITIES

One of failures of Mikhail Gorbachev was certainly his handling of inter-ethnic relations. From the time of his accession in 1985, as several commentators have already mentioned, Gorbachev repeatedly showed himself to be blind and insensitive to ethnic issues.[49]

Even worse, Gorbachev and his team, trying to avoid the dismemberment of the Soviet Union, started at the end of the 1980s to play the card of the rights of minorities in recalcitrant constituent republics against the so-called titular nations of these republics who had, according the 1977 Soviet Constitution, the right to secede from the Soviet Union. But there was no procedure provided for the implementation of this right. When first the Baltic republics and later different political forces in other parts of the USSR started to claim the implementation of this constitutional right, central authorities in Moscow tried to make secession practically impossible.

The Law on Secession which was passed in 1990 stipulated that in those regions of a constituent republic seeking secession, where minorities lived side by side, the votes should be counted separately.[50] The Law was ambiguous as to what exactly this clause meant, but obviously in a case where the results of voting in a republic as a whole and in a region where a minority held sway were different, the minority would seem to have acquired some basis for claiming secession from the breakaway republic in order to stay in the Union.

Though issues regarding the protection of minorities in new states which emerged after the collapse of the Soviet Union are real, and I will devote a chapter to them, the tactics used by the Soviet leadership did nothing to alleviate these problems. On the contrary, the methods used by Gorbachev and his team to prevent the dissolution of the USSR aggravated the situation, setting, at least in some republics, the titular nation against their minorities. Majorities began to see their minorities (sometimes rightly, sometimes wrongly) as the fifth column of the Kremlin.

When newly born political movements in some constituent republics (e.g., Popular Fronts in Estonia and Latvia, Rukh in Ukraine or Sajudis in Lithuania) started to claim sovereignty and independence from the centre, Moscow encouraged counter-movements either in autonomous republics or among ethnic minorities, which were usually called inter-movements.

Certainly, there were sincere and sometimes well-founded apprehensions among minorities in many republics. But the centre fully exploited these inter-ethnic frictions, instead of curing them, in order to prevent republics from leaving the Union, and thereby wound up even further the time-bomb which soon exploded in many regions of the USSR.

But the leaders of some of the republics were no wiser in dealing with their minorities. Georgia, under Zviad Gamsakhurdia, succeeded in alienating almost all the numerous Georgian minorities. Stephen Jones writes:

> The government elaborated a theory of minority rights based on the assumption that members of minorities with a relatively recent history of settlement in Georgia, such as Ossetians or Azerbaijanis, qualified neither for an inalienable right to residence in the republic nor to equal status with the dominant ethnic group.[51]

The abolition of the South Ossetian autonomy in December 1990 led to the war between Georgians and Ossetians.[52]

A dangerous historical dispute between some Georgian and Abkhazian historians is rather illustrative of how history is used or, to put it more correctly, abused for political ends. While Abkhazians claim that they have been in Abkhazia for two millennia, Georgian historians assert that Abkhazians had settled there only 300 years ago.[53]

From the point of view of the rights of the Georgians or the Abkhazians both these arguments are equally irrelevant. There are few territories in the world which have not been populated at different times by different ethnicities. Therefore such disputes, if they go beyond pure historical research and enter the realm of politics, are extremely dangerous and harmful.

It is often difficult to say in a minority – majority dispute which is the chicken and which is the egg, but under international law it is a responsibility of governments to undertake at least minimum measures for the protection of minorities, as provided for by the relevant international instruments.

Suppression and then denial of the existence of inter-ethnic problems in multi-ethnic countries can neither heal these painful problems nor do away with them. Suppression, to be effective, should be permanent and total, which means that such a country as a whole can never be democratic.

In some countries a kind of vicious circle on minority issues has emerged. On the one hand, minorities which are oppressed, discriminated against or simply feel that their identity is threatened or at least cannot be fully developed because of the policy of the government, demand more autonomy or even complete independence. On the other hand, governments are denying minorities their minority rights or do not take into account their specific problems and interests because of the fear that simple recognition of the existence of minorities, let alone protection of their rights and interests, may jeopardize the territorial integrity of the country. Actions and claims of minorities lead to denial of the existence of minorities, while repressions or different degrees of discrimination resulting from such a denial radicalize the claims of minorities. This was the situation in the initial phases of the conflict in Nagorno Karabach, in the Trans-Dniestr region of Moldova and in many other countries and regions.

It seems that the situation of the Kurds in Turkey rather clearly illustrates the point that the main reason for denial of minority rights is the fear of secession. Graham Fuller writes that:

> Turkey has been the most repressive in cultural policy toward the Kurds, denying their existence as a separate nationality within Turkey until very recently. Yet Kurds in Turkey can and regularly do rise to the highest positions within the state – on the condition that they ignore their Kurdish heritage and accept assimilation as Turks.[54]

Former President T. Ozal had Kurdish blood, and Foreign Minister H. Cetin is a Kurd.[55]

We may conclude that when a minority is denied its rights and is oppressed and discriminated against, it is thereby rejected by the majority. The majority rejects and alienates the minority leaving it outside the society. Thereby the minority becomes not simply ethnically or religiously distinct (this distinctiveness always belongs to it), but also socially, economically and politically different from the majority. We may say that the minority, due to the policy of the majority which does not permit the minority to fully develop its identity, acquires characteristics similar to those of colonial peoples. It can survive as a distinct group only independently of the majority. Therefore, the principle of the self-determination of peoples becomes directly relevant to such minorities.

When minorities are discriminated against or their identity is threatened by majority policy (though at first glance these policies may seem contradictory, in fact they go hand in hand, because denial of identity can only be achieved through discrimination), the minority is not participating together with the rest of the population in the ever-continuing and ongoing process of self-determination (it is though, of course, doubtful whether even the majority of the population under such a regime can always freely enjoy the right to self-determination). This means that the minority can realize its right to self-determination not in the society as a whole, together with the rest of the population, but only separately.

The Vienna Declaration and Programme of Action of 1993 particularly emphasizes the right to the self-determination of peoples: (a) under colonial domination; (b) under other forms of alien domination; (c) under foreign occupation. At the same time this document, like other international instruments, stresses that the principle shall not be construed as authorizing or encouraging dismemberment of sovereign and independent countries which respect the principle of the self-determination of peoples.[56]

It is clear, as we saw, what self-determination meant for the colonial peoples. It is more or less clear also what it means when a people is under foreign occupation. For example, the Kuwaitis, while occupied by Iraq, were denied their right to self-determination (though, in fact, it is doubtful whether they enjoyed much of it either before or after the Iraqi occupation).

What is less clear is what is meant by 'other forms of alien domination'. In my opinion, this should in any case include minorities which are discriminated against, are alienated by the majority, and are therefore under its domination.

TERRITORIAL AUTONOMY: A REMEDY AGAINST OR A ROAD TO SECESSION?

If all the ethnicities in a country are minorities then the Ukrainians, the Georgians and the Latvians in the former USSR, and the Serbs, the Croats or the Slovenes in the former Yugoslavia were all minorities in these states. But why in that case did they succeed in their claims for independence while 'minorities in minorities' (such as the Bosnian Serbs or the Ossetians and the Abkhazians in Georgia or the Tartars in Russia or the Gagauzes in Moldova) had to be content with a lesser degree of autonomy or are still fighting for their independence and are not finding much support or even simple understanding from the world community of states?

Did it make any difference that the Ukrainians or the Georgians had some degree of formal autonomy previously and that the Tartars' autonomy was of a lower degree, while the Gagauzes in Moldova did not previously enjoy any autonomy at all?

Such a conclusion would mean that those minorities which already enjoy certain administrative autonomy in clearly defined administrative borders have stronger claims to independence, and that those who do not enjoy any autonomy at all are in this sense disadvantaged. Such an approach would be extremely dangerous and often counter-productive to the interests of minorities because in such cases all devolution arrangements and grants of more autonomy to minorities, which often help to resolve inter-ethnic problems, would at the end of the day really endanger the territorial integrity of existing states and therefore would be rejected by governments. There is no doubt that one of the reasons why some governments (for example, those of Turkey, India and Sri Lanka) refuse to grant greater autonomy to the Kurds, the Kashmirians or the Tamils, respectively, is their apprehension that this would be a step towards the break-away of these parts of their respective countries.

Therefore it is extremely dangerous to support the secessionist claims of some groups on the ground that they already enjoy some degree of acknowledged autonomy within clearly defined administrative borders and have thereby become even more distinctive among the rest of the population. Moreover, such administrative boundaries are often arbitrary or have meaning only in so far as these administrative units belong to one and the same state.

For example, from 1940–56 Karelia enjoyed the status of a constituent republic in the USSR. In 1956 its status was down graded to the level of an autonomous republic in the Russian Federation.[57] Had not this happened, at the moment of the dissolution of the USSR in 1991 the Karelians probably would have had claims equal to those of the Ukrainians or the Byelorussians to independent statehood. It seems illogical that haphazard facts such as this should play an important role in resolving crucial issues of the existence of states.

On the contrary, effective territorial autonomy of ethnically distinctive groups must be seen as an expression of the efforts of the government in the resolution of inter-ethnic issues and consequently as an additional reason for the protection of the territorial integrity of that state.

Therefore the reason for the dissolution of the USSR lay not in its federal structure, which in any case was only formal, but in its imperial features.

USE OF FORCE AND SELF-DETERMINATION

Even in the case of the dissolution of the USSR no state supported claims for independence of the republics (the Baltic states were a special case because most Western countries had not *de jure* recognized incorporation of these states into the USSR in 1940[58]) until they had already achieved their independence (perhaps a bit unstable or uncertain, but nevertheless independence). Nor was there support for the claims of the republics of Yugoslavia until federal authorities in Yugoslavia had used military force in order to suppress moves towards independence in Slovenia and Croatia. Therefore, one may conclude that the Serbian nationalists and Soviet putschists using or trying to use military force in order to keep together these states, in fact made a substantial contribution to the dissolution of these countries.

It is necessary to emphasize that the use of force by secessionists, as well as by the authorities against secessionists, is one of the important issues in the assessment of self-determination claims.

Western states, being against the dissolution of the Soviet Union and Yugoslavia, nevertheless strongly warned leaders of these countries against use of military force against secessionist republics. Michael Beschloss and Stroub Talbott tell us, for example, that President Bush and Secretary Baker constantly reminded Gorbachev and Shevardnadze of their promises not to use force against the Baltic republics.[59]

Use of force by authorities against secessionist claims, if secessionists themselves do not resort to violence, speaks heavily against authorities and in favour of secessionists and gives credence to their claims for independence. Use of force against non-violent separatist movement amounts to repression and discloses the non-democratic character of the regime. It is difficult to imagine that, for example, the Canadian authorities would use military force to prevent Quebec's secession.

But on the other hand, as Lee Buchheit writes,

[a] group living in a democratic, non-discriminatory society that undertakes a campaign of terrorism merely to draw attention to its claims or to coerce its governors into accepting its demands – thus compelling the authorities to enforce security measures – cannot be seen as the victims of 'oppression'.[60]

This all seems to indicate that the world community in its assessment of and reaction to secessionist claims has to take into account the use of force by authorities against secessionists as well as its use the other way around.

In the case of the former USSR and Yugoslavia there was a dissolution of undemocratic, unrepresentative states, while the seceding parts promised immediately to undertake democratic reforms and protect human rights, especially the rights of minorities in their territories.

This, together with the fact that efforts to preserve the territorial *status quo* in Yugoslavia would probably have had an equally or even more damaging effect on the stability of the region, and would probably have been futile in any case, explains why the world community eventually came (after the use of military force by central authorities in Slovenia and Croatia) to recognize and support the claims of the Yugoslavian republics to independence.

In the case of the Soviet Union the August 1991 *coup d'état* attempt had as one of its aims the suppression, if necessary by military force, of not only the ongoing dissolution of the USSR but also of the democratic reforms and market-oriented changes in the economy. The failure of the putschists prevented the development of 'the Yugoslavian version' in the Soviet Union and in September Moscow recognized independence of the Baltic states; in December the USSR peacefully ended its existence.

Therefore, in the practice of the dissolution of either the USSR or Yugoslavia it is impossible to find anything which would support the thesis that different ethnicities or nations have the right to secede from existing states under international law.

The situation is, of course, different in the case of the occupation and annexation of territories in violation of the norms of international law prohibiting the use or threat of force. This was what happened in the Baltic states which were occupied by the Soviet Union in 1940. This is also the case, for example, with Tibet which has been occupied by China since 1951.[61] Strictly speaking, in such situations we are not dealing with secession but with the necessity to rectify violation of the norms and principles of international law. In such cases we have the violation of both principles: non-use of force and the self-determination of peoples.

But the prohibition of the use of force in international relations crystallized as a norm of international law only in the period between the two world wars. There is no doubt that all occupations and annexations in violation of the principle of the non-use of force after the adoption of the UN Charter in 1945 are illegal. But what about those committed earlier?

Certainly, the principle *nullum crimen, nulla poena* is also applicable in international law. Otherwise we would have endless claims to almost all territories.

Allen Buchanan writes that 'there must be a moral statute of limitations. To fail to acknowledge a moral statute of limitations would produce unacceptable disruption of the international order, with endless recriminations about ancient wrongs vying for priority.'[62]

There is such a statute of limitations in international law: occupations and annexations can be considered illegal if committed after the legal prohibition of the use of force or threat of force in international relations. However, I am afraid that such a conclusion cannot be considered absolute. On the one hand, occupation may be a continuous violation, especially if the population is resisting the occupation. On the other, though the principle *ex iniuria ius non oritur* is certainly applicable in international law so that illegal occupation and annexation cannot create legal situations, in international relations there is a tendency for long-lasting factual situations, even if initially illegal, to crystallize into legal situations at the end of the day (*ex factis ius oritur*).

For example, in January 1978 the Australian Minister for Foreign Affairs, Mr Peacock, said that Australia had decided to accept East Timor as part of Indonesia, even though it deplored the use of force by Indonesia. He stated, that this is 'a reality with which we must come to terms'.[63] Similarly, in July 1977 US Deputy Legal Adviser G.H. Aldrich stated before the Sub-committee on International Organizations of the US House of Representatives' Committee on International Relations that

> the integration [of East Timor to Indonesia] was an accomplished fact, that the realities of the situation would not be changed by our opposition of what had occurred, and that such a policy would not serve our best interests in light of the importance of our relations with Indonesia.[64]

Such explanations, given only a few years after the occupation of East Timor by Indonesia, are rather unfortunate and are dictated by narrow political interest. It is not possible, of course, to leave a situation in limbo forever and non-recognition of a factual situation, even if created by an illegal act, may bring inconveniences to third states. But the latter should consider not only their own inconveniences, but look at the situation in a wider context. The attitude of the occupied population, its relationship with the occupying power, and the damaging effects of the easy recognition of results of illegal acts are among the weighty factors which should be taken account of. Historical as well as ethnographic arguments may also play a role in the decision-making process (issues of non-recognition of illegal acts are dealt with in some detail in Chapter 4).

TOTALITARIANISM, INDEPENDENCE AND DEMOCRACY

For peoples, the attainment of independence – like freedom for the individual – is not only a means of achieving such values as, for example, economic prosperity or cultural identity, but is also an important value itself. James Mayall rightly notes that '[w]hat is claimed is freedom and independence for its own sake and not merely as a means of securing a more equitable distribution of income'.[65]

But independence is not the only thing that matters. There are other values which are at least of equal importance: human life and well-being, individual freedoms, etc. There is no sense in sacrifing these values in the name of the search for independence for nations or ethnic groups. There are about 8,000 identifiably separate cultures and languages in the world (this does not include dialects).[66] There are less than 200 states. Already the comparison of these numbers reveals that the state and the nation are far from being congruent.

When the absence of independence is an obstacle for the enjoyment of other important values it really becomes necessary to fight for independence. By that I am not asserting that independence in itself is not a value at all. It certainly is. Peoples, nations and ethnic groups, like individuals, want not only to be materially prosperous but they also want to have the possibility to determine their lives freely. They also want to preserve and develop their identity and culture.

At the same time, ethnic groups, like individuals in a society, must accept for their own and general well-being certain limitations to their freedom of choice. And this they usually do. That is why international law does not support claims for secession, though at the same time it does not prohibit them. But the absence of the right to secession means that other states cannot, without violating the norm of non-interference in internal matters of states, support secessionist claims. This would also be an encroachment on the territorial integrity of a state, not by the secessionist movement, of course, but by an interfering state.

On the other hand, not everything that happens in the territory of a state constitutes an internal matter. Oppression of the population, including ethnic minorities, or specific oppression of minorities is clearly a flagrant violation of international law. Other states and the international community as a whole acting through international organizations are authorized to undertake measures against such regimes. And a possible outcome would not only be the end of the repressive regime but also independence for suppressed minorities. However, I agree with Morton Halperin and David Scheffer that

> a group claiming a right to self-determination must come to understand that if it seeks the assistance of the United States [the authors deal mainly with a US approach to the issue] and the world community, it first should seek an accommodation of its interests within existing state borders . . .;[67]

and that 'the international community – including governments and multilateral institutions – must be involved early on in the process to seek to satisfy the demands of self-determination short of creating a new state'.[68]

It is interesting to note that totalitarianism rarely, if ever, succeeds in integrating a multi-ethnic society, though the Soviet leadership tried to standardize such a society and often spoke of the monolithic unity of the Soviet people. Therefore the end of totalitarianism in multi-ethnic countries often precipitates the disintegration of these countries.

This may sound like an argument against democratization, because it is not only democratic states which are relatively stable – totalitarian authoritarian ones are too. The danger of instability is greatest in the process of transition to democracy and concerns not only the social, economic and political life of the nation, but also inter-ethnic relations and, consequently, is fraught with the disintegration of the country. Proponents of totalitarianism or authoritarianism may say: look at what has happened in the former Soviet Union and Yugoslavia after *perestroika* and *glasnost*. Do you want a kind of Bosnia, Tadjikistan or Nagorno-Karabach in our territory?

It is certainly true that the dissolution of the USSR, Yugoslavia and Czechoslovakia did not happen while the lid of totalitarianism was still firmly in place. Only when it was lifted a bit by Gorbachev did inter-ethnic conflicts emerge on the surface. But is this necessarily an argument against lifting the lid?

I think that the Soviet, as well as the Yugoslavian, experience shows that it is impossible indefinitely to deprive peoples of their right to self-determination, and that it is better that they exercise this right sooner rather than later. Though totalitarian states may be stable, the quality of this stability is different from that of democratic states. It is, as they say, the stability of a powder keg, that is, until an explosion. On the other hand, these experiences show that in multi-ethnic societies inter-ethnic issues are most important and delicate, and that without the efforts of the democratic forces in the country, and timely and adequate external help, the processes of democratization may be very painful or may be put at risk altogether. This is all the more important because opponents of democratic reforms often try to use inter-ethnic frictions for their own ends.

THE WORLD COMMUNITY'S RESPONSES TO SECESSIONIST CLAIMS

The above analysis shows that neither the principle of the self-determination of peoples nor the principle of the territorial integrity of states provides definite solutions to all cases where secession may be at issue.

Unfortunately, interested sides usually, if not always, take only one of these principles as a guideline for their claims and actions. Taking into account that secessions of existing minorities most often create new minorities which in their turn start to seek independence (the cases of Bosnia-Herzegovina as well as of many former Soviet republics may become classic examples of this), and that this is fraught with dangers not only for international and regional stability but also for basic human rights and the world community, one certainly cannot encourage secessions from existing states. International law therefore simply cannot contain a norm granting such a right to any ethnic group. The reason for this is that states, as creators of international law, are understandably reluctant to recognize norms which may undermine their own territorial integrity. Human suffering in inter-ethnic conflicts following some recent cases of secession should induce every responsible person to think twice before speaking in favour of any secession.

The report of the Saskatoon symposium asserts that if international law were to subordinate territorial integrity to the right of 'all peoples' to self-determination by recognizing a principle that the members of a cohesive social entity within a sovereign state are entitled to freely determine their political status, the impact would be quite remarkable.[69]

I am afraid that this beautiful formula is a bit naïve and is detached from reality in many cases. Ethnicities do not live in isolation, in clear-cut units or territories. Secessionist claims and even ethnically based claims for autonomy practically always conflict with other claims and interests. For example, the claims of Quebecois for independence conflict with the claims of the indigenous peoples who live in Quebec. Minorities within minorities usually prefer to belong to a bigger unity than to be left with their immediate majority. This is one of reasons why there is conflict in the Caucasus. Though Rodolfo Stavenhagen is absolutely right that 'the violence we see around us is not generated by the drive for self-determination, but its negation'[70] (especially if by self-determination is meant the right to democratic participation rather than secession), it is no consolation to know who is right and who is guilty (or often more guilty and less guilty) when we see thousands of children, women and elderly killed by all sides in the Bosnian conflict.

However, situations involving issues of self-determination and the territorial integrity of states are so diverse and have such varying political, humanitarian, economic and other contextual facets that there can be no definite set of rules for every particular situation. This, certainly, does not mean that international law does not provide guidelines for self-determination issues. But, as in many politically sensitive issues in world affairs, different, often conflicting and controversial, factors have to be taken into account and therefore the policy oriented approach to legal issues becomes particularly relevant. I think that we may agree with Professor Lung-Chu Chen who writes that

> the test we recommend to determine whether to grant or reject a demand for self-determination is not whether a given situation is 'colonial' or 'non-colonial' but whether granting or rejecting the demands of a group would move a situation closer to goal values of human dignity, considering in particular the aggregate value conse-quences on the group directly concerned and the larger communities affected. In other words, the basic question is whether separation or unification would best promote security and facilitate effective shaping and sharing of power and of all the other values for most people. A proper balance between freedom of choice and the viability of communities must be maintained.
>
> It is essential to examine alternative consequences of either granting or rejecting claims for separation or unity. Specific con-sideration should be given to the following: (1) the degree to which the demanding group can form a viable entity, both in terms of its internal processes and its capacity to function responsibly in its relations with other entities; (2) the probable consequences of independence [separation] for the remaining people in the entity of which it has been a part; and (3) the consequences of demanded independence [separation] or unity [unification] for the aggregate pattern of value shaping and sharing for the peoples of the surround-ing communities and for the world at large.[71]

This means that decision-makers dealing with secessionist claims should take into account at least the following factors: the character of the state from which secession is sought (democratic, representative of the whole population or undemocratic, unrepresentative); the character of the secessionist movement (whether they represent the whole group seeking secession, what methods they use in order to achieve their ends, etc.); the status of the ethnic group claiming secession in the society as a whole; the potential viability of a new state if formed; the conse-quences of the secession for neighbouring states and regional stability; and the possibility of meeting the demands of the group within the existing state.

Preferably, decisions should be made by the international community as a whole via the UN or regional organizations and it is important that decisions should be made, as proposed by Halperin and Scheffer, at the earliest possible stages – not as a peace-keeping measure but as an act of preventive diplomacy.[72]

Taking into account the necessity to consider such a variety of factors in the decision-making process, most of which are of an extra-legal character, one may ask whether international law and the principle of the self-determination of peoples have played any role in the dissolution of the USSR or Yugoslavia. One may even question the applicability of legal principles to such sensitive political issues as the dissolution of states.

I think that international law, including the principle of the self-determination of peoples, has certainly influenced the events in the former Soviet Union as well as in Yugoslavia. A pure positivist, on the contrary, may come to the conclusion that everything which happened in these territories was outside the realm of international law, since policy considerations certainly played a predominant role in decision-making, not only by all the sides involved in these events but by other states as well.

The international law principle of the self-determination of peoples was claimed by independence movements in all the republics of the former USSR (the Baltic republics, of course, stressed the necessity to put an end to illegal occupation, but even they did not neglect the principle of self determination, especially as in their case both arguments worked in favour of independence). It was surprising how frequently international law arguments were used by forces seeking independence. Leaders of different entities in the former Soviet Union (and now some in Russia) spoke more often about the international legal personality of their entities than about their economic prosperity. Different forces in the centre, trying to hold together the Union almost at any cost, nevertheless never denied the existence of the right of peoples of all republics to self-determination, including even secession. It is interesting to note that the central authorities in the USSR did not use the argument that international law did not grant to any of the republics the right to secede. This was probably due to the fact that the Soviet Constitution contained such a right and that the self-determination of nations up to secession was Lenin's formula.

I think that the fact that Western countries, though never encouraging the dissolution of the Soviet Union in any way, and sometimes even strongly warning against nationalistic tendencies in different repub-lics,[73] at the same time opposed any attempts to suppress independence movements by force, illustrates and confirms the idea that self-determination is not the right to secession, but the right of peoples themselves – not only the right of their leaders – to freely determine their present and future.

SELF-DETERMINATION AND NATIONALISM

It becomes more and more obvious that in the post-Cold War world, instead of the nuclear threat one of main threats to the peace and security of mankind comes from inter-ethnic conflicts where often issues of self-determination or the rights of minorities are at stake. All these issues are closely linked with the phenomenon of nationalism.[74]

When an oppressed ethnic minority seeks secession, nationalism becomes an inevitable concomitant of the liberation struggle. Not only independence, but questions of national identity, development of culture and language become driving forces and slogans of this struggle. But nationalism, being a driving force for national liberation, if not tamed, inevitably becomes destructive.

In none of the inter-ethnic conflicts or tensions concerning the territories of the former Soviet Union or Yugoslavia can one find a blameless side. Most disturbing also is the fact that very rarely, if at all, are reasonable voices acknowledging faults and mistakes, to say nothing of crimes committed by one's own side, heard. The reason for this, as Ernest Gellner put it, is 'that the political effectiveness of national sentiment would be much impaired if nationalists had as fine a sensibility to the wrongs committed by their nation as they have to those committed against it'.[75] The accuracy of this assertion has now been proved in Eastern Europe and the erstwhile USSR. In some places in these territories it has become difficult, both physically and especially psychologically, not to behave like a nationalist, just as in countries permeated by religious fanaticism it was (or still is) difficult and even dangerous to be a heretic.

Often nationalistic sentiments are exploited by political leaders for their own ends, which further increases inter-ethnic tensions. This creates a vicious circle: to gain political power a politician has to exploit nationalistic sentiments thereby exacerbating them. To stay at the head of a movement or even a state he or she has then to become even more nationalistic.

Francis Fukuyama speaks of cultural factors that inhibit the establishment of a stable liberal democracy. The first of these factors has to do with the degree and character of a country's national, ethnic or racial consciousness. He writes:

> The desire for national independence and sovereignty can be seen as one possible manifestation of the desire for self-determination and freedom, provided that nationality, race, or ethnicity do not become the exclusive basis for citizenship and legal rights. An independent Lithuania can be a fully liberal state provided it guarantees the rights

of all citizens, including any Russian minority, that choose to remain.[76]

The desire for national independence and self-determination played a positive role in the events of 1991 in the former Soviet Union. It was directed against a totalitarian state and as the dissolution of the Soviet Union was as inevitable as was the end of 'traditional' empires, different nationalisms played historically progressive roles.

But once independence is achieved, nationalism turns mainly into a destructive force. Ideas of national (read ethnic) unity or national (read ethnic) exclusiveness cannot play any positive role in newly born multi-ethnic societies. Political will to create nation-states in such societies is counterproductive to the development of democracy. Fukuyama is correct in writing that:

> The Soviet Union could not become democratic and at the same time remain unitary, for there was no consensus among the Soviet Union's nationalities that they shared a common citizenship and identity. Democracy would only emerge on the basis of the country's breakup into smaller national entities.[77]

Now some of these smaller units are in turmoil and on the verge of breakup. There is no consensus between ethnic majorities and minorities. Democracy is equally unattainable under these circumstances. Does this mean that a new series of breakups is inevitable?

I am sure that this logic will not apply, though in some cases negotiated territorial rearrangements may be necessary. But as a rule, there is only one way towards democracy. Democracy and the observance of internationally recognized human rights are attainable only if newly born states recognize the rights and the equality of their minorities.

Moldova or Georgia cannot become really democratic states having such hotspots on their territories as the Trans-Dnestr region or South Ossetia and Abkhazia. It is necessary either to heal them or to cut them off – that is, to let them separate. Efforts to suppress the discontent in these regions would create everlasting wounds which would also become an insurmountable obstacle on the way to democracy. But I do not think at all that it is possible to qualify those seeking secession in the above cases as innocent victims. The Abkhazian conflict shows very clearly that the formula proposed in the Saskatoon paper is detached from the reality in that part of Georgia.

Taking into account that in most cases territorial rearrangements or secessions are politically unacceptable and would lead to the emergence of new minorities, the only way forward, other than permanent tension or civil wars, is by way of compromise, with respect for the rights and interests of the minorities.

If we use Ernest Gellner's definition of nationalism as a theory which requires that ethnic boundaries should not cut across political ones,[78] then its realization is simply impossible in that part of the world due to the intermingling of ethnic groups in almost all the states which have emerged after the collapse of the USSR. That is why efforts aimed at the creation of nation-states can lead only to inter-ethnic strife and tension, which will be the main obstacle for democracy and human rights.

CONCLUDING REMARKS

I assume that for some people my views on self-determination will sound rather statist because of my emphasis on the territorial integrity of states and my negative attitude towards secession. Some would probably even think that I am downgrading the rights of peoples, subordinating the right of peoples to self-determination to the right of states to territorial integrity. But are not all secessionists the strongest statists? Is not their aim to create new states with bureaucratic mechanisms and presidential, prime-ministerial, ministerial and ambassadorial posts for leaders of secessionist movements?

In many cases this is unfortunately so. Furthermore, rarely are secessions peaceful and I have grave doubts whether it is justifiable to sacrifice thousands of lives today in order to have a brighter future for millions tomorrow. Lives are sacrificed today and in reality, the brighter future is usually doubtful. Therefore, M. Kampelman is right that 'the price of war and violence associated with secessionist movements seeking sovereignty is too high for the participants to pay and for the international community to tolerate'.[79] Therefore, it is a humanitarian and not a statist component of the principle of the self-determination of peoples which speaks against secession and emphasizes the right of everybody to take part in the conduct of public affairs, thereby contributing to determination by the peoples themselves and not only by the leaders of their political, economic and social and cultural systems.

It may sound paradoxical, but the experience of the dissolution of the USSR and Yugoslavia has also show that minorities seeking secession are themselves often the strongest opponents of self-determination, which in their interpretation means secession. Senator Moynihan writes that the US had hardly gained independence when the union 'almost came apart in a disastrous civil war over slavery in which one section of the United States asserted the right to self-determination'.[80] The Senator continues: 'That should have taught a lesson; it did not. The lesson that minorities not infrequently seek self-determination for themselves in order to deny it to others. *Homo homini lupus.*'[81]

Leaders of some ethnicities simply lack Rawls's 'veil of ignorance' and in their own ignorance think of themselves as leaders of peoples while all others living in the same territory are thought to be minorities. Or, even worse, they have, as President Gamsakhurdia of Georgia called on the South Ossetians, to return to their 'real homeland in neighbouring North Ossetia' and, naturally, are not taking their territory with them.[82]

On the basis of the above analysis I would like to draw a few short conclusions concerning the current status of the principle of the self-determination of peoples.

1. The right to the self-determination is not confined to colonial peoples. It is an ongoing right of all peoples.
2. Self-determination and secession are different things. In the colonial context accession of a colony to independence was not strictly speaking a secession since the territories of parent states and the colonies were different. In the non-colonial context self-determination is an entitlement to the democracy, the right of participation in democratic process.
3. For the purposes of self-determination under international law, peoples are to be defined as populations of states, while different ethnicities in their territories constitute minorities.
4. The 'right to secession' is very similar to the 'right to revolution'. In the case of gross violations of human rights by a state, the population may overthrow the government and liberate itself from tyranny. In the case of gross violation of minority rights the minority may either overthrow the government or secede from the oppressive regime. In both cases (and they usually go hand in hand as democratic states would hardly grossly violate rights of minorities) such a state is in flagrant violation of international law and the world community has the right to intervene. Of course, it is difficult to determine the degree of interference (economic sanctions, humanitarian intervention, etc.), as this will depend on the circumstances, but in the case of a violation of minority rights such an interference may consist, *inter alia*, in the recognition by the world community of the right of the oppressed minority to secession.

3 Minorities in Eastern Europe and the former USSR
Problems, trends and protection

HISTORICAL REMARKS ON THE PROBLEM

Even before the dissolution of the USSR, Yugoslavia and Czecho-slovakia, issues concerning minorities and the protection of their rights and interests had become topical once more. Now these problems have overshadowed many other issues concerning the protection of human rights and fundamental freedoms. An early wave of attention to issues of minorities was concerned with the protection of religious minorities in different European countries in the seventeenth century. The Treaty between the King of Hungary and the Prince of Transylvania of 1606 accorded to the protestant minority in Transylvania free exercise of its religion.[1] One of the most famous treaties of that time – the Treaty of Westphalia, concluded in 1648 between France and the Holy Roman Empire and their respective allies, granted religious freedoms to the Protestants in Germany in terms of equality with Roman Catholics.[2] This wave of attention to minority issues was aimed at the protection of respective Catholic and Protestant religious minorities in countries where the majority religion was different.

At approximately the same time European powers started to conclude treaties with the Ottoman Empire in order to protect their respective religious minorities. Article 7 of the Austro-Ottoman Treaty of 1615 reads as follows:

> Ceux qui proffessent être le peuple de Jésus-Christ et qui obéissent au Pape, de quelque dénomination que le soit, écclesiastiques, moines, ou Jésuites, auront le droit de construire les églises dans les Etats du sérénissime Empire des Turcs où ils pourront d'après leurs usage, conformément au statut de leur ordre et d'après l'antique rite, lire l'évangile, se réunir en assemblées et vaquer au service divin.[3]

It is interesting to note that already in the nineteenth century the recognition of new states was linked with their treatment of minorities. The contracting parties to the Treaty of Berlin of 1878 (Austria, France, Germany, Great Britain, Italy, Russia and Turkey) declared that they would recognize Romania and Bulgaria provided that the following requirements were met:

> The difference of religions, creeds and confessions shall not be alleged against any person as a ground for exclusion or incapacity in matters relating to the enjoyment of civil and political rights, admission to public employments, functions and honours, or the exercise of the various professions and industries in any locality whatsoever. The freedom and outward exercise of all forms of worship shall be assured to all persons belonging to the State, as well as to foreigners, and no hindrance shall be offered either to the hierarchical organization of the different communities, or to their relations with their spiritual chiefs.[4]

In the context of the current discussion on whether minorities consist only of nationals of a state or also of foreigners, it is necessary to underline that in this Treaty religious rights were granted to both nationals and foreigners.

Further regard to the plight and protection of minorities came after World War I and was due mainly to the redrawing of the political map in Europe and the emergence of new states following the dissolution of the Austro-Hungarian and Ottoman empires. The experience of the League of Nations' period of the protection of minorities has been the subject of lengthy studies,[5] which exempts me from the necessity to give a detailed analysis of the modest achievements of the League of Nations' minority protection system as well as an explanation of the reasons for its general failure.

However, there were, certainly, some instructive elements in the League of Nations' system of protection of minorities which are of interest nowadays. For example, special minority treaties contained stipulations regarding the acquisition of nationality. These stipulations provided that the nationality of the newly created or enlarged country should be acquired by persons habitually resident in the transferred territory; or by persons born in the territory of parents domiciled there at the time of birth, even if they were not themselves habitually resident there at the coming into force of the treaty. The treaties also provided that nationality should be *ipso facto* acquired by any person born in the territory of the state, if he or she could not prove any other nationality.[6]

A clause in a resolution of the Assembly of the League of Nations on 21 September 1922 also sounds quite up to date, declaring:

While the Assembly recognises the primary right of the minorities to be protected by the League from oppression, it also emphasises the duty incumbent upon persons belonging to racial, religious or linguistic minorities to co-operate as loyal fellow-citizens with the nations to which they belong.[7]

It has been rightly argued that the ultimate failure of the League's system of minority protection was caused not by shortcomings in the system itself, but by the overall situation in the world and especially in Europe.

The League of Nations' system for the protection of minorities was but a part of the world structure established at Versailles, adopted to meet particular conditions arising from the territorial settlements there. Inevitably the minorities system depended on the general state of international order and relations, and when that order disintegrated the system necessarily collapsed with it. According to T. H. Bagley:

The between-war world was witness to an appalling phenomenon of retrogression, a backsliding of morals and politics. Dictatorships replaced democracies, hate and intolerance flourished, power overrode reason, and passionate nationalism crushed the growing bloom of international cooperation. That minorities should suffer in such a climate was inevitable; in fact it was quite natural that they should be the first to suffer therefrom.[8]

After World War II other issues overshadowed the problems concerning the protection of minorities, though they were not, of course, completely ignored. In the human rights domain the UN put the main emphasis on the elaboration of norms relating to the protection of the rights of individuals and the right of colonial peoples to self-determination. One of the reasons for such a neglect of minority issues was not only the modest results of the League of Nations' efforts, but, as James Mayall writes, that 'the concept of minority rights fell further into disrepute after Hitler had justified his assaults on Austria and Czechoslovakia in terms of the right of self-determination for their German-speaking populations'.[9]

The only tangible, but nevertheless rather, important achievement in the domain of the protection of minorities was the adoption of article 27 of the International Covenant on Civil and Political Rights,[10] which will be discussed below (see pp. 105–11).

But even before the problems of minorities achieved great prominence following the 'Big Bang' in the former communist world, issues concerning minorities had become topical in the UN as well as in the CSCE (Conference on Security and Cooperation in Europe) process.

The UN Commission on Human Rights was working on the draft Declaration on the rights of persons belonging to national or ethnic, religious and linguistic minorities which was finally adopted by the General Assembly in December 1992.[11] The Sub-Commission on the Prevention of Discrimination and the Protection of Minorities appointed a Special Rapporteur to prepare a study on 'Possible ways and means of facilitating the peaceful and constructive solution of problems involving minorities'.[12] The Copenhagen Document of the CSCE process of 1990[13] devoted considerable attention to minority issues. And in 1992 the CSCE High Commissioner on National Minorities was appointed.[14] In November 1992 the Council of Europe opened for signature the European Charter for Regional or Minority Languages[15] and at the time of writing the preparation of either a convention for the protection of minorities or a protocol to the European Convention on Human Rights and Fundamental Freedoms is under consideration.[16]

This high profile accorded to minority issues is to a certain extent a reaction to the processes of integration in the world. Integration and unification in certain domains (especially economic integration) tend to make countries uniform and similar. This causes powerful counter-tendencies aimed at the maintenance of cultural and other identities of countries, or even those of ethnic groups in different states. On the other hand, politicians, lawyers and other specialists have correctly come to the conclusion that even an effective protection of individual rights is not always in itself a solution for all problems relating to minorities.

MINORITY ISSUES IN THE USSR AND EASTERN EUROPE BEFORE THE 'BIG BANG'

There are two good reasons to look at minority issues in the USSR and Eastern Europe before the collapse of communism. First, in order to understand current and future developments it is necessary to know their roots. Second, nowadays and especially in those countries, there is a tendency to explain all difficulties, problems and violations of human rights as being a result of the communist past. Of course, there is often much truth in it. But sometimes the main linkage with the communist past lies in a black and white vision of the world. Then, all difficulties were explained away either as the bourgeois hangover or as intrigues of world imperialism. Now the communist past has to be blamed. In reality, the roots of most minority problems, which in the context of Eastern Europe and the former USSR often mean inter-ethnic conflicts, lie much deeper. The ideology and practice of communism undoubtedly influenced them and often made their resolution more painful. But it rarely created them.

My point is that there is no direct correlation between the social system existing in a country and the attitude of the authorities to minorities living in the territory of the state. On occasion, even the most undemocratic countries have achieved some progress in the resolution of minority issues. The attention given by some former socialist countries to minorities, while individual rights were severely suppressed, has, I believe, something to do with the collectivist approach of these states to social problems. They rightly saw in individual rights and freedoms a clear and certain threat to their power. But granting some language or cultural rights to minorities did not threaten them. Of course, when they saw in minorities even the slightest threat to their territorial integrity they were usually more ruthless than were other countries.

Consider, for example, the description in the World Directory of Minorities of the situation of the Sorbs (Wends) in the former German Democratic Republic. The Sorbs numbered approximately just over 70,000 people and so presented no threat to the territorial integrity of the GDR.

> The Government . . . since 1948, has clearly done a great deal to protect the identity of the minority: the principle of the 'Law for the protection of the Sorbian Population's Right', passed on March 23 of that year, providing for instruction in Sorb, has not been fundamentally changed. There are many schools with Sorb as the language of instruction at all levels, and a course in the language and history of Lusatia at Karl Marx University in Leipzig.[17]

What follows may sound ironical at a time when internecine war rages in the former Yugoslavia, but the same Directory rated highly the efforts of the Yugoslavian Government in the protection of minorities. Speaking of the Hungarian minority in Vojvodina, the Directory notes:

> the handling of this and other minorities in the province by the Yugoslav government since World War II has been highly creditable . . . To satisfy the various national traditions there are five official languages in the province: Serbo-Croat; Hungarian; Slovak; Romanian and Ruthenian.[18]

In the former USSR some ethnicities obtained their written language during the Soviet period. More books, journals and newspapers than before were published in the national languages of most ethnicities living in the USSR, though, according to communist party instructions, all culture in the former Soviet Union should have been national only in form, but socialist in substance. This meant that while, for example, the languages may have been national, the content of a book, movie, painting or even music should have been in conformity with the socialist realism as interpreted by the Communist Party of the USSR.

But alongside this there are many examples of horrendous crimes which were committed against not only individual human rights but also against whole ethnicities in communist countries. In the Soviet Union the Chechens, the Ingushies, the Crimean Tartars, the Volga Germans and the Meskhetian Turks were all deported under Stalin. During the assimilation campaign of 1984–5 in Bulgaria the authorities even denied the very existence of ethnic Turks in the country and inhabitants of Turkish villages were forced literally at gunpoint to change their names from Turkish-Islamic ones to those deemed more Bulgarian.[19] It would be easy to find more examples of this kind. My point is that there is nothing specifically socialist or communist in this attitude to minorities.

Consider, for example, capitalist Greece, the neighbour of socialist Bulgaria. In 1953 the Greek Government issued Decree No. 2536 designed to effect the colonization of the northern territories populated by Macedonians 'with new colonists with healthy national conscious-ness', and in 1959 'the inhabitants of certain villages were asked to confirm publicly that they did not speak Macedonian.'[20] And the reader will hardly need to be reminded of the violations of minority rights which have taken place in many non-communist authoritarian Third World countries.

One of main ideas of the Soviet leadership on ethnic issues was that eventually all ethnic differences would disappear or become at least non-substantial, and that there would be a new social entity – the Soviet people. This policy is not unique. Many countries have pursued assimilationist policies designed to achieve national unity. Only the methods have differed: from denying to minorities education in their own language to physical extermination of persons belonging to these groups.

The main difference between democratic countries and authoritarian states in this issue is that the former – even when they have serious problems with their minorities (for example, Canada), or even when they deny the very existence of minorities notwithstanding the obvious existence of them (for example, France[21]) – do not use violent methods of resolution of these problems.

The point which I wish to emphasize is that the attitude of states to minorities depends to a great extent on whether the authorities see in the minorities a threat to their national unity and territorial integrity. In this situation, as I wrote in the previous chapter, a kind of vicious circle emerges: the denial of rights, and especially repression, leads to claims for more autonomy or even independence and the latter exacerbates the negative attitude of the authorities.

The real way in which communist ideology and practice in the Soviet Union exacerbated tension in inter-ethnic relations was the very denial of the possibility of the existence under real socialism or communism of any inter-ethnic tension or conflicts. Existing problems were concealed rather than being healed and remained simmering under the surface. The fact that, along with most individual rights and freedoms, national sentiments and also nationalism were suppressed, contributed to the resurrection of nationalism in the former USSR and Eastern Europe. Nationalism as an ideology is now seen by many in that part of the world as something which has unjustly suffered in the Soviet Union and Eastern Europe and therefore needs rehabilitation and even compensation as a victim of communism.

ETHNIC DIVERSITY OF NEW STATES IN THE FORMER USSR

So-called nation-states in Western Europe, in contradistinction with states in most other parts of the world, emerged through, in some respects, a natural course of events which more often than not included long and bloody wars. But even now most of them contain substantial ethnic and linguistic, as well as religious, minorities, while some (Belgium, Switzerland) are in substance multi-ethnic states.

The emergence of states instead of empires in Eastern Europe and the former Soviet Union was a process which involved much artificiality. The redrawing of the political map of Eastern Europe after World War I, as I have already shown, demonstrates that any attempt to create nation-states, while perhaps resolving some ethnic problems, inevitably engenders new ethnically related ones. The dissolution of the USSR, Yugoslavia and, to a lesser extent, Czechoslovakia had the same effect.

When in Western Europe contemporary states emerged, the use of force in inter-state relations was accepted and nobody had heard of international standards of human rights or universal organizations charged with maintaining international peace and security and the protection of fundamental rights and freedoms.[22] Nation-states were often carved out in the process of long and bloody wars.

At the end of the twentieth century the world community of states would hardly accept that 100-year or 30-year wars will eventually resolve problems relating to the creation of nation-states in the Balkans or the Caucasus.

The new states which emerged in place of the USSR, Yugoslavia and Czechoslovakia are not, with some exceptions (for example, Slovenia) less multi-ethnic than their predecessors. Consider, for example, Russia. This, the biggest among the Soviet successor states, has more ethnically based sub-units, called republics, than the Soviet Union had. There are twenty-one republics,[23] including such recalcitrant ones as Tartarstan and Chechnia, which are among the smallest. There are also ten autonomous districts, some of which are territorially considerably larger than most Western European states. These units, which are mostly based on distinct indigenous populations, nevertheless all contain substantial Russian and other minorities or even majorities.

The republics of the Caucasus are well-known for their ethnic and religious diversity. In Georgia, for example, there are sizeable minorities of Armenians (448,000 or 9 per cent), Russians (372,000 or 7.4 per cent) and Azeris (256,000 or 5.1 per cent). Ossetians living in South Ossetia (160,000 or 3.2 per cent), Abkhazians in Abkhazia (85,000 or 1.7 per cent) and Adzharians who are Shiite Muslims of Georgian ethnic origin, live side by side in regions which formerly had some degree of political autonomy.[24]

The new states in Central Asia are in the same situation. The Russian newspaper *Nezavisimaya Gazeta* called Central Asia a ticking time-bomb of the Kremlin cartographers.[25] In 1924 new states were created quite artificially by a decision of the Central Executive Committee of Turkestan: today there are about ten contested territories.[26] Political struggle in these countries is often only camouflaged with terms such as democracy, socialism or even Islam, being in substance inter-tribal or inter-ethnic conflict. For example, the armed conflict in Tadjikistan was not only, or even mainly, between democrats and communists but between different tribes.

Ethnic diversity is common also at the opposite end of the former Soviet Union – in the Baltics. In Estonia in 1989 there were approximately 62 per cent of ethnic Estonians and 30 per cent of Russians.[27] In Latvia 48 per cent of the population is ethnically non-Latvian.[28] Lithuania is more homogeneous, though it does contain sizeable Polish and Russian minorities.

In many of the new states such ethnic diversity has existed for centuries. Some of this diversity is due to the creation of or changes in territorial boundaries during the Soviet years, and especially to the labour migration as well as to the deportation of entire peoples. But whatever the precise cause of this ethnic diversity the future of all these new states depends to a great extent on how they resolve the problems of their minorities.

NATIONALISM AND ETHNIC MINORITIES

It is notable that many treatises and articles on nationalism ignore the question of the relationship between nationalism and human rights, especially the rights of minorities. Nationalism is analysed mainly, if not exclusively, in the context of the congruence between a nation and a state. Therefore Ernest Gellner defines nationalism as

> a theory of political legitimacy, which requires that ethnic boundaries should not cut across political ones, and in particular, that ethnic boundaries within a given state – a contingency already formally excluded by the principle in its general formulation – should not separate the power holders from the rest.[29]

In similar fashion Anthony Smith, speaking of the ethnic revival in the contemporary world, emphasizes that

> as an ideological movement, nationalism seeks to attain and maintain autonomy, unity and identity of a social group, some of whose members conceive it to constitute an actual or potential nation. The aim of nationalism is always the creation of 'nations' or their maintenance or reinforcement.[30]

Most authors writing of nationalism concentrate on the nationalism of ethnicities, which are deprived of their nation state and strive for it. Therefore they put an emphasis on the nationalism of minorities.[31] J. Breuilly writes that in his book he is 'concerned with significant political movements, principally of opposition, which seek to gain or exercise state power and justify their objectives in terms of nationalist doctrine',[32] and that 'nationalism is usually a minority movement pursued against the indifference and, frequently, hostility of the majority of the members of the "nation" in whose name the nationalists act'.[33]

These are certainly very important characteristics of nationalism. But nationalism is not confined to ethnicities which are deprived of their nation-states and strive for it. A widespread form of nationalism is the nationalism of dominant majorities, especially in states engaged in nation-building. For example, the Croatian or Georgian nationalisms did not evaporate after those states gained their independence. They simply took different forms and, to a certain extent, found other addressees. Serbian nationalism exists not only in Bosnia–Herzegovina or Croatia where Serbs are trying to break away. It is quite functional and instrumental in Serbia proper. The Russian nationalism did not become less vociferous after the creation of the independent Russian state.

In some states governmental nationalism manifests itself not only in attitudes towards minorities at home but also towards ethnic brothers and sisters in other states. Hungary, for example, in article 6(3) of its Constitution recognizes its 'responsibility for the fate of Hungarians living beyond its borders.'[34]. The Macedonian Constitution (art. 49) declares that the Republic 'cares for the status and rights of those persons belonging to the Macedonian people' who live in the neighbouring countries.[35] These constitutions have in mind not citizens of the state living abroad, but ethnic Hungarians or Macedonians. Such constitutional clauses and practices are fraught with serious inter-state frictions and even conflicts.

Nationalism is, of course, a phenomenon which one can find in most countries where different ethnicities live together, but in former communist countries, which are practically all multi-ethnic states, nationalism has a particularly fertile soil. One of the reasons for that consists in the fact that nationalism, like communism, is a collectivist ideology. Both subordinate an individual and his rights and interests to the interests of society: be it defined in terms of a nation or a class. In Chapter 6, which is devoted to human rights in post-totalitarian societies, I will deal in some detail with the relationship between individualism and collectivism as philosophical categories. Therefore here I would like only to emphasize that individualism, defined by Hayek as 'the respect for the individual *qua* man, that is the recognition of his own views and tastes as supreme in his own sphere',[36] is incompatible with both communism and nationalism, as well as with their strange mixture – national-socialism. This may help to explain the ease with which many communist leaders have became hard-line nationalists. That is why this so called 'red–brown' alliance in Russia – an alliance between former communists and extreme nationalists – is not so surprising, though internationalism was always one of the tenets of communism.

One can find very interesting observations on this issue in an article by the former Marxist, and now Russian nationalist, philosopher Alexander Tsipko who wrote:

It is characteristic that a dogmatic Marxist, who has learnt by heart like a parrot textbook dogmas of Marxism, can adopt a nationalistic point of view and open his soul to national feelings, can be proud of his people and its culture. Kravchuk, Brazauskas, Nazarbayev [presidents of Ukraine, Lithuania and Kazakhstan respectively] easily and naturally transformed from party officials into national leaders. This could happen only because their Marxism was not deeply rooted in their souls, but was only instrumental, serving their career purposes.[37]

But if they could embrace Marxism for the sake of their careers why should they be more sincere in embracing nationalism? It is true to say that these leaders are rather moderate nationalists, if nationalists at all. Ukraine, Lithuania and Kazakhstan have resolved their inter-ethnic issues relatively well, and without excessive nationalistic fervour, at least up until now.

But Tsipko seems to be a real nationalist accusing, for example, 'Democratic Russia', (DR) – a political movement supporting President Yeltsin – of not embracing Russian nationalism. According to him the matter is that 'DR does not believe in the absolute value of state, nation and religion'. Instead democrats, writes Tsipko, believe in the absolute value of law, as if law can be higher than nation, state, God, and the individual human being.[38] The order of these values should be noted, as should the fact that only three of them are absolute. The party is substituted for God; the individual is not in the list of absolute values.

John Goetz writes that:

> President Gorbunovs [of Latvia] has survived his embarrassing past as a functionary of the Latvian Communist Party by mimicking the radical nationalists. He has gone along with every shift to the right the nationalist movement has taken. On the 50th anniversary of Blutsonntag, when the murder of 85 000 Latvian Jews is remembered, Gorbunovs said Latvia's Jews should take responsibility for their own role in the massacre.[39]

When working closely with the former Chairman of the Supreme Council of Estonia, A. Rüütel, I personally witnessed this subtle but quick transformation in him also. Being a moderate communist leader of Soviet Estonia, he, after 1988, made a significant contribution to the smoothness of the independence process in Estonia. But because of his communist past he probably felt obliged to reiterate time and again his loyalty to the Estonian nation and to make compromises with extreme nationalists, who finally out-voted him in the Parliament during the presidential elections, though in the popular vote he had obtained a clear majority but fell short of obtaining 50 per cent of the votes.

The Prime Minister of Estonia, Mart Laar, in December 1992 proudly declared in his interview with the Russian newspaper *Megapolis-Express*: 'Yes, we are rightists, yes, we are nationalists.'[40] John Goetz in *The Guardian* writes that since 'the collapse of the Soviet Union, Latvia's political spectrum has moved steadily toward radical nationalism' and 'Latvia may be the only place in the world building monuments to the SS; 19 have been erected so far.'[41] In Hungary 'as in the rest of eastern Europe, prejudice is reasserting itself now that communist oppression has gone' and the 'generally unsympathetic climate is making it more difficult for Hungary's resident Slovak, Romanian, Serbian Croatian and Jewish parents to manage their own schools. Even more worrying for these communities is the fact that racist intolerance is creeping into the curriculum.'[42]

These are countries where people do not kill each other because of their ethnic differences as in the former Yugoslavia or in Georgia and Nagorno-Karabach. These are really the luckiest among post-communist countries, where economic reforms have already brought about not just hardships to the majority of their populations but also some positive achievements and structural changes.

A specific feature of nationalism is the attitude towards other nations and ethnicities and especially towards neighbours. This attitude has more to do with the methods used by nationalists in furthering their aims than with the aims themselves. Nationalism is always – and this is sometimes forgotten – not only for something or somebody, but also against something or somebody. Nationalism cannot exist in an abstract form (i.e. not being directed against a specific ethnicity or ethnicities).

Nationalism is always instrumental. When a minority struggles for autonomy or independence its nationalism is directed against the majority which objects to that autonomy or independence. And nationalism cannot be rational; it has to be simple and emotional in order to mobilize mass support. Nationalism has to be directed not only against those among the majority who oppose the aspirations of the minority, but against the majority as a whole. In turn it engenders a superiority complex, which very often is a reaction to a previous inferiority complex, and even hatred towards those against whom it is directed.[43]

Although manifested in different ways, what is clear is that nationalism creates negative feelings in one part of the population which are directed against another. This may involve a vicious circle. Oppression, denial of rights or even insufficient attention to the problems of minorities stimulate minority nationalism, which in its turn supports and enhances majority nationalism. And here, of course, the minority is most often the weaker side, whose rights and interests suffer most.

In his study for the UN Sub-Commission on the Prevention of Discrimination and the Protection of Minorities, Asbjorn Eide writes that ethno-nationalism[44] 'can be expansionist, exclusivist and/or secessionist.'[45] In all of these forms nationalism is detrimental to minority rights. In its expansionist form, it either tries to unite members of one and the same ethnicity scattered in different states (attempts to create 'Greater Serbia' is one of the more notorious examples), or, by taking too close an interest in defending the rights and interests of its ethnic brethren in other countries, starts to interfere in the domestic affairs of those states. Of course, these are often two sides of the same coin.

In its exclusivist form nationalism may give rise to different forms of 'ethnic cleansing'. In all cases it tries to eliminate minorities by excluding them either from the political life of the country (for example, through restrictive citizenship legislation), or by discriminating against them in other spheres of social life. For example, when Sri Lanka became independent, the Tamils, who had come to the island generations ago, were denied citizenship. This contributed to the ethnic explosion there.[46] Estonian and Latvian citizenship policies have also played a role in aggravating inter-ethnic tension in those countries.

We may conclude that nationalism is hardly conducive to the enjoyment and protection of minority rights, nor to human rights in general. According to Snyder, 'nationalism has always been associated with warfare and the warrior traditions. The struggle was always the insider against the foreigner, against those who spoke different languages and had disparate traditions and an alien culture.'[47]

Of course, not every nationalism necessarily and automatically leads to grave violation of human rights. But even non-governmental nationalism may adversely affect human rights as well as inter-state relations, if the government does not take prompt and decisive measures, including the criminal prosecution of those who spread and incite racial and ethnic hatred.

Speaking in January 1992 UN Secretary-General Boutros-Ghali observed:

> Civil Wars are no longer civil, and the carnage they inflict will not let the world remain indifferent. The narrow nationalism that would oppose or disregard the norms of a stable international order and the micronationalism that resists healthy economic or political integration can destruct a peaceful global existence . . . Nationalist fever will increase ad infinitum the number of communities that lay claim to sovereignty, for there will always be dissatisfied minorities within those minorities that achieve independence. Peace, first threatened by ethnic conflict and tribal warfare, could then frequently be troubled by border disputes.[48]

It has been correctly said that 'the hopes of cosmopolitans everywhere seem further than ever from being realized, and ethnic ties and national loyalties have become stronger and more deep-rooted than ever'.[49] It is also true that 'the very economic and industrial trends' which were assumed to undermine 'tribalism and nationalism, have instead tended to reinforce ethnic and national divisions and loyalties'.[50] But nevertheless I think that these trends, as well as the democratization of the world, which do enhance nationalistic feelings and actions in some countries or regions as a kind of counter-reaction, also work to undermine nationalism or tribalism. The paradox is that because of this undermining and weakening of nationalism it sometimes becomes more aggressive and even stronger.

The struggle for national liberation was (and in some cases continues to be) the struggle of oppressed ethnicities. Professor Mayall is right that 'the creation of states during the nationalist era must be viewed as an integral part of the history of liberty'.[51] The collapse of empires, the development of democracy, and the increase in the number of democratic (including multi-ethnic) countries in the world means that although the number of ethnicities is not diminishing, the number of oppressed ethnicities certainly is. Therefore, nationalism, as an ideology of the struggle for national liberation – which is a positive side of the ideology – is losing its ground. What this means is that the role of the nationalistic ideology and nationalistic movements is becoming more and more destructive and negative. The correlation between the benign, libertarian side of nationalism and its xenophobic, destructive component has changed with the changes in the world. Incarnations of nationalism are no longer Garibaldi or Mahatma Gandhi, but Hitler, Milosevic, and ETA terrorists.

Nationalism is in some aspects rather similar to religion. It is based on a belief in something irrational, even mythic. Like religion, it may also serve benign purposes or create intolerance and hatred. Like religion, nationalism can be moderate, resulting, for example, in economic protectionism or claims for cultural autonomy. But it can be fundamentalist, leading to discrimination, wars and terrorism. If mankind in the foreseeable future probably has to live with nationalism it should not surrender to and appease fundamentalist nationalism.

INTERNATIONAL LAW AND TECHNIQUES FOR THE RESOLUTION OF THE PROBLEMS OF MINORITIES

It is now time to look at the current status of international law on minority issues and how its requirements can be implemented in the countries of Eastern Europe and the former USSR. As there are many important controversial legal problems relating to the protection of minorities generally, these also will be dealt with in some detail.

The most comprehensive norm of international law currently in force relating to the protection of minorities is article 27 of the Covenant on Civil and Political Rights (CCPR).[52] This article provides that:

In those States in which ethnic, religious or linguistic minorities exist, persons belonging to such minorities shall not be denied the right, in community with the other members of their group, to enjoy their own culture, to profess and practice their own religion, or to use their own language.

In the field of education, the UNESCO Convention against Discrimination in Education of 1960,[53] which entered into force in 1962 is also relevant to minority protection. Convention No. 107 of the International Labour Organization (ILO), which dates from 1957, concerns the Protection and Integration of Indigenous and other Tribal and Semi-Tribal Populations in Independent Countries,[54] is of special interest for such populations, though the Convention is ratified by only twenty-seven states. Countries such as Russia, the USA, Canada and China, with sizeable indigenous populations, are not parties to the Convention.

The CSCE meetings and documents have paid much attention to minority issues. Not only were many important recommendations made, but the post of the CSCE High Commissioner on National Minorities was created. The creation of this post and its mandate shows that minority issues in the CSCE context are seen not only as human rights problems, but also as important security matters. The Helsinki Decisions provide that the

High commissioner provides 'early warning' and, as appropriate, 'early action', at the earliest possible stage in regard to tensions involving national minority issues that have the potential to develop into a conflict within the CSCE area, affecting peace, stability, or relations between participating states.[55]

The newest document on the issue is the UN GA Declaration on the Rights of Persons Belonging to National or Ethnic, Religious and Linguistic Minorities, adopted in December 1992,[56] which contains a series of recommendations on how to resolve minority problems.

At first sight it may seem surprising that, notwithstanding lengthy formulations which describe how minority issues may be resolved in different countries, all these documents have not added significant new normative elements to the brief formulation of article 27, which does not mean that these documents are superfluous or unimportant. They clarify various points and, more importantly, they make the positive experience of different countries available for other states to consider. However, article 27 already contains practically all that is necessary and possible at the universal level for minority protection. The requirements of the article simply need to be implemented.

My own view is that the UN Declaration on minorities, as well as the relevant CSCE documents, is highly reminiscent of the General Comments which are prepared by the Human Rights Committee on specific articles or issues of the Covenant on Civil and Political Rights.[57] These Comments clarify points which are unclear or controversial in the Covenant and show what has been done or could be done in order to better implement concrete requirements. But they do not and cannot in principle go beyond the requirements of the Covenant itself.

The reason for the situation is that minority issues vary considerably and that even in a single country various minorities (for example, Gypsies and Hungarians in Slovakia) face different problems, the solutions to which are also necessarily different. Therefore at the universal level and in the legally binding form it would be very difficult, if not impossible and maybe even counter-productive, to create more detailed requirements concerning the protection of minorities. I doubt whether even at the regional (e.g. European) level it would be possible or desirable to adopt a document binding on states which goes far beyond article 27.

It is difficult to foretell, of course, the future effectiveness of the European Charter for Regional or Minority Languages which has been recently open for signature and ratification by European countries.[58] But the flexibility of the instrument giving the participating states the freedom to choose among proposed measures of development and protection of regional or minority languages in the domains of education, justice, administration, mass media, culture and economic and social life seems to be the only possible approach even at the regional level. State parties have to choose at least 35 measures from the 100 listed in the Charter. It has to be noted that this instrument deals with only one, though very important, aspect of the protection of minorities – language.

Such a flexibility is necessary not only because of each country's differing available resources and the reluctance of some states to go far enough in the protection of regional and minority languages, but also stems from the non-identical needs and claims of the minorities themselves in different countries.

Therefore, I have doubts concerning the expediency or advisability of further international standard-setting in relation to the protection of minorities. The world needs more effective mechanisms with an early warning capacity. It also requires the political will of the world community to become involved in various ways, often on the basis of confidentiality, in simmering inter-ethnic tensions and problems. The

French plan for a new European stability pact, aimed at forestalling any future conflict over national minorities in Eastern and Central Europe, considered by the European Community summit in Copenhagen in June 1993, may be a step in the right direction.[59]

PROTECTION OF MINORITIES UNDER CUSTOMARY INTERNATIONAL LAW

I believe that article 27 requirements have become part and parcel of universal customary international law. It is not, of course, due only to the fact that by the end of 1993 there were 124 state-parties to the CCPR.

The first requirement of article 27, that minorities must not be discriminated against, is also covered by articles 2 and 26 of the same Covenant, as the prohibition of discrimination based on grounds such as race, colour, language, religion and national origin is absolute. This prohibition is enshrined in the UN Universal Declaration of Human Rights, as well as in the International Convention on the Elimination of All Forms of Racial Discrimination of 1965 and in many other universal and regional instruments. The work of the UN Commission on Human Rights also confirms the universal character of the non-discrimination requirement. The General Comment of the Human Rights Committee on non-discrimination says that 'Non-discrimination together with equality before the law and equal protection by the law without any discrimination, constitute a basic and general principle relating to the protection of human rights'.[60]

The situation is less clear with the second requirement of article 27: that persons belonging to minorities shall not be denied the right, in community with the other members of their group, to enjoy their own culture, to profess and practise their own religion, or to use their own language. This right does not have such clear support as the non-discrimination requirement in international documents or in practice. Nevertheless I would argue that this aspect of minority rights also has the character of a customary norm of international law of a universal nature and my arguments are the following.

A closer look at article 27 and its practical implementation by different states permits the conclusion that article 27 does not grant any privileges to minorities in comparison with the majority. As Gudmundur Alfredsson and Alfred de Zayas write, the '[s]pecial rights [of minorities] should not be seen as privileges since such rights are rooted in the principle of equality just as in non-discrimination'.[61] The only exception is indigenous peoples, whose protection may need some special measures giving them certain privileges or advantages in specific areas. The second requirement of article 27 appears to be simply another aspect of the requirement of non-discrimination. Majorities and minorities have an equal right to their identity. Non-discrimination means that everybody should be equal with everybody else as to his or her rights and this also covers the right to remain different and to preserve and develop one's identity.

A special provision aimed at the protection of the right of minorities to preserve and develop their identity is needed because the majority may (and in practice often does) threaten the identity of the minority, even if the majority does not pursue a special policy aimed at the assimilation or exclusion of the minority. And as the majority and the minority have an equal right to their identity, this part of article 27 is in essence a prohibition of discrimination by a stronger party against a weaker one in the right to their identity.

Confirmation of my view that article 27 is a customary norm of international law may be found in the Document of the Copenhagen Meeting of the Conference on the Human Dimension of the CSCE. In this document the participating states reaffirmed: 'that respect for the rights of persons belonging to national minorities as part of universally recognized human rights is an essential factor for peace, justice, stability and democracy in the participating States'.[62]

One very important element of the protection of minorities under article 27 is the issue of whether states fulfil their obligations by simply not denying minorities their right to identity, or whether states have to take positive action in order to guarantee the implementation of that right. This issue was partly clarified in the Copenhagen Document of the CSCE as well as in the UN Declaration on Minorities.

Paragraph 33 of the Document establishes that the participating states will create conditions for the promotion of the identity of minorities. Article 4 of the UN Declaration requires that states shall take measures to create favourable conditions to enable persons belonging to minorities to express their characteristics and to develop their culture, language, religion, traditions and customs, and that states should take appropriate measures so that, wherever possible, persons belonging to minorities have adequate opportunities to learn their mother tongue or to have instruction in their mother tongue.

This approach has to be applauded. Clearly, without state support of culture and education those rights would most often remain unfulfilled. It also fits with the non-discrimination requirement which obliges a state to create equal opportunities for minorities as well as for the majority.

MINORITIES AND PERSONS BELONGING TO MINORITIES

The reader may have noticed that I am not paying too much attention to whether I use the term 'minority' or 'persons belonging to minorities'. Some authors have devoted pages to it,[63] and states have always been keen to speak of the latter and not the former. Does the reference in official documents to 'persons belonging to minorities' mean that minorities as such are not protected by these documents and these rights are only individual rights and not collective ones as well?

In article 27, the reference to 'persons belonging to minorities' as those who are protected by the article and not to minorities themselves, is well balanced by the indication that such persons should be free to exercise this right in community with other members of their group. This means that via the protection of the rights of persons belonging to the minority the rights of the minority as a group are also protected.

The reference in article 27 to persons belonging to minorities is beneficial for minorities as it permits individuals to use the procedure of individual communications under the Optional Protocol to the CCPR, which otherwise would have been closed to them just as it is closed to peoples under article 1 of the Covenant.[64]

This does not mean that the Covenant does not protect minorities as a group. As the experience of the Human Rights Committee shows, it is impossible to protect individual members of minorities against discrimination, or to guarantee to them their right to identity, without securing the same for the minority as a group. Consider, for example, the communication No. 167/1984 (*Chief Bernard Ominayak and the Lubicon Lake Band* v. *Canada*). The Human Rights Committee declared the communication admissible because it emanated from a person belonging to the minority (Chief Bernard Ominayak). However, in its final views on the case the Committee concluded:

> historical inequities, to which the State party refers, and certain more recent developments *threaten the way of life and culture of the Lubicon Lake Band* [emphasis added], and constitute a violation of article 27 so long as they continue. The State party proposes to rectify the situation by a remedy that the Committee deems appropriate within the meaning of article 2 of the Covenant.[65]

It is to be noted that the Committee does not speak of persons belonging to the Band or of Chief Ominayak whose way of life may be threatened, but of the Band itself. I would have found it quite artificial to say in the views of the Committee, for example, 'that recent developments threaten the way of life of Chief Ominayak', and actually no member of the Committee expressed his or her views in such words. What this means is that the Committee found a violation of the rights of the minority as such – not only of those of the author of the communication.

When considering reports of state parties on the implementation of the Covenant, the Human Rights Committee does not distinguish between minorities as such and persons belonging to minorities. Violation of the rights of minorities as a group would inevitably result in violation of the rights of persons belonging to that group, while violation of special minority rights of persons belonging to minorities is most often an indication of the violation of the rights of minorities as a group.

In short, the difference between individual and collective rights is not so absolute. In turn, article 27 is not so different from certain other articles of the same Covenant. For example, freedom of religion (article 18) can in most cases be fully exercised by an individual only in community with others. It hardly needs saying that freedom of assembly (article 21) and freedom of association (article 22) cannot be exercised by individuals alone.

MINORITIES AND CITIZENSHIP

One of the controversial issues concerning the position of minorities is whether only citizens of a given country can be categorized as persons belonging to minorities or whether the concept extends to foreigners and stateless persons as well.

In his study, Capotorti defines persons belonging to minorities only as nationals (citizens) of a given country.[66] The Report of the CSCE meeting of experts on national minorities held in Geneva in July 1991 does not clarify the issue directly, although the formulation of some clauses gives the impression that only citizens were to be included. For example, according to Part III of the Report participating states respect 'the right of persons belonging to national minorities to effective participation in public affairs'.[67] It is well known that article 25 of the CCPR speaks of the right of citizens only to participate in the conduct of public affairs. It may be concluded that, as persons belonging to minorities have the right to participate in the conduct of public affairs, they have to be citizens. This conclusion seems to be confirmed by Part IV of the CSCE Report. It is stated that 'the participating states affirm that persons belonging to a national minority will enjoy the same rights and have the same duties of citizenship as the rest of the population'.[68] However, article 27 of the CCPR is silent on the matter. Furthermore, the UN Declaration of December 1992 avoided this issue. It is the case that different views are held by states as well as among experts.[69]

It is true that legislation in all states distinguishes between citizens and non-citizens, and that the former usually have not only more rights but more obligations as well. But this difference between citizens and non-citizens is not and should not be based on ethnic criteria. Therefore, it is natural that different persons belonging to the same minority may have a different status in any given country depending on their citizenship. The status of foreigners may depend also on whether they are permanent or temporary residents of a country.

But the differentiation between the legal status of citizens and non-citizens has no direct bearing on minority rights as they are defined in international law. My view is that there is no reason why the rights enshrined in article 27 of the CCPR should be confined to citizens. Foreigners or stateless persons permanently resident in a country should be able, along with other members of their group, to enjoy their own culture, to profess and practise their own religion, and to use their own language. There is no good reason why these minimum requirements should not be extended to foreigners and stateless persons as well.

Of course, the minimum required by international law is not always sufficient for the resolution of minority problems. We know that if in some cases it is enough to have local newspapers in minority languages or places of worship for religious minorities, in other cases the resolution of minority issues requires the establishment of territorial autonomies. Good examples are South Tyrol in Trentina Alto Adige in Italy or the Aaland islands in Finland. The implementation of article 27 at the national level requires a variety of different measures depending on local conditions.

International law does not prescribe the forms of implementation of article 27 of the CCPR. Much depends on the size, historical traditions, area of habitation and other characteristics of minorities. States may, and often probably have to, go much further than the minimum required by international law. And in that case a state may and probably should take into account whether a minority consists of foreigners permanently resident in the country, or whether it has populated the region for centuries. In the latter case, thought may be given to territorial autonomy, but in the case of foreign residents that would scarcely be possible.[70]

In some countries where foreigners are excluded from minority protection one should ask: why it is done, what is the reason? It would also be necessary in such cases to look into the citizenship legislation. Are not persons belonging to certain ethnic groups first denied citizenship and then as a result also denied the protection under minority rights clauses? This question arises, for example, in relation to the restrictive citizenship legislation of Estonia and Latvia where a substantial percentage of the non-indigenous population became stateless persons.[71]

MINORITIES AND THEIR 'MOTHERLANDS'

Minorities very often have their so-called 'motherland' state where their ethnic brethren live. Such a situation often creates difficult problems. The situation is particularly grave in Eastern Europe and in territories which formerly were part of the Soviet Union. For not only are minority problems of a very serious character in many of these countries, but also the 'motherlands' often take too close an interest in their ethnic brothers and sisters in other countries. Previously, reference was made to the constitutions of some Eastern European states which, as specified in article 6(3) of the Hungarian Constitution, establish that the state has a responsibility to look after the recognition of the rights of ethnic brethren living outside the state boundaries. At the time of writing Russia is showing particular interest in Russian minorities in all the states of the former USSR.

In June 1992 the Defence Minister, Pavel Grachev, declared that the army would defend the 'honour and dignity of the Russian population' in any region.[72] Two important points have to be noted here: first, that it is the *army* which will defend, and second, that it will defend *ethnic* Russians rather than the citizens of Russia.

In August of the same year several members of the Council for foreign and defence policy, a private organization established by the deputy director of the Institute of Europe, Serguei Karaganov, published a document which, *inter alia*, stressed that the presence of the Russian diaspora in the 'near abroad' gives Russia 'political, economic and social trump cards of significant potential power'.[73]

Such arguments do not increase trust towards Russia in the states which once belonged to the Russian and Soviet empires. They are certainly counter-productive for the protection of the rights of ethnic Russians living beyond the frontiers of Russia. Moreover, such statements feed nationalists in the countries of the 'near abroad'.

However, it would certainly be unrealistic to think that states would completely ignore the plight of their ethnic brethren in other countries. Therefore, an important question arises. What are the responsibilities of these 'motherland' countries towards their ethnic brothers and sisters who live abroad and are not its citizens?

From the point of view of international law, their lawful interest in these matters is the same as that of any other country. International law permits states to exercise diplomatic protection of their citizens abroad. Citizens of other countries or stateless persons, whatever their ethnic origin, are under the protection of international human rights law and not that of the state where their ethnic brethren live. Thus, Russia has no more right to interfere on behalf of the Russian minority in Estonia than the United Kingdom has.

Equally, it would be unrealistic to expect 'motherlands' to remain indifferent in the face of real violations of the rights of their ethnic brothers and sisters in other countries. The way to deal with such understandable concerns is not through unilateral diplomatic demarches or unilateral constitutional provisions extending the protection of a state to foreign citizens on the basis of their ethnic origin or threats, which are usually counter-productive. The best way would be to resolve such issues through bilateral negotiations and the conclusion of relevant treaties. Another way is through adequate international mechanisms and procedures like the CSCE, Council of Europe or UN.

MINORITIES AND CONSOCIATIONAL DEMOCRACY

As minority situations vary so widely, states have to use different modalities for the resolution of their problems. The range of tasks relating to the protection of minorities extends from, for example, how to finance schooling in a minority language, to negotiating a cease-fire between warring factions. The point, of course, is that whether the latter ever happens or not may depend on the resolution of the former.

In his speech to Atlantic College on 15 February 1993, UK Foreign Secretary Douglas Hurd spelt out different possible options for the resolution of minority problems such as some form of autonomy for minorities within a state, freedom from discrimination or assimilation, the right to speak one's mother tongue and the right to pursue one's culture and religion.[74] There are many other different ways of resolving these issues.

One of the ways of dealing with minority issues in many newly born countries, or even in old countries in Eastern Europe which are undergoing drastic reforms, is the establishment of some elements of so-called consociational democracy. Some political scientists have argued that this may be a solution for plural societies including multi-ethnic ones.[75] According to Lijphart

> it is in the nature of consociational democracy, at least initially, to make plural societies more thoroughly plural. Its approach is not to abolish or weaken segmental cleavages but to recognize them

explicitly and to turn the segments into constructive elements of stable democracy.[76]

There are, indeed, as Lijphart indicates, only three principle possible ways of dealing with minorities: assimilation, separation and the recognition of minority problems, and the resolving of them in everyday life.[77]

Policies of assimilation are usually counter-productive. Measures aimed at assimilation engender or enhance nationalism among minorities. Snyder speaks of Napoleon:

> Instead of unifying Europeans under his banner, the Corsican, without actually desiring the consequences, extended the force of nationalism into a dominant position in the nineteenth century in Europe. From there it spread its tentacles throughout the world.[78]

The same happened in the Soviet Union, where the authorities tried to create a uniform entity – the Soviet people. History, we may observe, is now repeating itself in some newly born states of Eastern Europe and the former USSR.

Assimilation is also clearly contrary to article 27 of the CCPR which emphasizes the right of minorities to their identity, and the 1992 UN Declaration on minorities is simply imbued with anti-assimilationist spirit.[79]

Separation or secession are usually accompanied by bloody wars and in most cases should be resorted to only as a last resort, as was spelled out in the previous chapter.

Dealing with complicated minority issues, especially if minorities are numerically large, may, indeed, necessitate recourse to elements of consociational democracy, the main features of which are: government by a grand coalition of political leaders of all significant segments; the mutual 'veto', which serves as an additional protection of vital minority interests; proportionality as the method of political representation; and a high degree of autonomy for each segment to run its own affairs.[80] The experience of various countries shows that consociationalism succeeds if favourable conditions for its success exist. Switzerland, the Netherlands, Austria, and Belgium may be referred to as the most successful examples. There have been some equally prominent failures such as Lebanon and Cyprus.[81]

In Colombia elements of consociationalism were used after a long period of civil war (1948–64) which became known as La Violenca,[82] and leaders of the Conservatives and the Liberals understood that these arrangements for power-sharing formed the only alternative to the Hobbesian *bellum omnium contra omnes*.

The failure of the consociational systems in Lebanon and Cyprus may be due, if not entirely then at least to a great extent, to foreign factors.

Certainly, it is not in all newly born countries of Eastern Europe and the former USSR that favourable conditions for consociational democracy exist (or for any type of democracy at all). But introduction of some elements of consociationalism may not only be desirable but even necessary for democratization in at least some of new states.

For example, territorial or cultural autonomy for ethnic minorities in many countries of the former Soviet Union may become necessary. The creation of two-tier parliaments where in one house minorities would have equal or proportional representation, the encouragement of the participation of representatives of minorities in the government and civil service, and other such measures should be explored.

Democracy formally means rule by the majority. But one of the important indicators of its quality is how the majority protects the rights and takes into account the interests of minorities. The world as a whole, and especially newly born countries, is still far from realizing this truth. That is why issues concerning the protection of the minorities are so important. Democracy, if not completely non-existent, will at least be deficient in society as a whole if the rights of minorities are denied or grossly violated. Democracy in any domestic society, like peace in the world society, is indivisible. In Europe, where the keyword is integration and the importance of international frontiers is diminishing, the approach of individual countries to their minorities should also be integrationist and not assimilationist or segregationist. Democracy in a multi-ethnic society means much more than one person – one vote.

4 Law and politics in the recognition of new states

INTERNATIONAL LAW ON THE RECOGNITION OF STATES

The emergence of new states in Eastern Europe and the former Soviet Union has raised issues relating to the recognition of states and has once more engendered discussions on whether such recognition is a political or legal phenomenon or whether it has a declaratory or constitutive nature.

Recognition is, first of all, as events in Eastern Europe and in the former Soviet Union have confirmed, certainly an act of high political importance and its grant or refusal are basically dictated by political considerations. But at the same time, it is not only governed, at least to a certain extent, by international law but also always has important (both domestic and international) legal consequences. *Oppenheim's International Law* (9th edn) states that

> while the grant of recognition is within the discretion of states, it is not a matter of arbitrary will or political concession, but is given or refused in accordance with legal principle. That principle, which applies alike to recognition of states, governments, belligerents or insurgents, is that, when certain conditions of fact (not themselves contrary to international law) are shown to exist, recognition is permissible and is consistent with international law in that it cannot (as may recognition accorded before those facts are clearly established) be considered to constitute intervention; and that, while recognition is accordingly declaratory of these facts, it is also constitutive of the rights and duties of the recognized community in its relations with the recognizing state.[1]

Some states have expressly and officially formulated their views concerning the recognition of states. The official position of the UK Government, for example, is as follows:

The criteria which normally apply for the recognition of a state are that it should have, and seem likely to continue to have, a clearly defined territory with a population, a Government who are able of themselves to exercise effective control of that territory and independence in their external relations. There are, however, exceptional cases when other factors, including relevant United Nations resolutions, may have to be taken into account.[2]

The US Government holds that:

International law does not require a state to recognize another entity as a state, it is a matter of judgement of each state whether an entity merits recognition as a state. In reaching this judgement, the United States has traditionally looked to the establishment of certain facts. These facts include effective control over a clearly defined territory and population; an organized governmental administration of that territory; and capacity to act effectively to conduct foreign relations and to fulfil international obligations. The United States has also taken into account whether the entity in question has attracted the recognition of the international community of states.[3]

These rather lengthy quotations were necessary to see to what extent different states followed these rules or doctrines in recognizing new states in the former USSR and Yugoslavia.

The European Community member-states adopted, in December 1991, 'Guidelines on the recognition of new states in Eastern Europe and in the Soviet Union'.[4] This document, referring to traditional international standards of recognition of new states, also established some new criteria and conditions which have to be fulfilled by new states before recognition is granted. These new requirements are rule of law, democracy and respect for human rights; guarantees for the rights of ethnic and national groups and minorities in accordance with commitments subscribed in the framework of the CSCE; acceptance of existing boundaries and compliance with international obligations in the domain of disarmament and state-succession. An analysis of the significance and implementation of these Guidelines will be given below.

Chronologically one may distinguish between the recognition of the Baltic states in August–September 1991, of other former Soviet Republics at the end of 1991 and the beginning of 1992, and of the republics of the former Yugoslavia as independent states some time later.

But more important than the chronological distinction of respective acts of recognition is the difference in the political and legal contexts within which they occurred.

RECOGNITION OF THE BALTIC STATES

Even before the failed August coup in the USSR the Baltic republics had sought some kind of recognition of their struggle for independence.

Though most Western countries had not recognized the annexation of these countries by the Soviet Union in 1940, and had expressed sympathy with their independence claims, they naturally could not recognize the Baltic republics as independent states before they could be considered as such.

The failed coup was a gift for democratic forces and especially for the Baltic republics. The dissolution of the USSR and the consequent independence of the Baltics was, no doubt, foreseeable, but without the coup the process would have been certainly more painful and possibly incurred more casualties. When Estonia (on 20 August) and Latvia (the next day) declared their independence,[5] the correlation of forces in the USSR had already drastically changed, and they could therefore realistically hope that these declarations would be recognized by other states.

As the recognition of new states in doubtful cases depends to a great extent on the position of the parent state, the Chairman of the Supreme Council of Estonia, Arnold Rüütel, the Chairman of the Foreign Relations Committee of the Parliament, Indrek Toome, and myself flew immediately to Moscow after the failed coup in order to secure at least recognition by President Yeltsin of Russia or, at best, recognition by President Gorbachev of the USSR. We could more realistically, of course, count on recognition by Russia as in article 1 of the Treaty on Fundamentals of Inter-State Relations between Estonia and Russia of 12 January 1991 in which both states had agreed to 'recognize each other as sovereign states and entities under international law, simultaneously recognizing the right of the other *to realize its sovereignty in whatever form it chooses*' [emphasis added].[6]

One may, of course, say that Russia itself was still a part of the Soviet Union and did not consider, at least openly and officially, secession from the USSR at that time which would have meant, of course, the dissolution of the latter. But as early as June 1991 (i.e. three months before the attempted coup), I gathered from my conversations with Minister Andrei Kozyrev and his deputies Andrei Kolossovsky and Georgii Kunadze that, though these ambitious young Russian diplomats did not contemplate any secession of Russia from the Union at that time, they certainly ascribed to the future Union only secondary functions – at least in the field of its foreign relations. Immediately after the failed coup the real power centre in the USSR was not in the Kremlin, but in the White House on the Moscow River where Yeltsin and the Russian Parliament sat. Therefore, the calculations of the Estonian leadership to seek recognition from Russia had, I think, some political justification.

We spent almost the whole day in the White House in order to obtain a Decree of President Yeltsin on the recognition of Estonia. As everybody was either too busy or away I had, together with Mr Kolossovsky, to draft a document which was then signed by Yeltsin as a Decree which (a) recognized the independence of Estonia, (b) required the Foreign Ministry of Russia to start negotiations with Estonia on the establishment of diplomatic relations, (c) called on President Gorbachev to recognize the independence of Estonia, and (d) called on the world community of states to recognize the independence of Estonia.[7]

A few hours later a Decree, with analogous content, was handed over to the Latvian delegation headed by the Chairman of the Supreme Council of Latvia, Anatolis Gorbunovs.[8] The situation concerning Lithuania was different because Russia and Lithuania had, after Lithuania had declared independence on 11 March 1990, concluded a Treaty in which the High Contracting Parties recognized each other as 'sovereign states', specifically mentioning the Lithuanian declaration of independence.[9] Russia had signed similar treaties with Estonia and Latvia but these states had not by then declared their independence, though, as I already mentioned, they had started transitional periods which had to end with independence.

These treaties and decrees of recognition were documents of immense political importance though their legal nature was doubtful. But I think that it was doubtful only at that time. Future political developments conferred legality upon these and some other documents with rather unclear legal force. Had the August coup succeeded, however, these documents would no doubt have had only minor historical value. But the success of democratic forces and the dissolution of the USSR invested these documents with the authority of valid international treaties and acts of recognition retrospectively.

Denmark recognized the Baltic states on 26 August, other EC countries on 27 August,[10] and by 30 August about forty states had been granted recognition.[11] Most Western countries did not recognize the Baltic countries as newly born entities but as states having restored their independence.

But President Gorbachev, who after his confinement in Foros (Crimea) had become somewhat out of touch with reality, on 27 August at the session of the Supreme Soviet of the USSR still insisted that republics which wanted to secede from the USSR had to do so in accordance with the Soviet Law on secession passed in 1990.[12] But on 4 September the

USA recognized the restoration of the independence of the Baltic states[13] and on 6 September the newly created Council of the Federation, which was composed of leaders of all the republics of the Soviet Union, finally recognized the independence of the Baltic states.[14]

This sequence of acts of recognition is rather interesting. Recognition by the Western countries was certainly prompted by their non-recognition of the incorporation of the Baltic states in 1940 into the USSR. But the illegality of the incorporation in itself was certainly not enough for recognition of these entities as independent states. In autumn 1991 these countries were not in control of their territories, and the parent state (i.e. the Soviet Union) had not yet recognized their independence. Therefore, in late August, President Bush wrote President Gorbachev a letter urging him to recognize the Baltic states as soon as possible and said that the US would follow suit.[15]

This sequence of events shows that the recognition by Russia was politically very important. Ukraine followed suit on 26 August.[16] These recognitions by non-recognized entities, parts of the parent state which still refused to recognize, played a unique role in the history of the recognition of states.

In the case of the restoration of the independence of the Baltic states recognition was certainly not a simple act of declaration of fact. The fact of independence, though foreseeable, was not certain at all. In this case recognition undoubtedly contributed to the achievement of this fact. Therefore, we may conclude that these acts of recognition contained strong constitutive elements.

I will concentrate on issues of premature the recognition below when analysing the recognition of Yugoslavian republics. But a question of prematurity of recognition naturally always arises when a parent state has not yet granted its recognition and the criteria of independent statehood are not met, and this was in fact the situation which the Baltic states were in. However, one factor which speaks against prematurity of recognition of the Baltics is that we are here dealing with a case of illegally annexed territories. James Crawford, speaking of the recognition of Guinea-Bissau and Algeria, writes that 'self-determination will operate to legitimize recognition that would otherwise be premature'.[17] Similarly, in the case of the Baltic states the illegality of their incorporation into the USSR in 1940 played a role in justifying their recognition in August–September 1991.

The second and more important factor was, of course, the foreseeable imminence of the independence of these countries. Western countries had not recognized Estonia, Latvia and Lithuania as independent states before the failed coup though the majority of them had always supported their right to independence. Even Lithuania's independence, declared in March 1990, was rightly not recognized by other states (except Iceland[18]) as this independence was not only *de facto* absent but its achievement in the future was also at that time rather doubtful. But at the end of August 1991 independence of the Baltic states was imminent and significant steps had already been undertaken to achieve the declared status. The position of Russia was very important, if not legally then at least politically. Therefore, the recognition of these countries by other states contributed to the objective process already well under way and helped to avert a reactionary backlash.

As the Baltic states had been incorporated into the USSR in violation of international law and this illegal act was not validated by subsequent recognition, one important element or consequence of premature recognition – namely, that it would have been an interference in internal affairs of the Soviet Union – was absent here, as issues relating to internationally wrongful acts cannot be considered as domestic affairs of a state.

The process of the recognition of the restoration of independence of the Baltic states also confirms the importance of the non-recognition of the consequences of illegal acts.

In international law illegal acts may create legal situations or even new international law in accordance with the maxim *ex factus ius oritur* (e.g., emergence of exclusive economic zones which in the beginning were created by some states in violation of freedoms of the high seas). In order to prevent this maxim having effect in a concrete case and to guarantee the effect of another maxim – *ex iniuria ius non oritur* – it is necessary that states and international organizations explicitly refuse to recognize the legality of such acts. As Hersch Lauterpacht wrote: 'the principle of non-recognition fulfils in the present stage of international organization an important function in the maintenance of the authority of law'. It is directed 'against the law-creating effects of facts'.[19]

On the other hand, as Kristina Marek rightly observed, 'non-recognition can be no more than temporary. At risk of creating a "paralysie juridique" it cannot be upheld *ad infinitum*.'[20] This is one of the difficult dilemmas which often confront states (e.g., the case of the so-called Turkish Republic of Northern Cyprus, East Timor, etc.).

RECOGNITION OF THE OTHER REPUBLICS OF THE FORMER USSR

In some ways recognition of the independence of other republics of the former Soviet Union was closer to recognition of the republics of the former Yugoslavia. In both cases this was a matter of the recognition of newly born states and not the recognition of restoration of independence. Historically, of course, some of them had at one time or other been independent and sovereign states, but it seems that the dust of history had already settled on their lost independence.

Also, unlike in the case of the Baltic republics, the European Communities 'Guidelines on the recognition of new states in Eastern Europe and in the Soviet Union' had already been adopted and were applied in the recognition of other Soviet republics and the republics of the former Yugoslavia, I think, however, that it would be proper to deal with these Guidelines in the context of the recognition of the republics of the former Yugoslavia, as most of the controversial issues arise in relation to them.

In contrast to the recognition of the republics of the former Yugoslavia, the question of recognition of the former Soviet republics only arose after the decision on the dissolution of the USSR had already been taken by all the constituent republics of the Union, and when even the President of the USSR had reluctantly acquiesced in his statement of resignation on New Year's Eve.

On 28 December 1991 Japan recognized the independence of the other ten former Soviet republics which had signed the Commonwealth agreements, having recognized Russia a day before; on 28 December Italy recognized Ukraine and announced that it would recognize other republics once they met the criteria set by the EC; on 31 December the EC announced that its twelve member states would recognize all the CIS (Commonwealth of Independent States) member-states except Kyrgystan and Tajikistan once they had given assurances that they would comply with the EC Guidelines on such issues as human rights, disarmament, and nuclear non-proliferation.[21]

Georgia was recognized on 23 March by EC countries and the next day by the USA, and was admitted to the CSCE the same day. This was an acknowledgement of the Georgian State Council's Chairman Eduard Shevardnadze's professed commitment to democracy, human and minority rights, and free-market economy.[22]

Thus recognition of these republics took place *ex post facto* – that is, only after independence was not only declared by them but also when it was already recognized by the parent country. Therefore, compared with the situation in the Baltics, here a strong constitutive element of recognition is absent. Nevertheless, it is hardly possible to deny any constitutiveness at all in these acts of recognition. More often than not the recognition of new states takes place in a situation when newly born entities have not yet consolidated their independence and are rather feeble and unstable. Therefore, recognition of most newly born entities by the world community of states always contributes to the strengthening of their legal and political status, not only externally but also internally.

I think that *Oppenheim's International Law* states correctly the minimum of what recognition means:

> Recognition, while declaratory of an existing fact, is constitutive in its nature, at least so far as concerns relations with the recognizing state. It marks the beginning of effective enjoyment of international rights and duties of the recognized community.[23]

Often recognition by the world community of states, and not only by some individual states having special interest in recognizing a new entity as an independent state, is necessary to make the acquired independence irreversible and to constitute a new entity as a subject of international law.

When the republics of the former USSR or Yugoslavia asked for recognition immediately after their declarations of independence, they did not really have the long-term implications of their recognition by other states in mind very much, if at all (for example, immunity from the jurisdiction of foreign courts, recognition of their legal acts or even the possibility of entering into multifarious bilateral relations with recognizing states). They were simply trying to consolidate and secure their recently acquired feeble independence.

Therefore, though recognition does not, of itself, create states, it is often, if not always, much more than a simple declaration of existing facts, and will inevitably have important legal consequences. A contemporary state can normally exist and very often even survive only when accepted by the world community of states. Therefore, I think that recognition by the world community of states is: first, a statement and acceptance of the fact that a new entity corresponds to the criteria of statehood; second, an element in the process, if not always of the Constitution then at least of the consolidation of a new entity as a state and especially as a subject of international law; and third, a necessary basis for the establishment of multifarious relations between the recognized and recognizing states, for the recognition of the legal acts of the former.

Quincy Wright distinguished between 'particular' recognition (i.e. recognition by individual states) and 'general' recognition by the community of nations.[24] I think that this distinction is still relevant. While 'general' recognition may consist of a series of 'particular' recognitions, which all constitute a basis for bilateral relations between recognizing and recognized states, only 'general' recognition (including admission to international organizations, such as the UN) means that a new entity has become a true member of the international community and can realize in full its international legal personality.

In the cases of the recognition of former Soviet and Yugoslavian republics we saw what Hersh Lauterpacht called 'the collectivization of the process of recognition'.[25] Collective acts of recognition had taken place also after World War I. For example, the Note of 16 January 1921, addressed by the President of the Inter-Allied Conference at Paris to the President of the Estonian delegation stated: 'Le Conseil Supreme des Puissances alliées, prenant en consideration les demandes presentées à divers reprises par votre Gouvernement, a decidé, dans sa seance d'aujourd'hui, de reconnaitre l'Esthonie comme Etat de jure.'[26] And as Lauterpacht observed, 'diplomatic practice shows that, as in the case of recognition of governments, recognition of states, even when granted separately, is often preceded by negotiations aiming at establishing a common line of action'.[27]

This collective (as in the case of the EC countries) or coordinated recognition occurred in the case of the recognition of the republics of the former USSR and Yugoslavia. As the international community of states becomes more cohesive the trend towards collective or at least coordinated recognition of new states may introduce (or one may say, is already introducing) some changes into the very character of the recognition of states. For example, constitutive elements, already present in an act of recognition, may become even more prominent, existing states and their organizations may introduce new criteria of recognition besides traditional standards of statehood.

RECOGNITION OF THE REPUBLICS OF THE FORMER YUGOSLAVIA

Most difficult and controversial issues of recognition arise in the Yugoslavian case. There are at least two reasons for this. First, the secessionist republics did not have the consent of the federal authorities at the time when recognition was sought and even when it was granted. Second, significant minorities in two of these republics – Croatia and Bosnia-Herzegovina – were against the separation, wishing either to remain in Yugoslavia or to join Serbia or even to become independent themselves. And third, because of these two reasons, Croatia, and especially Bosnia-Herzegovina, did not exercise full control over their territories at the time of the recognition. Therefore controversial issues such as the criteria for recognition and the question of premature recognition are especially conspicuous here. Analysis of the significance and practical implications of the EC Guidelines on the recognition of new states in Eastern Europe and the Soviet Union is also especially relevant in the Yugoslavian case.

Though this is not the place for a detailed political and social research into the Yugoslavian conflict, the inseparability of politics and law in this case, as in the case of the recognition of the republics of the former USSR, necessitates the introduction of significant political elements into our analysis.

It is important here to refer, very shortly of course, to some developments which took place before the declarations of independence by Croatia and Slovenia and the subsequent use of force by the federal authorities against these recalcitrant republics.

Slovenia and Croatia declared their independence on 25 June 1991,[28] which was then suspended for three months by both republics and confirmed by them on 8 October 1991. Macedonia held a referendum in September 1991 which favoured Macedonian sovereignty and independence.[29] The Parliament of Bosnia Herzegovina adopted a resolution on the sovereignty of the country on 14 October 1991.[30]

These were legal landmarks, but the process of the dissolution of Yugoslavia had started much earlier and there were different trends and options open to the sides involved in these conflicts as well as for third parties. Not only were terrible crimes being committed (and at the time of writing still are being committed), but also tragic political mistakes were made which led to many of these crimes.

The Serbian-dominated federal authorities were against the proposals of different republics to transform Yugoslavia into some kind of looser entity like, for example, a confederation.[31] This intransigence of Serbian-led federal administration, and rising Serbian nationalism instigated and exploited by such politicians as Milosevic, led to demands by Croatia and Slovenia for total independence. But probably Slovenia was the only republic of the former Yugoslavia which could realistically hope to leave the Federation without serious difficulties. In the case of Slovenia the most serious problems were created by direct acts of the federal leadership and the Yugoslav People's Army, which used military force against the republic.

But neither Croatia nor especially Bosnia-Herzegovina could realistically leave Yugoslavia without resolving the issues concerning their minorities, especially the Serbian ones. Here I do not refer to oral or written promises, or even to clauses in legal acts of these republics which were introduced in response to the requirements of Western countries. What was necessary were real practical measures and guarantees. Some acts of the Croatian leadership, however, simply fuelled the Serbian nationalism of Milosevic and played into his hands. The unilateral withdrawal of Croatia also left little, if any, choice for the Bosnian leadership.[32]

Therefore, I think that though by the summer of 1991 the federal leadership, dominated by Serbia, Milosevic, and the commanders of the YNA, had already committed massive human rights violations in Slovenia and Croatia, using military force against the civilian population which led to arbitrary killings, torture, and destruction of cities and villages, the Croatian leadership also has to share the responsibility for what has happened and is happening in the former Yugoslavia.

As Misha Glenny writes:

> The spiral of nationalist violence between Serbs and Croats began before the war. The HDZ's [Croatian Democratic Union] campaign of sacking Serbs was in some regions accompanied by the confiscation of rented accommodation. From about May 1991 onwards, Serbs' property, especially in the crisis regions under Croat control, became the target of regular bomb attacks while the Serbs who remained were frequently ostracized by the Croats. In Croat nationalist strongholds like Split, open intimidation was reported much earlier ... Even before the war began, the government was concerned to hush up nationalist-motivated crimes against its Serb population while when applying for recognition, its police and soldiers were involved in the slaughter of innocent Serbs in Gospic, Sisak, Karlovac, Daruvar, Virovitice, Zagreb and elsewhere.[33]

In post-World War II Yugoslavia Tito's regime, which was probably the less repressive and certainly the most open to the outside world in comparison with other communist regimes, had created a balance of inter-ethnic relations which should have been handled with the utmost care and caution. Not only had nationalism (among many other things) been suppressed, but a system of checks and counterbalances had been created which, when incautiously dealt with, exacerbated the inter-ethnic tension.

Tito's 1974 Constitution was in a sense a clever piece of work. A Muslim nationality was created, Bosnia-Herzegovina became a republic, Serbia was split into three constitutional units, with the provinces of Vojvodina and Kosovo becoming *de facto* republics,[34] Montenegrins also obtained their republic. Macedonia, which was earlier dubbed simply as Southern Serbia, also become autonomous. In order to diminish Serbia, some territories, together with their inhabitants, were given from Serbia to Croatia etc.[35] But as Glenny wrote: 'the system could only function with two absolute political taboos: overt nationalism and the active participation of masses in politics. It was these two taboos which Milosevic smashed in 1987.'[36] There were realistically no hopes that politicians intoxicated by nationalism would be able cautiously and calmly to disentangle this Gordian knot. To try simply to cut it would have meant to cut across human lives, which in reality is what happened.

This short excursion into these political events was necessary because they are inseparable from the respective legal problems and because the recognition of states in most cases, as we have already seen, is not a purely legal act but is first and foremost a politically motivated decision, especially if the situation is rather murky.

The world community's concern with and involvement in issues of the self-determination of peoples, protection of minorities or massive violations of human rights means that states do not passively stand by observing what is happening and waiting for the results of these events in order then to recognize them. The world community is, and should be even more, actively involved in these issues at early stages of their development in order to avoid the calamities which not only some individual states face but which the world community as a whole now faces.

The recognition of states may be one of the elements of such an involvement, but it has its own requirements. Therefore, even if a population of a territory has, from the point of view of individual states or even their organizations, the right to independence, this does not mean that it would be possible to recognize something representing this population as an independent state if the criteria for statehood are not met. Such steps would not only be illegal but also politically counter-productive. Therefore, in my opinion, when in spring 1991 in the US Senate the resolution proposed by Jesse Helms demanding immediate US recognition of Lithuania failed by a vote of 59 to 36 the White House felt, rightly, relieved.[37] Recognition of Lithuania, which really deserved its independence, when the independence was still in serious doubt, would have only aggravated the situation and may have led to something similar to the Yugoslavian situation.

Turning now to concrete issues concerning the recognition of independent states in the former Yugoslavia it will be necessary to concentrate on the following issues. Were all the traditional criteria for the recognition of new states met in the cases of the recognition of Yugoslavian republics? Was recognition premature, at least in some cases? What was the role and significance of the EC Guidelines on the recognition of new states? What were the political motives and implications of recognition in these cases?

According to Hersch Lauterpacht the conditions for the recognition of states 'are identical with the requirements of statehood as laid down by international law, namely, the existence of an independent government exercising effective authority within a defined area'.[38] Kristina Marek concluded that 'there is a state in the international law sense, when there is an independent legal order, effectively valid throughout a defined territory with regard to a defined population'.[39]

Emphasis is put by most authors on actual independence among the criteria of statehood. 'The first condition of statehood is that there must exist a government actually independent of that of any other State, including the parent State',[40] wrote Lauterpacht. The attitude of a parent state is extremely important. Recognition by a parent state of a seceding entity as an independent state, as I have already noted, speaks heavily in favour of recognition by third states. But I think that Lauterpacht is right in asserting that 'a community may have succeeded in shaking off the allegiance to the mother country, but if it is in a condition of such internal instability as to be deprived of a representative and effective government, it will be lacking in a vital condition of statehood'.[41] Therefore, though recognition by a parent country is important evidence of the independence of a new state, it is not on its own a sufficient basis for its recognition by other states.

Here I would like to note, though only in passing because this is not the topic of my analysis, that in cases of the recognition of new states recognition of the government is also always at issue. Though the recognition of states and governments differs, and a problem of recognition of governments may arise quite independently from that of recognition of states, it is impossible to recognize a state without recognizing its government currently in power because an effective government is one of the conditions of statehood and, consequently, of recognition.

I am also not going to dwell upon forms of recognition. Most often recognition is in the form of a special official act whereby states declare that they have decided to recognize a new entity as an independent state. This was done in most of the cases of recognition of the republics of the former USSR and Yugoslavia. But some states considered that their voting in the UN for admission of the new states to the UN membership was an act of recognition.[42] Establishment of official (especially diplomatic or consular) relations with a new state is also a form of its recognition.

The EC Guidelines on recognition, putting forward a number of political and humanitarian conditions for the recognition of new states in the former Soviet Union and Eastern Europe, nevertheless affirmed the readiness of the EC countries to recognize these states 'subject to the normal standards of international practice and political realities in each case'.

But analysis of the processes of the recognition of new states in the Balkans leads me to conclude that in the cases of the recognition of Croatia and Bosnia-Herzegovina neither 'the normal standards of international practice' nor even the new conditions established by the Guidelines were fully met.

The Croatian Government did not exercise effective authority over its territory and population and was heavily involved in military conflict with federal forces and local Serbs.[43] As to the special conditions put forward by the Guidelines even the Commission of Arbitration of the Conference for Peace in Yugoslavia in its Opinion of 11 January 1992, after formal comparison of the Guidelines and respective Croatian Acts, found that not all these conditions were met.[44] But most importantly, there had been and were continuing, grave violations of the rights of ethnic Serbs in Croatia, and even the Constitution passed later introduced important and unacceptable differences between citizens of Croatia who were ethnic Croats and others.[45] Croatia, like Serbia, used military force against Muslims in Bosnia-Herzegovina.

Alongside the constant emphasis on the historical rights of the Croatian nation, 'including the inviolable right to secession' (if this is the case, I wonder why the Serbs in Croatia do not have the same inviolable right), the Preamble of the Constitution declares that 'the Republic of Croatia is hereby established as the national state of the Croatian nation and a state of members of other nations and minorities who are its citizens: Serbs, Moslems, Slovenes, Czechs, Slovacs, Italians, Hungarians, Jews and others, who are guaranteed equality with citizens of Croatian nationality'.[46] The Human Rights Committee which supervises the implementation of the International Covenant on Civil and Political Rights, while considering the Croatian report on civil and political rights in November 1992 found such a distinction in the Constitution between ethnic Croats and other citizens unacceptable.[47]

There were voices claiming that recognition was necessary because of Serbian aggression and because it would transform the internal conflict into an international one, thereby making it possible for the international community to undertake measures against the crimes committed by the Serbian authorities, the YNA, and Serbian irregulars in Croatia and Bosnia Herzegovina.[48]

Though such atrocities were undoubtedly committed, I do not think that such an argument stands up well. It is manifestly inconsistent with any practice concerning the recognition of states. Theoretically this would mean that recognition really creates states and would be tantamount to the acceptance of the extreme constitutive theory of recognition. In practice such an approach would serve as an encouragement for all secessionist movements to start to seek recognition, and if the world community of states wants to be consistent it would have to recognize all oppressed minorities claiming their independence as independent states in order to be able to interfere to protect them.

The world community of states should neither remain indifferent to massive violations of the rights of minorities, nor can or should it recognize minorities as states in order to be able to interfere. What the Yugoslavian authorities and the YNA did in Slovenia, Croatia and later in Bosnia-Herzegovina could never have been considered as an internal affair of Yugoslavia by the world community of states. Ethnic cleansing, massive and indiscriminate bombing of cities and the other atrocities committed by the Serbian leadership and military in Slovenia, Croatia and Bosnia-Herzegovina cannot nowadays be considered internal affairs. Already on 25 September 1991 in its Resolution 713 the UN Security Council pointed out that 'the continuation of this situation constitutes a threat to international peace and security,'[49] which meant that even without the recognition of individual republics the world community could have dealt with the situation under Chapter VII of the UN Charter. The Yugoslavian crisis once more powerfully reminds us of the necessity to reconsider issues of humanitarian intervention (see the first chapter of this book).

It would be extremely naïve and legalistic, in the negative sense of this term, to think that a simple act of recognition can transform a civil war into an international armed conflict. This would be tantamount to the assertion that it is an act of recognition which creates states.

Though I think that the recognition of Croatia was premature and that Croatia realistically had no hope of leaving Yugoslavia peacefully without striking a deal with the Serbian minority,[50] there were no serious doubts that Croatia would be a viable entity which could be recognized as a state at the end of the day. But the most damaging effect of the premature recognition of Croatia fell on Bosnia-Herzegovina. Here I would like once more to quote Glenny, whose analysis of the conflict in the former Yugoslavia is, it seems to me, both impartial and profound. He writes:

> The final factor provoking war was the international community's approach to recognition. Once Croatia and Slovenia had been granted international recognition, Izetbegovic had no option but to seek the same, as to remain in Yugoslavia dominated by Milosevic and Belgrade would have been simply unacceptable to all Moslems and

Croats in the BiH. Izetbegovic was thus forced by German led EC policy into the same mistake that Tudman had made voluntarily – he embarked upon secession from Yugoslavia without securing prior agreement from the Serbs.[51]

I do wonder though whether such an agreement would have been possible at all and whether Bosnia-Herzegovina could have been considered a viable entity ready to be recognized as a state.

Bosnia-Herzegovina asked for EC recognition in a letter of 20 December 1991 to the President of the Council of Ministers of the EC.[52] The Commission of Arbitration in its Opinion No. 4 on 11 January 1992 found that in the circumstances of the case it was not possible to consider that the will of the population of Bosnia-Herzegovina to establish a sovereign and independent state was completely established. The Commission referred to the absence of the expression of the will of the Bosnian Serbs to create an independent and sovereign Bosnia-Herzegovina and their declaration on 9 January 1992 of the Serbian Republic of Bosnia-Herzegovina. But the Commission of Arbitration said in the same Opinion that its conclusion could be modified in the case of a referendum in which all the citizens of Bosnia-Herzegovina were called to participate.[53]

Bosnia-Herzegovina held a referendum on 1 March 1992. Most Serbs boycotted the poll but nevertheless almost 63 per cent of the electorate opted for independence.[54]

What strikes me in reading the Opinions of the Commission of Arbitration is that the Commission, being guided by the EC Guidelines on recognition, analysed only the formal conformity of legislative acts with the new requirements set out in the Guidelines and took for granted, it seems, that these entities fulfilled the traditional standards for recognition required by international law, and that laws which had been passed and promises which had been made would or could be implemented.

Recognition of Croatia as well as Bosnia-Herzegovina was prompted certainly by the brutalities committed by the YNA and Croatian and especially Bosnian Serbs, and by the perception that the new regimes in Croatia and Bosnia-Herzegovina were committed to democracy and a market economy while the Yugoslavian and Serbian leadership was the incarnation of the old communist regime. There is some truth in such a perception, but only some. But, certainly, in any case, this is not enough for recognition.

There are in the same part of the world some situations which have strong parallels with the cases just analysed. South Ossetia and Abkhazia have declared their independence from Georgia and are effectively fighting Georgians. They exercise some control over their territories. In Serbia the case of Kosovo may be pending. The Easy recognition of Croatia and Bosnia-Herzegovina may nourish the hopes of Albanians in Kosovo that if they start armed struggle for their independence (and they really are oppressed by Serbian authorities) they would be recognized by the world community of states. Albania has already recognized the self proclaimed Republic of Kosovo.[55] This would be fraught with large-scale war in the Balkans. President Bush, at the end of his term in the White House, warned the Serbian leadership that in the event of 'any military action in Kosovo caused by Serbian action, the United States will be prepared to employ military force against the Serbians in the Kosovo and in Serbia proper'.[56] But such threats, if not supported by proper actions and if used selectively, can only undermine the credibility of future threats.

The fact that recognition is first of all a political act and is even subject to abuse is confirmed by the long-standing non-recognition of Macedonia.

The Arbitration Commission of the International Conference on Yugoslavia had already (on 11 January 1992) found that the Republic of Macedonia satisfied the tests set up in the Guidelines on the Recognition of New States and the Declaration on Yugoslavia adopted by the Council of the European Communities on 16 December 1991.[57] But Macedonia was not recognized because of the resistance of Greece, which objected to the name of the new state. The non-recognition, naturally, made the situation in this newly born country even more difficult.

If premature recognition is contrary to international law, I think that such non-recognition of a state, which has come into being without any violation of international law and which conforms not only with the test of statehood but even with the special conditions put forward for its recognition by the EC, constitutes an abuse of the right not to recognize a new state. This is especially so if one compares this non-recognition with other acts of recognition of former Soviet and Yugoslavian republics. If recognition is to a great extent within the discretionary powers of states, they should be at least consistent in exercising this power.

The practice of the recognition of new states in Eastern Europe and the former Soviet Union confirms that recognition remains an important and sometimes powerful political and legal instrument in the hands of existing states. But like any important and powerful instrument, recognition should be used wisely and, naturally, in conformity with international law.

The first lesson to be learned is, probably, that notwithstanding the establishment of new requirements for recognition – a step which in itself is quite permissible – the traditional criteria for recognition should be observed. Though states, in recognizing new entities as independent states usually took into account only the criteria of statehood, there have been cases when recognition was granted under certain conditions. So, paradoxically, the Congress of Berlin 1878 linked recognition of the independence of the Balkan states to their adherence to the principle of non-discrimination towards their religious minorities.[58] Great Britain, on the initiative of its Foreign Secretary George Canning, made it clear to Brazil and Mexico that it viewed the abolition of the slave trade as a precondition for recognition, and Britain's recognition of Brazil in January 1826 was followed by a treaty providing for abolition of the slave trade in November 1826.[59]

I think that the conclusion that the first criterion for recognition is the existence of statehood, remains true notwithstanding the fact that acts of recognition may carry rather strong constitutive elements. But the presence of constitutive elements does not mean that recognition can create states. Recognition can consolidate and strengthen recently acquired and feeble statehood, and can help to make independence irreversible. But recognition, if premature, may also add fuel to internal conflicts, which often accompany the processes of the dissolution of states or secessions.

One of the mistakes of the world community of states, represented mainly by the UN and EC, in its approach to the Yugoslavian crisis was its lack of comprehensiveness. In December 1991, shortly before Germany announced its recognition of Slovenia and Croatia, the UN Secretary-General wrote:

> I believe that the Twelve were correct when they reiterated, at their special European Political Co-operation Ministerial Meeting held at Rome on 8 November, that the prospect of recognition of the independence of those republics wishing it, 'can only be envisaged in the framework of an overall settlement'.[60]

The second interesting development has to do with the new criteria for recognition put forward by the EC countries. Application of such requirements corroborates the point of view, held by most states and academics, that there is no obligation to recognize an entity even if all the requirements for independent statehood are met. But normally, new states which fulfil the usual requirements of statehood are sooner or later recognized, and non-recognition is used as a sanction against entities which have come into existence in violation of the norms of international law or whose behaviour does not conform to basic human rights. This was the case, for example, with the Ian Smith regime in Southern Rhodesia, which came into existence in violation of the right to self-determination.[61] The world community of states is also refusing to recognize the so-called Turkish Republic of Northern Cyprus, which was established as a result of the use of force by Turkey.[62] The UN adopted several resolutions calling for the non-recognition of so-called independent bantustans in South Africa.[63]

In the territory of the former Yugoslavia there are some so called 'self-proclaimed' states (this dubbing of entities which call themselves states, but are not recognized by other states, as 'self-proclaimed' states, shows that recognition really validates states as subjects of international law) which are not and should not be recognized by the world community – the Serbian Republic of Krajina which proclaimed its independence on 19 December 1991 in what amounts to almost one-third of Croatia's territory,[64] or the Serbian Republic of Bosnia and Herzegovina proclaimed on 7 April 1992[65] (note that these proclamations coincided with the recognition of Croatia and Bosnia-Herzegovina respectively).

These entities came into being in violation of international law not because Bosnian Serbs and Croats, or Croatian Serbs, had less right to independence than Croats, Slovenes, and others in the former Yugoslavia. They were all equal under international law. As I have already written in the chapter on secession, international law neither provides for the right to self-determination nor prohibits it. Violation of international law in the cases of the establishment of these entities was due to the methods they used in the furtherance of their aims (e.g., 'ethnic cleansing' through which Bosnian Serbs and also Croats have been trying to secure their territories in Bosnia-Herzegovina). The same applies to Serbs in Krajina also. Another violation of international law has been perpetrated by that part of Yugoslavia (Serbia and Montenegro) which actively supported the Serbs in Croatia and Bosnia.

CONCLUDING REMARKS

From my point of view, the attempt by the EC countries as well as by other states to link recognition with democratic reforms in countries seeking recognition is a step in the right direction; nevertheless it failed.

There are at least two reasons for that. First, all additional conditions for recognition (of a humanitarian nature, related to succession to treaties, etc.) should not dampen traditional requirements of statehood: population, territory and government in control of both. Second, such conditions of recognition should be taken more seriously. Now, all newly born entities have been recognized, other countries being content with promises of democratic reforms and the protection of minorities, which were taken at face value. But practices in many newly born states have been quite different.

The report of the Special Rapporteur of the UN Commission on Human Rights, T. Mazowiecki, prepared at the end of 1993, reports grave human rights violations by all parties to the Yugoslav conflict. Serbia and Croatia are both accused of ethnically based crimes. Not only in Serbia, but also in Croatia the situation of the media 'is affected in many respects by the prevailing climate of national and religious hatred which is often encouraged through misinformation, censorship and indoctrination' (E/CN.4/1944/47, 17 November 1993, para. 133).

In the case of the former Yugoslavia the policy of applying non-recognition as a stick and recognition as a carrot has had little, if any, practical influence on the situation within recognized states. This does not mean that the world community of states should remain indifferent as to the internal situation in newly born states. The Yugoslav tragedy has many roots and certainly was not created by the world community's approach. It could hardly have been completely avoided had the world community chosen another approach. The Serbian and Croatian national-isms are the main causes of the crisis. There are no innocent politicians in this fratricidal war, there are only innocent victims. But the absence of a comprehensiveness on the part of the world community certainly aggravated the situation and made its disentanglement even more difficult.

5   Issues of continuity and the succession of states

INTERNATIONAL LAW ON THE SUCCESSION OF STATES

The birth and death of states involving issues of state succession do not occur every day or even every year. Usually after a wave of the emergence of new states (for example, Latin American states at the beginning of the nineteenth century, Eastern European states after World War I, decolonization in the 1960s, and the dissolution of the USSR and Yugoslavia in the 1990s), there are long periods during which no state emerges or disappears. Also, every wave is unique. This rarity of events which occur in different political contexts is also a reason for the existence of mutually exclusive theories and of even more controversial practices.

The two Conventions on state succession[1] have many clauses which pertain more to the progressive development of existing customary international law than to its codification. As representatives of several states noted in the Sixth Committee of the United Nations General Assembly commending the work of the International Law Commission (ILC) on the draft articles on the succession of states, '[t]he draft was the more remarkable because the task of codification was particularly difficult in a field where there was no general doctrine and State practice and custom had not yet produced well established and consistent precedents'.[2] Both Conventions were, however, under the influence of the then latest wave of the emergence of new states and concentrated too much on the succession of states emerging in the wake of decolonization.

The succession of states, which in both Conventions is defined as 'the replacement of one State by another in the responsibility for the international relations of territory',[3] always occurs in highly sensitive political contexts. This means that conflicting interests influence decision-making in the processes of state succession. These interests are in general terms reflected in two extreme doctrines on the succession of states. First, the theory of universal succession asserts that '[t]he ensemble of rights and obligations devolves ipso jure from the one sovereign to the other without exception and without modification'.[4] As a reaction to this theory, which does not and never did correspond to international practice, another extreme doctrine asserts that the extinguished State's rights and obligations no longer have a subject, and that its creditors have lost their debtor.[5]

Because issues of state succession are of high political sensitivity, the principles governing them cannot be as detailed as the rules governing, for example, the rights and duties of states in exclusive economic zones or the rules concerning diplomatic privileges and immunities, which have been applied in everyday practice over the centuries. In addition, the law of state succession is a very special part of international law in the sense that, even if codified in international treaties, it can govern many, if not most, cases of the succession of states only as a set of generally recognized norms of customary international law. Even if both Conventions on state succession were in force and ratified or adhered to by many states, they would not be obligatory for new states as new subjects of international law. Rather, only those norms of the Conventions which had become part of customary international law would be obligatory for newly born states. By that, I am not attempting to suggest that new states[6] are clean slates as regards the treaty obligations of their predecessor states, but only that such obligations would be based on customary international law.

As already mentioned, many of the norms in the two Conventions on state succession – which are not in force and in the near future certainly will not acquire the necessary number of ratifications to enter into force – were not the result so much of the codification of existing norms as of the creative development of international law by the ILC. Because of the lack of any practice or the presence of some scarce but controversial practices, these norms certainly have not since become norms of customary law. This means that in any case only the norms of customary international law can govern issues of state succession involving new states. Thus, it is true that new states would be clean slates in relation to treaty norms governing state succession, even if there were such norms.[7]

Still, an interesting question arises here: how really new are these 'new' states? The adherents of the clean-slate doctrine emphasize state sovereignty as a reason for a new state not to be bound by the obligations of its predecessor. They also stress that succession in domestic law, where the successor assumes the rights and obligations of the predecessor, is different from succession in international law, where sovereign states are the main actors. Certainly, state succession is quite different from succession in domestic law, but it seems to me that some aspects of this comparison indicate that there are at least good theoretical grounds in cases of state succession for a successor state to assume a substantial part of the rights and obligations of a predecessor state.

In cases of succession in domestic law, a predecessor and a successor exist at one and the same time *de facto* and *de jure* (that is, physically and legally), as two different and distinct subjects. At a certain moment one subject (the predecessor) ceases to exist and his rights and obligations devolve to the other subject (the successor). Hence, a predecessor and a successor are different entities.

In cases of the emergence of new states in international law, on the contrary, these states always conserve some elements of their predecessor states. There is necessarily a certain *de facto* continuity in cases of state succession. A predecessor state simply cannot completely disappear, except in cases like that of the legendary Atlantis. Of the three elements of statehood – population, territory and authority – parts of the population and territory remain the same in cases of the emergence of new states resulting from the secession or dissolution of existing states. Their newness, therefore, is always relative. Although new subjects of international law, they are not at the same time completely new entities. A new state *de facto* succeeds a predecessor state, and this *de facto* succession is a basis for succession to certain rights and duties of a predecessor state.

RUSSIA – A SUCCESSOR TO THE SOVIET UNION OR ITS CONTINUATION?

One of the important legal questions which has practical consequences in the case of the dissolution of the USSR is whether there was a dismemberment of the former USSR or whether there were secessions from the existing state while it continued to exist, albeit with a different territory and population. As James Crawford writes

> there is a fundamental distinction between State continuity and State succession: that is to say, between cases where the 'same' State can be said to continue to exist, despite changes of government, territory, or population, and cases where one State can be said to have replaced another with respect to certain territory.[8]

This differentiation between cases of state succession and the continuation of states, notwithstanding changes in territory, population and authority, is especially important in light of the uncertainties in the law of state succession.

Certainly, from the point of view of politics, economics and social structures, what has happened and is still happening in the erstwhile Soviet Union is a deep social revolution. The communist ideology and policy in many new states are being replaced by a free market economy and liberal ideas. Democratic reforms are under way in different parts of the former communist empire. Some in the former USSR have attempted to use Soviet diplomacy and Soviet legal doctrine to show that social, and particularly socialist, revolutions disrupt the existence of states and that therefore there is no state succession in cases of social revolutions. This approach, however, has been rejected both in legal doctrine and in the practice of states. Accordingly, even deep social changes are irrelevant for determining whether or not a state continues to exist.

To determine whether from the point of view of international law there was a dismemberment of the Soviet Union, whereby no entity continues the existence of the former USSR, or whether one of the former republics of the USSR continues its existence, we have to take into account objective as well as subjective factors. These factors tend to indicate that, at least for the purposes of determining the international legal personality of states existing in place of the former USSR, we have a case of the separation of parts of the territory of the USSR while its core – Russia – continues to exist as a continuation of the Soviet Union. What then are these factors?

First, geography, demographics and sheer size indicate that Russia continues the existence of the former Soviet Union. Even after the dissolution of the Union, Russia remains much bigger than all the other former Soviet republics taken together. Although fourteen republics separated, and from a political point of view we can speak of the dissolution of the Union, geographically and demographically, Russia remains one of the biggest states in the world. Second, Soviet Russia after 1917 and especially the Soviet Union after 1922 were themselves continuing states of the Russian Empire. In a sense, current changes are more profound than changes after the 1917 revolution. The socialist revolution, though of course changing in many respects the nature of Czarist Russia, did not abolish its imperial character. Even the national anthem of the Soviet Union started with the words 'unbreakable union of free republics united forever by Great Russia'.

The preceding are objective factors, but, as Crawford correctly observes, '[w]here there are substantial changes in the entity concerned, continuity may depend upon recognition (as in the case of India after 1947)'.[9] This means that in such cases subjective factors become important. Though Crawford implies recognition by other states, I think that equally important is how the state concerned considers itself. Thus, in cases of substantial changes in the state concerned, such that there are doubts as to the continuous existence of the state, it seems to me that both the behaviour of the state itself and the factor of recognition by third states become relevant.

The Foreign Minister of the Russian Federation has written that 'Russia, as a continuing state of the USSR, intends to promote in every possible way the strengthening of the United Nations . . .'[10] In his letter of 24 December 1991 to the Secretary-General of the United Nations President Yeltsin stated, moreover, that 'the membership of the Union of the Soviet Socialist Republics in the United Nations, including the Security Council and all other organs and organizations of the United Nations system, is being continued by the Russian Federation (RSFSR) with the support of the Commonwealth of Independent States'.[11] In the Decision by the Council of Heads of State of the Commonwealth of Independent States (CIS) on 21 December 1991, these states indeed decided that '[t]he States of the Commonwealth support Russia's continuance of the membership of the Union of Soviet Socialist Republics in the United Nations, including permanent membership of the Security Council, and other international organizations.'[12] Russia's continuance of the USSR's membership in the United Nations and other international organizations was also accepted by other states and by these organizations. Russia, as a continuing state of the USSR, was not obliged to apply for membership in these organizations, as other former Soviet republics which were considered successor states to the Soviet Union had to do.

The question of UN membership was in this case resolved identically to that of the Indian and Pakistani memberships in 1947 after the dissolution of India into two states, India and Pakistan. In 1947, the UN acted on the basis of the 4 August 1947 legal opinion by the Secretariat which concluded that 'from the point of view of international law, the situation is one in which a part of an existing State breaks off and becomes a new State'.[13] This had no effect on the international status of India, which continued to be a member of the UN. However, 'the territory which breaks off, Pakistan, will be a new State; it will not have the treaty rights and obligations of the old State, and will not, of course, have membership in the United Nations'.[14]

I omit here any further comments concerning the absence of any treaty rights and obligations of a new state, but as a rule there is no succession to membership in international organizations. This principle may be considered as a customary norm governing matters of state succession. If a state is still a member of international organizations after substantial changes, this presumably means that it continues its own membership rather than succeeding to somebody else's membership.

Therefore, these factors – both objective and subjective – suggest that Russia really does continue the existence of the Soviet Union, albeit in diminished borders and with a diminished population. Similarly, Russia's approach concerning the USSR's property abroad and the USSR's armed forces stationed outside of the CIS countries also indicates that Russia considers itself to be a continuation of the former USSR and that other states either expressly recognize it as such or at least acquiesce. While the reasons for recognition are varied and are not all necessarily of a legal nature, the consequences of such recognition or acquiescence nevertheless have legal importance. For example, the permanent members of the Security Council did not want to open the discussion concerning permanent membership in the Security Council. Similarly, the Baltic countries were happy that there was somebody who would be in charge of the armed forces of the former USSR stationed in their territories and with whom they could negotiate about their withdrawal. Thus, recognition of Russia as a continuation of the erstwhile Soviet Union, even if it was to a certain extent a legal fiction, made the lives of existing states less complicated. In legal terms this means that Russia has assumed all of the treaty and other international obligations, as well as the rights, of the Soviet Union.

Although Russia is a continuing state of the USSR and generally continues to hold the Soviet Union's rights and obligations, this does not mean that these rights and obligations remain intact. Substantial changes of circumstances have led to certain adjustments of these rights and obligations. For example, Russia, unlike the USSR, is not able to fulfil all the treaty obligations of the former Soviet Union concerning delimitation or cooperation in the Baltic Sea because its Baltic coastline has greatly diminished. Later, I will consider in more depth the implications of the doctrine of *rebus sic stantibus* in cases of state succession. Here, I would like to stress only that although, as Crawford writes, 'acquisition or loss of territory does not *per se* affect the continuity of the State' and that '[t]his may be so even where the territory acquired or lost is substantially greater in area than the original or remaining State territory',[15] substantial territorial and demographic changes require use of the doctrine *rebus sic stantibus* in adjusting the international legal relations of the state.

All this said, it is necessary to make some qualifications. Russia's continuation of the USSR does not mean that the other former republics have nothing to do with the USSR's rights and obligations. They are successor states to the Soviet Union and their status affects Russia's international rights and obligations. The CIS countries have signed a series of agreements and have made decisions at the level of heads of states and governments on issues of state succession.[16]

Already on 4 December 1991, before the dissolution of the USSR, eight republics signed (in fact all of the former Soviet Republics were invited to sign) a Treaty on Succession to the USSR's State Debt and Assets.[17] On 30 December 1991, the heads of the CIS countries agreed that 'every one of them has the right to a relevant fixed just share of the property of the former USSR abroad'.[18]

On 20 March 1992, a Decision of the Council of Heads of States–Members of the CIS was adopted in Kiev, on the many complex issues relating to the succession to treaties in which the CIS states have mutual interests, as well as to state property, state archives, and to the debts and assets of the former USSR.[19] In this document the heads of state decided to recognize that all state-members of the CIS are successors to the rights and obligations of the former USSR. They also decided to establish a Commission of representatives with full powers for negotiations and preparation of propositions on issues of state succession.

None the less, resolution of the succession issues has been extremely difficult. For example, on 15 May 1992 the heads of the CIS countries in Tashkent signed a Protocol concerning the work of the Commission established on the 20 March Decision and obligated it to activate its work.[20] Then, on 9 October 1992 they adopted a Decision on the work of the Commission in which they suspended the Commission and decided to resolve 'issues related to succession on matters of debts and assets of the former USSR on a bilateral basis'.[21]

As to the international treaties of the former USSR, the heads of the CIS states signed, on 6 July 1992, a Memorandum on mutual understanding on issues of succession to treaties of the former USSR having mutual interest.[22] The Memorandum contains some interesting points which are worthy of discussion. In the document the heads of the CIS states reached an understanding that

> in practice all multilateral treaties of the former USSR have general interest for the state-members of the Commonwealth. At the same time these treaties do not require any joint decisions or actions of the state-members of the CIS. Participation in these treaties will be decided in accordance with principles and norms of international law by every state-member individually depending on the specificity of every concrete case on the character and content of each treaty.

The Memorandum also establishes that as to the bilateral treaties of the former Soviet Union which are of interest to two or more state-members but not for all, decisions and actions on them should be made by those states to which such treaties are applicable, and that 'methods of negotiation accepted in international legal practice and a search for mutually acceptable decisions should be on the basis of this work'. The Memorandum refers specially to treaties establishing borders, which should stay in force in any case.

The difficulty of resolving succession issues is demonstrated by several failures of the CIS countries to agree on these matters. For example, on 16 June 1992 in Minsk, these states decided to establish a Commission for the preparation of an agreement on the division of non-military maritime vessels of the erstwhile USSR.[23] Yet then, on 9 October 1992 in Bishkek, they concluded that because of non-participation in the work of the Commission of representatives of the former Soviet republics which are not members of the CIS but have big non-military navies, there was no sense in the continuation of the Commission.[24]

Furthermore, in the Treaty on Succession to the USSR's Debt and Assets of 4 December 1991, the CIS countries agreed in article 4 on their respective shares in debts and assets of the USSR.[25] For example, the Treaty provided that Russia would be responsible for 61.34 per cent, and the Ukraine for 16.37 per cent.[26] On 6 July 1992, the CIS heads of states signed an agreement on the division of the property of the former USSR abroad whereby the same percentages were agreed upon.[27] Later, a new understanding was reached between Russia and the other CIS member-states, except the Ukraine, that Russia would take over all international debts as well as all assets abroad. The Ukraine accepted 16.37 per cent of the debts and assets. However, at the beginning of January 1993, the Ukraine announced that it would not continue with the debt-repayment deal concluded with Russia.[28] But at the end of July of the same year the Vice Premier of Russia, Alexander Shochin, declared in an interview that soon an agreement with Ukraine providing for the 'zero' option (i.e. no foreign debts, no foreign assets for Ukraine) would be signed.[29]

These developments demonstrate that when the vital interests of states (for example, finances, assets, debts, property held abroad, and naval or other military forces and bases) are at issue, long and difficult negotiations are necessary in order to reach an agreement between successors. Successor states decide whether the international treaties of a predecessor state will apply more or less independently of each other. Often, third-party states, or the world community as an interested party, will have to take a position. Indeed, with respect to the resolution of these issues, there are few customary rules of international law which can guide states.

THE SPECIAL CASE OF THE BALTIC STATES

Estonia, Latvia and Lithuania were occupied by the Soviet Union in 1940 but their incorporation into the USSR was not, at least *de jure*, recognized by most Western countries. Therefore, their struggle for independence, which developed in 1988, was fought not so much under the banner of self-determination as to end the illegal occupation. Lithuania declared its independence from the Soviet Union on 11 March 1990, and Estonia and Latvia declared transitional periods which were to end with independence. The Soviet authorities imposed economic sanctions against Lithuania, and in January 1991 tried to suppress Lithuania's drive for independence by military force. This show of force, which was meant as a warning to all three Baltic countries, did not succeed thanks to the decisive actions of the populations and political leaders of the Baltic countries and the support of democratic forces all over the Soviet Union, especially those in Moscow and Leningrad. Crucial also was the role of Boris Yeltsin who undertook several measures in support of the Baltic countries. On 12 January 1992 a Treaty between Russia and Estonia was concluded whereby the parties recognized each other as subjects of international law.[30] That same day the Presidium of the Supreme Soviet of Russia passed a Declaration on the events in the Baltic countries.[31] The Declaration stated that '[u]se of military force against peaceful citizens in the Baltic republics is intolerable' and '[u]se of the army against legally elected state authorities is illegal and anti-constitutional'.[32] Especially important and a cause of protests on the part of the military was a statement that the use of Russian citizens serving in the army in the territories of other republics was illegal.[33]

During the *coup d'état* attempt in the USSR in August of 1991 the Parliaments of Estonia and Latvia, following Lithuania, declared that their independence was restored.[34] Thus, these republics did not secede from the USSR but rather restored their independence lost in 1940.

Western countries, who had recognized the Baltic states before World War II and had established diplomatic relations with them at that time, in 1991 recognized the restoration of their independence and renewed diplomatic relations (see Chapter 4). This implies that from the point of view of international law the Baltic countries reverted to sovereignty. Charles Alexandrowicz defined reversion as a legal presumption that a State which lost its sovereignty but reverted to it (before the dust of history had settled), recovers a full and unencumbered sovereignty. The interpretation of rights and obligations connected with such sovereignty would therefore be in favour of the reverting State.[35]

This is what Professor Crawford called '[i]dentity without continuity'.[36] Here, it is also necessary to refer to Kristina Marek, who in 1954 and 1968 wrote that '[t]here can still be a relation of identity and continuity between the independent Baltic States of 1940 and such Baltic states as will recover their effective freedom before an overwhelming normative pressure of facts will have brought about their final extinction. . . .'[37]

In 1991 the Baltic countries indeed restored their independence and therefore do not consider themselves successor states to the USSR. This means that the USSR's rights and obligations do not extend to them. On the other hand, some rights and obligations of the pre-World War II Baltic states have been reacquired by them. For example, the United Kingdom and Estonia resumed their visa-free travelling regime which had been established before World War II but which had not been applicable for more than fifty years,[38] and Estonia and Finland renewed, through an exchange of notes the application of their Treaty on cultural cooperation.[39] Still, most treaties concluded more than fifty years ago by the Baltic States have become obsolete. It is clear that *restitutio ad integrum* after more than fifty years is more often a legal fiction than a realistic option.

Although the newly independent Baltic states did not consider themselves to be successors to the USSR in practice, it has none the less been very difficult for them to neglect legal norms and juridical facts that occurred during the preceding years. For example, realistically it was very difficult, if not impossible, to neglect altogether treaties concluded by the Soviet Union. Therefore, Estonia and Finland, through an exchange of notes, agreed to use temporarily certain treaties, or parts of them, concluded between Finland and the USSR.[40] None the less, the Baltic countries refused to participate in the payment and servicing of the USSR's external debts and did not claim any property or assets of the USSR in foreign countries.

As I have already mentioned, *restitutio ad integrum* after more than fifty years of being a part of another state is often more a legal fiction than a reality, and attempts to put this reality into the Procrustean bed of legal fictions are fraught with grave problems. Marek wrote of such a situation:

To pretend that everything in an illegally occupied territory or under a puppet government is non-existent, is not only to press legal fiction beyond all reasonable limits, but to create a situation never to be disentangled in future [*sic*]. Apart from the sheer practical impossibility of enforcing such an extreme point of view, it would hardly be in the interest of the restored State itself to plunge the liberated country into endless chaos and anarchy.[41]

Marek hardly had in mind the Baltic states when uttering this warning, even though two pages earlier she wrote about these countries as possible examples of the reversion to sovereignty after many years of lost statehood. None the less, in some aspects an attempt to restore the situation which existed fifty years ago, but which does not correspond to new realities, is taking place in Estonia and Latvia.

For example, proceeding from the assumption that the Republic of Estonia, which declared its independence on 20 August 1991, is not a successor state to the Soviet Union but was in 1940 illegally occupied by the USSR, and that the Republic of Estonia of 1991 is a continuation of the pre-World War II Estonia, the Supreme Council of Estonia in February of 1992 restored the Estonian Citizenship Law of 1938.[42] This law provided *inter alia* that Estonian citizens are 'children whose father at the time of their birth held Estonian citizenship' or 'natural children whose mother at the time of their birth held Estonian citizenship'.[43] This means that only citizens of 1940 Estonia and their direct descendants on their father's side could become Estonian citizens in 1992.[44] All other residents who want to become Estonian citizens must go through the process of naturalization just as any other foreigner, notwithstanding how long they have lived in Estonia and whether or not they were born in Estonia.

Such an approach is politically doubtful and legally unsound. Although one has to agree that the Baltic states did not voluntarily join the USSR but were occupied in 1940, and one may therefore speak of the restoration of independence, this does not mean that it is possible to start rebuilding the country in 1991 on the assumption that the pre-war republic can be restored *ad integrum*. Not only have all Baltic countries changed, such that their demographics are completely different from before the war, but also the world community of states and the norms of international law, including international standards on human rights, are also quite different from what existed more than fifty years ago.

The Supreme Council of Estonia understood this, and it did not restore other old laws. Instead of reviving, for example, the 1938 Constitution of Estonia, a new Basic Law, corresponding to realities of the end of the twentieth century, was elaborated and adopted by the referendum.[45] This was, of course, the only reasonable option. Hence, it is apparent that it was a desire to obtain or at least to approximate to ethnic purity and not considerations of legal consistency that led to such an approach towards citizenship questions in Estonia.[46]

SUCCESSION TO BORDERS AND THE *UTI POSSIDETIS* PRINCIPLE

Another big problem which all three Baltic states face is the problem of borders and territories. During the fifty years of the Soviet Empire, their borders, which at that time were administrative, delimiting one constituent republic from another, were changed. The fact that Lithuania gained some territory from Poland and Byelorussia is not an issue. On the other hand, Estonia and Latvia lost some territory to the Russian Federation after World War II and now they claim those lost territories back. Article 122 of the new Constitution of Estonia provides that 'the land border of Estonia shall be determined by the Tartu Peace Treaty of 2 February 1920, and other international border treaties'.[47] Under the 1920 Estonian–Russian Tartu Peace Treaty, the border lay substantially more eastward than does the current border.[48]

Here, we have a situation rather dangerous in practical terms but theoretically interesting.

One of the few clear and non-controversial norms governing issues of state succession is a customary rule enshrined in article 11 of the Vienna Convention on Succession of States in Respect of Treaties, which provides that the succession of States does not as such affect a boundary established by a treaty.[49] With respect to succession and boundaries, it is not exactly a treaty which is succeeded to but rather the boundary itself as an objective reality having its own *de facto* and *de jure* existence regardless of whether the treaty itself is in force. Although this rule relates only to international boundaries established by international treaties, the dissolution of the USSR, as well as that of Yugoslavia, confirms the obligatory nature of this norm of customary international law.

In cases of the dissolution of states or of secession, a question of the boundaries of a new state with those of its predecessor (in cases of secession) or other breakaway states (in cases of dissolution), generally arises. This is not *stricto sensu* an issue of state succession because no international right or obligation concerning these issues could have existed before, but the problem is closely related to issues of state succession. The rule governing issues of the establishment of borders between new states or with the predecessor state – the *uti possidetis, ita*

possidetis (have what you have had) principle – establishes succession
to borders which were of an administrative nature. The *uti possidetis*
principle emerged in the context of the decolonization of Latin America
and was later applied in Africa. The Chamber of the International Court
of Justice in its Decision on the frontier dispute between Burkina Faso
and Mali of 22 December 1986 established that *uti possidetis* constituted a general principle which is logically related to the achievement
of independence wherever it occurs.[50] The Arbitration Commission on
Yugoslavia in its opinion of 11 January 1992 declared that in the
absence of an agreement stating otherwise, previous limitations acquire
the character of frontiers protected by international law:[51]

> This conclusion follows from the principle of respect for the territorial
> status quo and, in particular, from the principle of uti possidetis. Uti
> possidetis, though initially applied in settling decolonisation issues in
> America and Africa, is today recognized as a general principle, as
> stated by the International Court of Justice in its Judgment of 22
> December 1986 in the case between Burkina Faco and Mali. . .[52]

Though application of the *uti possidetis* principle may lead to quite
artificial borders in some cases, it has now become a customary rule.
Most international borders are, in any case, artificial. Attempts to
create natural borders, especially on the basis of ethnic or historical
criteria, are more often than not fraught with the danger of provoking
bloody conflicts.

In the dissolution of Yugoslavia, and also with respect to the territory
of the former Soviet Union, there have been claims of territorial
changes which have fuelled conflict and even bloodshed.[53] Generally,
however, the practice of dissolution by these countries confirms the *uti
possidetis* principle. New states, of course, may agree to have territorial
changes or adjustments. Otherwise though, after the achievement of
independence, existing delimitations acquire the protection of international law, and any subsequent changes must be achieved without the
use or threat of force and through peaceful means. During negotiations,
of course, parties may take into account other factors and, I think, even
in cases of third-party settlement it is possible for that party to take into
account other factors (e.g., of a historical, ethnic or economic nature),
especially when those involved agree to such a method.

A conclusion that *uti possidetis* has become an obligatory norm of
international law does not yet give a definitive answer to the question of
the borders of the Baltic states. They were illegally occupied and
annexed by the USSR, and these territorial changes occurred during the
illegal annexation. On the one hand, *uti possidetis* requires leaving

borders as they were at the moment of restoration of independence; on the other hand, the necessity to remedy the results of the illegal occupation and annexation means that frontiers existing before the loss of independence should be restored. Accordingly, we have a situation which is not rare in international law: two conflicting principles, both of which express real values, pointing towards different, even opposite, solutions.

Decision-makers (the term is used broadly here, and encompasses parties to the conflict, third-party decision-makers, international institutions, etc.) have to take into account not only these two principles, but, first of all, the prohibition against the use of force and the obligation to have recourse only to peaceful means for the resolution of international conflicts. In the process of the peaceful resolution of such conflicts, different extra-legal factors become very important. One such factor is the length of time which has elapsed since the illegal occupation. The longer the time, the more weighty are the arguments in favour of the recognition of current realities. A decision should be the outcome of two different legal maxims originating from the Roman law – *ex iniuria non ius oritur* (illegal acts do not create law), and *ex factis ius oritur* (facts have a tendency to become law).

ISSUES OF SUCCESSION IN THE CASES OF THE OTHER FORMER SOVIET REPUBLICS

Article 34(1) of the Vienna Convention on Succession of States in Respect of Treaties states that:

> When a part or parts of the territory of a State separate to form one or more States, whether or not the predecessor State continues to exist: (a) any treaty in force at the date of the succession of States in respect of the entire territory of the predecessor State continues in force in respect of each successor State so formed; (b) any treaty in force at the date of the succession of States in respect only of that part of the territory of the predecessor State which has become a successor State continues in force in respect of that successor State alone.[54]

This article is based on the premise of the continuity and stability of treaty relations in cases of state succession. Comparing the text of article 34(1) with that of article 17(1), which provides that 'a newly independent State may, by a notification of succession, establish its status as a party to any multilateral treaty which at the date of the succession of States was in force in respect of the territory to which the succession of States relates',[55] we see that article 34(1) means automatic succession. Even notification is not required.

The rule enshrined in article 34(1) is too rigid and does not correspond to international practice. It therefore cannot be considered a customary norm. In the case of bilateral treaties or multilateral treaties with a limited number of participants made by the former Soviet Union, only Russia continues to be a party. Other states have either discontinued their participation in such treaties or renegotiated them with the other parties. In order to show that the rule in article 34(1) is too rigid and simplistic, let us take the Strategic Arms Reduction Treaty (START), signed by the United States and the USSR. After the dissolution of the USSR special negotiations were necessary in order to reach a consensus on how to ratify the treaty. It was agreed that five states (the United States, Russia, Ukraine, Byelorussia and Kazahkstan) would sign a Protocol whereby not only Russia but also three other former Soviet republics would become parties to the START Treaty. It was made a condition of allowing them to join the Treaty as independent states that they promise to become parties to the 1968 Treaty on Non-Proliferation of Nuclear Weapons (NPT) as non-nuclear states while Russia continues the Soviet Union's participation in the Non-Proliferation Treaty as a nuclear power.[56]

Or let us take the NPT[57] itself. It contains the obligations of five nuclear powers not to transfer nuclear weapons or their control over them to anyone and not to assist any non-nuclear weapon state to manufacture or otherwise acquire them (article 1). Other states which are parties to the NPT are obliged to remain non-nuclear weapon states.

Does the succession to the NPT of the former Soviet republics mean that they will acquire the rights and obligations of the former USSR – that is, become independent nuclear powers?

This would be completely against the object and purpose of the NPT, whose aim is to contain the proliferation of nuclear weapons. Here the rule, contained in article 34.2 (b) of the 1978 Convention on succession in respect of treaties, saying that the continuity principle, enshrined in para.1 of the article, is not applicable if 'it appears from the treaty or is otherwise established that the application of the treaty in respect of the successor State would be incompatible with the object and purpose of the treaty' should be applied. If there are doubts as to whether para.1 of this article corresponds to the practice and is feasible, there are no doubts, it seems to me, that there should not be a succession to a treaty if this is contrary to the object and purpose of the treaty.

Difficulties of a similar kind arise in the case of succession to the Soviet–American Anti-Ballistic Missile (ABM) Treaty.[58] Does the succession to the USSR's rights and obligations under this treaty mean that all successor states have the right to build 100-missile ABM systems around their capitals?

Obviously, such a conclusion seems rather absurd. The US, certainly, when entering into these treaties with the USSR, did not expect that it would face multiple nuclear states with ABM systems around their capitals or missile launch sites.

Although the START Treaty, the NPT or the ABM Treaty are perhaps a bit too specific, many other treaties also support the view. It therefore seems to me that paragraph 2 of article 34 of the Convention looks, in the light of international practice, more like a general rule than does the first paragraph. Paragraph 2 states that:

> Paragraph 1 does not apply if: (a) the States concerned otherwise agree; or (b) it appears from the treaty or is otherwise established that the application of the treaty in respect of the successor State would be incompatible with the object and purpose of the treaty or would radically change the conditions for its operation.[59]

The Vienna Convention's treatment of unifying states is equally problematic. Already the reunification of Germany has shown that article 31 of the Convention, which is meant to govern issues of treaty succession in cases of the uniting of states and is also based on the continuity of all treaties, was not of great help. As Stefan Oeter writes:

> A careful examination of state practice . . . probably would prove that the traditional rules stated by most authors prior to the ILC's attempt at codification still reflect the relevant law of state succession in that respect. These rules differentiate between purely political treaties on the one hand, which are terminated by the extinction of the acceding state, localized treaties at the other extreme, which continue to apply, and ordinary treaties such as treaties of commerce, extradition etc., which have to be terminated or adapted to the changed circumstances by way of negotiations between the contracting parties.[60]

It is not that successor states are reluctant to accept the obligations of their predecessors – though international practice shows that this may also be the case – but rather that most treaties cannot automatically be applied unchanged because of the changed circumstances. Agreements between concerned parties and the principle of *rebus sic stantibus* therefore become general rules, especially in cases of bilateral treaties and multilateral treaties with a limited number of participants.

On the other hand, the dissolution of the USSR and Yugoslavia also shows that the world community of states was seriously concerned with the stability of international legal relations and, by pushing the newly born states, achieved acceptance by them of the most important obligations of their predecessors. This was the case with the START and the CFE (Conventional Forces in Europe) treaties. Furthermore, this was expressly provided for in the guidelines on recognition of new states in Eastern Europe and in the Soviet Union adopted by the European Community.[61] Though the specific treaty obligations had to be modified, successor states accepted the essence of these obligations. Hence, practice did not confirm so much the automatic succession to treaties but rather a procedure of negotiated and agreed readjustment of the international obligations of predecessor states.

Much depends on the characteristics of the treaty. It is interesting to note that while, for example, US courts have on several occasions upheld the view that bilateral extradition treaties are inherited by successor states,[62] the United States Restatement of Foreign Relations Law insists on the clean slate doctrine as to succession to international treaties for all successor states.[63]

Some bilateral treaties (extradition treaties, treaties on double taxation, etc.) are of such a nature that they can easily survive state succession. But even here political relations between states affect the application of such treaties by successor states.

Practical considerations of political, economic or humanitarian nature often play an important role in the resolution of issues relating to state succession. So after the dissolution of the Czech and Slovak Republic on 1 January 1993 its successor states had to apply anew for membership of international organizations, including the Council of Europe. Both states were admitted to the Council of Europe on 30 June 1993.[64] The Czech Republic and the Slovak Republic, by virtue of the respective declarations on succession of 1 January 1993 and the decision of the Committee of Ministers of the Council of Europe of January 1993, succeeded to the eight so-called 'open' (open also for non-members of the Council) conventions of the Council of Europe with effect from 1 January 1993.[65] This meant that for these states to succeed to the aforementioned conventions it was necessary to have the expression not only of their will but also of the will of the Council of Europe as well.

Even more interesting were the issues of succession to so-called 'closed' conventions (open only for members of the Council). Here the disruption in the membership of the Council of Europe should have, in principle, also disrupted the succession of the Czech Republic and the Slovak Republic to such conventions, particularly to the European Convention for the Protection of Human Rights and Fundamental Freedoms. But such an approach may have had a damaging effect on individual petitions to the Strasbourg bodies which may have been sent after 1 January 1993 and before the admittance of these states to the Council's membership (30 June 1993). Therefore the Committee of

Ministers of the Council of Europe decided on 30 June 1993 that such conventions which were obligatory for the predecessor state were in effect for the successor states from 1 January 1993.[66] Jiri Malenovsky rightly concludes that '[l]a pratique du Conceil de l'Europe dans les questions de succession prouve que c'est la liberté politique et la pragmatisme qui prevalent dans une large mesure dans les solutions adoptée jusqu'ici.'[67]

I would formulate the principle applicable to bilateral treaties or multilateral treaties which are not of universal character in the following way: a successor state is obliged either to succeed to the international obligations of its predecessor or to renegotiate in good faith with other parties to the treaty the terms of its application (or if other parties agree, of its termination), taking into account not only changed circumstances and the object and purpose of the treaty, but first of all the necessity to guarantee stability of legal relations.

SUCCESSION TO UNIVERSAL TREATIES AND HUMAN RIGHTS OBLIGATIONS

A special category of treaties are the so-called 'universal treaties'. Treaties codifying existing customary law such as the Vienna conventions on diplomatic, consular or treaty law and especially the UN human rights instruments, which are ratified by most states in the world, cannot be said to be non-applicable because of a change of circumstances. Nor can it be said that their application to new states is contrary to the object and purpose of such treaties. One may even say that the very object and purpose of such treaties can be achieved only if all states participate in them.

But even in the case of universal treaties, however, practice is not conclusive. It is clear that new states have the right to become parties to these treaties as successor states. For example, Slovenia on 6 July 1992[68] and Croatia on 12 October 1992[69] informed the UN Secretariat that as successor states they considered themselves bound by the international human rights treaties of the former Yugoslavia. Therefore, they were considered to be parties to these treaties from the moment of the succession and not after the lapse of several months as provided for by these instruments for those states which accede to it. Even here we saw a notification by the Governments of the successor states. But Azerbaijan, on 13 August 1992, notified the UN Secretary-General not of its succession to all of the Soviet Union's treaties, but rather of its accession to three human rights treaties, which had been obligatory for the USSR.[70] In any case such notifications of succession or adherence are rather rare in the case of the former Soviet or Yugoslavian republics. Lack of time or other priorities may have been some of the reasons for the lack of notification. Does this then mean that in the absence of any reaction from the part of successor states, they are considered not bound by universal treaties?

In answering this question, international practice before World War II is not of great help because of the lack of such universal treaties. The emergence of new states in the process of decolonization was a special case. Although most of them succeeded to the majority of international treaties of universal character, they did not consider themselves automatically bound by the treaties of their predecessors. For example, Okon Udokang recounts that Tanganyika declared in a note of 9 December 1961 by Mr Nyerere (its Prime Minister) to the Secretary-General of the UN that Tanganyika was fully conscious of the 'special character' of multilateral treaties and 'was prepared to deal with each multilateral treaty previously applicable within its territory by specific arrangements, that is by reviewing each [treaty] individually, and indicating to the depositary what step in each case, it wished to take in relation to the instrument'.[71] Udokang also noted that:

> Uganda, in its note of February 12, 1962, to the Secretary-General, and Kenya in a similar declaration indicated their intention to continue to honour existing treaty obligations within specified periods of varying lengths, during which the relevant instruments would be subjected to legal examination for the purpose of terminating those which, by virtue of the ordinary rules of customary international law, could not survive the change of sovereignty.[72]

In the case of new states emerging as a result of the secession or dissolution of states, there is a very strong argument in favour of their succession to universal as well as to regional multilateral human rights instruments. These treaties contain not only reciprocal commitments of states but also rights and freedoms of individuals under their jurisdiction, and these rights and freedoms constitute, in a sense, 'acquired rights' which a new state is not free to take away.

The Permanent Court of International Justice in the *German Settlers Case* held that:

> [p]rivate rights acquired under existing law do not cease on a change of sovereignty. . . [E]ven those who contest the existence in international law of a general principle of State succession do not go so far as to maintain that private rights including those acquired from the State as the owner of the property are invalid as against a successor in sovereignty.[73]

Of course, by 'acquired rights' the Permanent Court of International Justice meant only property rights, and in international law generally, 'acquired rights' are rights 'corporeal or incorporeal, properly vested in a natural or juristic person, and of assessable monetary value'.[74] I am not saying that human rights should be included in the category of acquired rights in the sense which these rights have usually had; therefore, I use quotation marks when speaking of human rights in cases of state succession as 'acquired rights'. Still, human rights treaty obligations are not only the obligations of a state *vis-à-vis* other state-parties, but are first and foremost the rights of individuals protected by relevant instruments. Human rights are no less important than property rights; moreover, the right to property has become one of the human rights. When international law started to protect acquired rights, there were no international human rights standards, but now the situation has changed. Most states participate in universal human rights instruments, and there are important regional human rights treaties. The populations of most states are covered by these treaties, and, though in many signatory states human rights are violated, participation in these treaties and monitoring mechanisms help to remedy violated rights and prevent new and graver violations. The non-participation of successor states in international human rights treaties signed by their pre-decessors would therefore leave the populations of these countries without the protection they had formerly enjoyed.

It interesting to note that the European Community's Declaration on the Guidelines on the recognition of new states in Eastern Europe and in the Soviet Union refers not only to a democratic basis and the rule of law as conditions for the recognition of these states but expressly states that recognition would be granted if a state has 'accepted the appro-priate international obligations' and commits 'to settle by agreement, including where appropriate by recourse to arbitration, all questions concerning state succession and regional disputes.'[75] The Commission of Arbitration of the Conference for Peace in Yugoslavia, in its opinion concerning international recognition of the Republic of Slovenia by the European Communities and its member states of 11 January 1992, states that the Republic of Slovenia in its request for recognition, as well as in its response to the questionnaire of the Commission, had agreed to succeed to the respective international treaties of Yugoslavia and had promised to accept international monitoring mechanisms on human rights.[76] Slovenia has indeed succeeded to Yugoslavia's inter-national human rights obligations.

This example shows that the international community is putting pressure on new states to guarantee the implementation of the international human rights obligations of predecessor states. Because great social upheavals, and even the peaceful break-up of states, are very painful events, it becomes especially urgent for the international community to monitor closely the human rights situations in various countries. The non-extension of the international human rights obligations of a predecessor state to its successor states would considerably weaken the possibilities of such a control and is therefore unacceptable. Events in Eastern Europe and the former Soviet Union show that even when the general trend of changes and long term prospects are beneficial for human rights, the immediate effect of changes may be rather painful. International control over human rights situations in newly born countries should accordingly become even more intensive, and in practice this is happening.

The International Human Rights Committee, monitoring the implementation of the International Covenant on Civil and Political Rights in the autumn of 1992 before its forty-sixth session, decided to request urgent special reports on specific issues under the Covenant from Bosnia-Herzegovina, Croatia and Yugoslavia (Serbia–Montenegro) as successor states to the former Yugoslavia. The Committee noted in its letters to these states that 'all the peoples within the territory of the former Yugoslavia are entitled to the guarantees of the Covenant'. All of the requested states appeared before the Committee and did not question the authority of the Committee to consider their reports, even though only Croatia (and it only after the request was sent by the Committee) had notified the Secretary-General on its succession to the human rights instruments of the former Yugoslavia. These states thereby acquiesced to be bound by Yugoslavia's obligations under the Covenant.

CONCLUDING REMARKS

The practice of state succession after the dissolution of the USSR and Yugoslavia has clarified some issues. First, it has shown the importance of distinguishing between the succession of states and the continuation of states, notwithstanding substantial changes in territory, population or political regime. The events have also stressed the concern of the international community of states with the stability of international legal relations and also with the acceptance by successor states of the obligations of their predecessors. At the same time, the practice of state succession has confirmed that the automatic acceptance of the obligations of predecessor states (except, of course, universal treaties) is often impossible. Negotiations and adjustments are necessary. The events also have indicated that much depends on fortuitous circumstances. Very often new states do not have sufficiently qualified personnel to differentiate between, for instance, succession to the obligations of the predecessor state and adherence to the same treaties. Often it is difficult for them to make competent decisions, especially under the time constraints they face. The positions of other states, and especially their concerted actions as well as the stance of international organizations, therefore become very important.

I think that the practice relating to the dissolution of Yugoslavia and the Soviet Union in terms of state succession indicates that even if new states do not consider themselves to be automatically bound by all their predecessors' treaties, they cannot simply unilaterally renounce their predecessors' obligations. Rather, they must negotiate in good faith the readjustment of these obligations. This applies, above all, to very complex arms limitation treaties, since the circumstances existing at their conclusion will usually be significantly changed as a result of the events which produce questions of state succession. However, the application of *rebus sic stantibus* here does not mean that successor states should have nothing to do with such treaties. In this interdependent world, the stability of international relations is of such high value that the world community of states cannot afford to have these relations completely broken as the result of the dissolution or secession of states. Oscar Schachter is absolutely right that 'it is unlikely that the Restatment's rule of a clean slate for new states will prevail in practice and theory'.[77]

As to universal human rights instruments, the practice of new states – though not unequivocal – and the position of third states, as well as doctrinal findings, seem to indicate that there is a tendency for new states to accept their predecessors' obligations in order to be accepted as members of the international community. New states should be born not only into general customary international law but also into those international human rights treaties which were obligatory for their predecessors.

It is interesting to note that though the Vienna conventions on state succession are not in force, and some provisions of them, as we saw, do not correspond to the actual state practice, many articles of them are referred to rather often in resolving issues of state succession. The Arbitration Commission of the International Conference for the former Yugoslavia in its opinions on issues of state succession drew rather heavily on some articles of these Conventions and especially on the 1983 Convention on succession to state property, archives and debts. So in Opinion No. 13 the Commission opined that in a case of the dissolution of a state articles 18, 31 and 41 of the 1983 Convention, which deal with succession to state property, archives and debts in cases of the dissolution of states, become relevant.[78]

It seems that in the case of succession to property located in the territory of a successor state a kind of *uti possidetis* principle has become a customary rule. This means that the property of a predecessor state is transferred to the successor state on the territory of which it is located. As to property and assets located abroad (assets of central banks as well as state debts) the equitable proportion principle seems to have become a customary norm. But though the principle is rather sound and is not contested by anybody, the devil is, of course, in the details of its practical application.

6 Human rights and democracy in post-totalitarian societies

As was shown in the first chapter, the character of the new international system will depend, to a great extent, on the success or failure of reforms in the new states of Eastern Europe and the former Soviet Union. There are two basic components which will determine the future of these states and, consequently, of the whole world: economic reforms and the process of democratization and the development of fundamental rights and freedoms. I have already dealt with certain aspects of the issues of democracy and human rights in Chapters 2 and 3; I will attempt to paint more comprehensive and detailed picture of the prospects and difficulties facing these societies.

FROM TOTALITARIANISM TO *PERESTROIKA* AND *GLASNOST*

In a totalitarian state, and the USSR was undoubtedly an exemplary one, it is hardly possible to speak of human rights at all. Human rights, which are often rights of the individual versus the state, presuppose the existence of a civil society and an autonomy of the individual *vis-à-vis* the state. This was not the case in the Soviet Union. The state and the Communist Party were omnipresent. Even when a Soviet citizen travelled abroad, for example, he or she was not exercising his or her liberty of movement – the state or the Communist Party had allowed him or her to travel as a special favour. Neither could there be also, for instance, any freedom of the press, as all mass media was state (Party) owned and controlled.

Absence of an independent judiciary meant that declared rights could not be guaranteed. Though executive and judicial branches might have had some independence from each other, they were both completely subordinated to the Communist Party. In the early 1970s Professor Piotr Galanza in his lectures on the history of law at the Moscow

University, used to emphasize that courts in the Soviet Union were most independent because they were subordinated to nobody but Party committees. He could probably afford such jokes, which were especially dangerous as they corresponded to reality, because of his age and more importantly because he had been a member of the Communist Party since March 1917.

Therefore, one could speak of violations of human rights in the Soviet Union only from the point of view of international human rights standards. In the international arena the Soviet Government was rightly accused of violating these standards, which did not penetrate 'the Iron Curtain', though the USSR had ratified most UN instruments on human rights. Under the Soviet legal system there were no human rights. There were privileges for proper and good behaviour and deprivations for bad or politically incorrect behaviour.

After March 1985, when Mikhail Gorbachev became the Secretary-General of the CPSU, new winds started, though very slowly, to blow. For example, it took several years for newspapers to start publishing materials which cautiously referred to the possibilities of introducing a multiparty system in the USSR. The mass media began to criticize some aspects of socialist ideas, but didn't dare to question the foundations of these ideas. Gorbachev himself and the Soviet mass media spoke only of a socialist democracy and a socialist rule of law state as aims of reforms.

It is interesting to note that when Gorbachev for the first time, and I think unwillingly, put in doubt one of the pillars of Marxism-Leninism – namely, the subordination of common human values to the interests of class struggle (or could one even say, the complete negation of the possibility of existence of such values) – he had to quote Lenin[1] (though there is probably only that one and rather vague reference in Lenin's works to the priority of common human values over the interests of the working class). On the other hand, one can find tens or maybe even hundreds of very clear remarks by Lenin and the other founding-fathers of Marxism-Leninism where they expressed contempt for democracy as such and derided common values because, according to them, every social class had its own values, morals and interests. But Gorbachev simply had to refer to Lenin, both because of his background and especially because of the conditions prevailing at that time in Soviet society, though he was in essence undermining the very foundations of Marxism-Leninism – the class approach to all social issues.

But, notwithstanding the fact that the processes unleashed by Gorbachev in 1985 were very slow to gain momentum, by 1991, the year of the demise of the USSR, the country had already undergone substantial changes. I think that it is necessary to pay tribute to the first and the last president of the Soviet Union for unleashing and leading these processes. One has to be courageous to start the processes of democratization in a totalitarian society and one has to be committed to democratization in order not to turn back and not to use methods which were only too familiar for every Soviet leader to safeguard the power of the Communist Party and its Secretary-General.[2]

Of course Gorbachev did not foresee what kind of forces he had unleashed. The developments and events had their own inner dynamic. What he wanted to reform had to be completely dismantled. And this dismantling concerned not only the communist ideology and policy but also the country. Not only was the ideology on which the communist regime was based utopian, the composition of the USSR was artificial as well. Gorbachev wanted to reform the state, to make it, according to his own words, a genuine federation, because, notwithstanding its official title, it had always been a very strong unitary state. Later the idea of a federation with some confederative elements was proposed, but here, as often happened, Gorbachev was too late.

All drafts of the Treaty of Union elaborated under Gorbachev's leadership were not only late but had one fundamental deficiency – they tried to combine the incompatible in various domains. In the political field such incompatible opposites were, for example, the maintenance of the leading role of the Communist Party in society and the democratization of society and the state. In the reform of the state structures such contradictions were the sovereignty of the constituent republics and the sovereignty of the USSR itself.

But now, looking retrospectively at those events, it seems that these inconsistencies were almost inevitable. They reflected the struggle which was going on between the new and the old, and they also reflected the level of development of the society at that time, as well as the correlation of the different political forces. Compromises, though short-lived, were, at the time, very often inevitable.

By the end of 1991 when the Soviet Union collapsed, some democratic changes had already been introduced. The main and one of the few tangible achievements of *perestroika* was *glasnost*, which may be said to be tantamount to the freedom of the press or freedom of expression, except that it existed in a chaotic and uncertain social environment and was therefore often without any limits but at the same time also without guarantees.

Laws on mass media, on freedom of conscience and religious organizations, on non-governmental associations and on the right to leave the country, though far from corresponding in all aspects to respective international standards (especially the last one), were passed by the Supreme Soviet of the USSR.[3] The Soviet Union also adhered to the Optional Protocol to the International Covenant on Civil and Political Rights.[4] Adoption of all these acts was achieved in the process of hard struggle between democratic forces and conservatives from the Central Committee of the Communist Party, the military industrial complex and the KGB.

In 1989 the two most odious articles, 70 and 190 of the Criminal Code of Russia, and the corresponding articles in the codes of other republics, under which most dissidents were sentenced, were repealed.[5] But even here the law repealing these articles contained new provisions intended to maintain at least some elements of the old articles. Only under the pressure of public opinion and influenced by articles published by some well known academic lawyers, which were highly critical of these provisions, did the Supreme Soviet change the law which had just been passed.

This shows on the one hand that *glasnost* had already played its positive role, but on the other hand it also indicates how difficult it was for the seeds of democracy and human rights to make their way through.

COLLECTIVISM, INDIVIDUALISM AND HUMAN RIGHTS

In order to better understand current problems and future prospects in the field of human rights in the new states which emerged after the dissolution of the USSR a short excursion of a theoretical nature is needed into the history of socialist ideas and the Soviet practice concerning human rights. I think that such an excursion may show something useful for some other countries as well.

Now there is probably no doubt that the most important ideas of Karl Marx, especially those concerning communism, were as utopian as had been the ideas of those who Marx, Engels and Lenin called the 'utopian socialists' (Campanella, More, Owen) and were considered by them to be the predecessors of 'scientific socialism' (i.e. Marxism-Leninism). Such basic ideas of Marxism as the elimination of market relations, socialism as the first stage of communism (communism being considered to be a completely new social formation), the role of the proletariat and its dictatorship, etc., all proved to be utopian.

It is interesting that Marks and Engels themselves warned that a massive growth of the productive force, and a high degree of development, were an absolutely essential practical precondition for the success of a socialist revolution, for without them only a widespread poverty would result; and in cases of extreme need, the struggle for essential objects would have to start all over again, which would mean that all the old abominations would have to rise again.[6]

In this warning Marx and Engels were right and wrong at the same time. They were right (probably not having it in mind at all) that for the acceptance of really viable socialist ideas economic, cultural and intellectual preconditions were necessary. They were right also in foreseeing what would happen in the case of a successful socialist revolution in an underdeveloped and poor country. But they were wrong in believing that a socialist revolution could be successful in highly developed societies.

It was only in the underdeveloped countries that there was a chance for the violent planting of the utopian ideas of Marxist teaching. In these countries there were no economic, social, or spiritual foundations for realizing the positive sides of socialist teachings. They therefore at the best remained slogans only, or frequently were perversely used for the suppression of the individual and his rights and freedoms. But at the same time only under these conditions could a socialist revolution be possible.

The records of many countries have shown that socialist ideas were perceived rather easily and put into practice in countries economically and socially underdeveloped. Thus it was in Russia in 1917, and thus it was in so-called 'countries of socialist orientation' in the Third World. Is this a coincidence? It seems not. As Lenin himself noted: 'for Russia in the concrete, historically extremely original situation of 1917, it was easy to launch the socialist revolution; but to continue it to the end in Russia will be far more difficult than in the European countries'.[7]

Those difficulties which Lenin probably had in mind were really, in any case, insurmountable, because the aims themselves were utopian. And in order to implement utopian ideas in Russia after 1917 violence was widely used (and how could one put into practice utopian ideas without violence?), not only against the overthrown so-called exploitative classes, who naturally desperately resisted the new power, but also against the peasants and the intelligentsia, as well as against representatives of the new ruling class itself (i.e., the working class).

In this regard it is appropriate to remind the reader of the words of Vladimir Korolenko, a brilliant Russian writer, who wrote to Lunacharsky, at that time the People's Commissar on Education: 'The very ease with which you managed to carry the masses of our people along with you, shows not our readiness to socialist construction, but on the contrary, the immaturity of our people.'[8] 'In our country, industrially backwards, with little developed capitalism, it will be easier to organize the economic life in accordance with the communist plan',[9] wrote another equally brilliant Russian philosopher Nikolai Berdyayev.

They were right, but as is often the case with those who are right and brilliant they were not heard but instead were sent far away. These first 200 Russian intellectuals were lucky. Lenin sent the best minds of Russia to the West, while Stalin some years later chose another direction – the East, Siberia.

There are several reasons why these ideas were accepted in under-developed countries. No doubt the socialist ideas were especially attractive to the oppressed people, who truly had nothing to lose except their chains. This, and also the susceptibility of the poor masses to the collectivist ideas, the ideas of equality and social justice in countries where individual rights and freedoms were unknown for the majority of the population. But in such countries these ideas acquire, as a rule, the most radical, extremist form, and a decisive, uncompromising fulfil-ment in practice.

In Western societies, where there are more developed and widespread individualistic concepts which place the individual at the centre of society and even of the world order, where the level of societal development has achieved such a degree that practically all of society's members have something to lose, ideas that call for the socialization of all the means of production and the violent overthrow of the existing structures do not find an especially fertile soil.

However, in underdeveloped countries, where the socialist ideas are more easily accepted, where, using Lenin's expression, 'it is easy to launch the socialist revolution', only the most utopian ideas and violent means of their implementation can be used. Here, the violent intro-duction of the utopian elements of the socialist teaching (nationalization of the means of production, the liquidation of the market, etc.) becomes possible, and at the same time truly valuable ideas (e.g., the guaranteeing of each person's social and economic well-being, free health care or education) cannot be realized in practice.

As a result, in those countries which announced the building of socialism and embraced the practical implementation of the ideas of socialism, considerable limitations and violations of human rights and freedoms always took place; the cults of party and the state leaders developed, and dictatorial regimes emerged.

And this no doubt is not coincidence. Where essential material preconditions for the acceptance of ideas of social security, free health care, etc. are lacking in a society, and where individual rights and freedoms remain undeveloped and where democratic traditions are completely absent, some aspects of socialist ideas receive one-sided interpretation and application while other aspects remain only slogans or are simply forgotten. In the name of a class, nation, or people which does not have sufficient political experience, leaders of different levels begin to run public affairs with the support of the bureaucracy.

This is why, when the attempt was made in Russia to put into social practice ideas which generally contradicted the tendencies of social development or which required for their implementation considerably more developed social relations, it was necessary to do it through violent methods.

However, the aim – a humane society – must be attained in a humane way, otherwise the aim becomes one with the means of its attainment in the sense that the final result will be forged by the character of the means applied. By this I do not wish to call for obedience to tyrants, the submissiveness of the oppressed, or to deny a people the right to overthrow a government not guaranteeing its rights and freedoms. However, the violence carried out in Russia after October 1917, not only in practice in the form of the executioner's excesses but also enshrined in instructions and even raised to the level of theory, repeatedly exceeded the measures necessary for overcoming the resistance of the overthrown classes.

As to the representatives of the overthrown classes, the Soviet Chekist (ChK was a predecessor of the KGB), M.I. Latsis, himself a victim of the Stalinist terror in 1928, wrote in 1918:

> We do not conduct a war against separate persons. We destroy the bourgeoisie as a class. Do not search amidst the investigation materials and proofs, for evidence of the fact that the accused acted in either word or deed against the Soviets. The first question which you must pose to him is to what class he belongs to, what is his background, his upbringing, his education or profession. And these questions must determine the fate of the accused. In this is the idea and the essence of the Red Terror.[10]

On 2 June 1921, V.A. Antonov-Ovseyenko and M.N. Tukhachevsky, both later shot by Stalin in 1939 and 1937 respectively, in conducting the struggle with Antonov's peasant revolt in the Tambov province, signed order No. 171, which, *inter alia*, declared:

1   Citizens refusing to disclose their names to be shot on site without trial.
2   Villages in which weaponry is hidden shall be sentenced by order of the authorities to seizure of hostages, who shall in turn be shot in case of refusal to yield the weaponry.
3   In cases of locating hidden weaponry, persons to be shot on the spot without trial.

4   Families which hide bandits shall be subject to arrest and eviction from the province, and all property to be confiscated. The elder worker in the family to be shot on site without trial.[11]

And finally, let us bring forth the opinion of yet another victim of the Stalinist terror, A.I. Rykov, in connection with the 'Shakhty Affair'. At the Central Committee Plenum in 1928, he said that the party must subordinate various legal processes to questions of policy, and in general not follow abstract principles of punishing the guilty according to justice; and that as regards the question of arrest, it was necessary to approach this topic not so much from the point of view of the interest of our criminal policy, as from the point of view of our 'over-all policy'.[12]

I have brought attention only to these three cases concerning four well-known revolutionaries and political and military leaders of the Soviet State, but the adherence to violent methods of struggle and the reign of terror instigated in response to resistance to the Bolsheviks, led to not only these people becoming victims of the Stalinist oppression, but the whole nation as well. If violence against violence can sometimes be justified as an unavoidable evil, then terror even in response to terror can never be justified, for terror is applied with the aim of striking fear, and its direct victims more often than not are innocent persons, as is well documented in the order of Antonov-Ovseyenko and Tukha-chevsky, especially in that part of the order which speaks of shooting hostages or the elder worker of the family.

After World War II, the Stalinist model of socialism was extended to the countries of Eastern Europe. Of course it was not everywhere that those in power committed such crimes against their peoples as was the case with Stalinism. However, restrictions and at times gross violations of individual rights and freedoms took place in all these countries. The attempts of some of them to change their Soviet model ended tragically. Yugoslavia was ostracized, and in Poland, Hungary and Czechoslovakia troops were brought in with the aim of putting down attempts to change the existing political order and democratize society.

The sad experience of the former socialist countries, not just in the area of economic development but also in the attempt to secure human rights and freedoms, inevitably raises the question of the future possibilities for socialism.

Socialism as it existed in its administrative-command or barracks form, that 'real socialism' or 'actually existing socialism' which existed in the Soviet Union and the Eastern European countries, is definitely dead, notwithstanding Castro's obstinacy or China's still playing around with the terminology.

Socialism, as a special social, economic and political system whatever may be meant by that (e.g., different versions of African socialism), which was based on Marx's teaching has also received a justified blow.

One of the specific features of Marxism-Leninism has always been its exclusiveness. Although the classics of Marxism-Leninism unquestionably relied on the achievements of mankind's previous social thought, as opposed to the works of most Soviet philosophers, there can be no doubt in the fact that the so-called founding-fathers of Marxism contrasted Marxism sharply with all other tendencies of social thought. Djilas, who certainly is familiar with the phenomenon from different sides, rightly notes that

> in the pretensions of contemporary communism of being, if not the unique and absolute, but in any case the highest science, based on dialectical materialism are hidden the seeds of despotism. The origin of these pretensions can be found in ideas of Marx, though Marx himself did not anticipate them.[13]

Such claims are distinctly discernible, for example, in the ideas developed by Lenin – that Marxism alone produced answers to all questions of social sciences from A to Z; that Marx's ideas cannot be revised in any way (and those who tried to do so were dubbed as revisionists, which was considered by Stalin to be not only a political error but also a crime); that they are all powerful and comprehensive and so forth.

However, socialist ideas are not limited to those of administrative–command socialism or to Marxism–Leninism and some have a direct bearing on human rights.

Even in Russia as early as 1906 a Russian lawyer Boris Kistyakovsky wrote:

> Thus, in the socialist state more than anything the system of subjective rights will be expanded and augmented; the rights of the individual and the citizen will receive in this system complete recognition and decisive formulation. To two categories of public rights, realized in the modern state based on law and order, that is, to the freedom of the individual in the narrow sense and to political rights, there shall be added a third category – socialist rights.
>
> These rights include the right to work, or the right of every person to the use of land or means of production, and the right of each person to participate in all material and cultural benefits; they will all be united by one general right to a worthy human existence.[14]

And most importantly, and what differentiates Kistyakovsky from Marxists, 'bourgeois' individual rights and freedoms will not be eliminated in a so-called socialist state. They will be supplemented by new rights. With this in mind the Russian scholar says that 'violence can never be justified. Political freedom is such a huge and valuable benefit, that it cannot be relinquished for one instant, nor for any temporary gains.' And he asserts that for the sake of realizing the power of the people, one can never, not even temporarily, turn to violence towards so-called 'enemies of the people'.[15]

In current terminology all this would mean that civil and political rights should be supplemented by social, economic and cultural rights, that ideas of individual rights and freedoms (i.e. civil and political rights) should be augmented by ideas of social justice and the welfare state. And one could forgive Kistyakovsky the use of the term – 'socialist state' because what he really described corresponds very much to a welfare state.

Ideas of socialism were born and developed in Western Europe, in countries where various philosophical and religious concepts, based on individualism, were widely accepted. Bhikhu Parekh writes that

> The view that the individual is conceptually and ontologically prior to society and can in principle be conceptualized and defined independently of society, which we shall call individualism, lies at the heart of liberal thought and shapes its political, legal, moral, economic, methodological, epistemological and other aspects.[16]

Individualism as an ideology recognizes the high value of a human being and the interests of the individual. In philosophy individualism is expressed as the consideration of the individual as the basic and central form of human existence, as the highest degree of expression of the nature of man. This contrasts with many other social, philosophical and religious teachings which attach basic importance to supra-individual forces: society as a whole, or some other human communality (nation, class, etc.). F. Hayek wrote: 'it is this recognition of the individual as the ultimate judge of his ends, the belief that as far as possible his own views ought to govern his actions, that forms the essence of the individualist position'.[17]

The absolute dominance of individualism as an ideology can and does have its negative points, especially if its extreme manifestations find expression in a public consciousness and if one speaks only of an individual's rights and freedoms without taking into account the interests of society as a whole, and, even more importantly, the interests and rights of other individuals. Rhoda Howard is right in concluding that '[t]he unbridled individualism typical of some sectors of the North American population is an indication that human rights are not being protected'.[18]

As one should not sacrifice the interests, rights and freedoms of the individual for the sake of the interests, rights and freedoms of any social entity (be it a nation, class or state as a whole), similarly the primacy of individual rights and freedoms over the interests of society should not be made absolute. Both extremes are identically unacceptable and dangerous. A wise compromise must be found between them.

In a society where the individual with his interests, rights and freedoms (both civil and political) is the centre of attention (if not always in practice, then at least in theory and in the public conscious-ness), the limited nature of individualistic views and practices must be overcome. This involves, as I see it, introducing certain ideas, which may be called 'socialist' as they were initially elaborated in the doctrines of Western social thought, and corresponding practical steps into public life. And this is the practice in most Western countries where the liberty of the individual, freedom of speech, the right to a fair hearing, etc. have been supplemented by different social benefits (free health care and other social programmes) which have taken the form of social and economic rights. I doubt, though whether it is possible to divide human rights into three generations (civil and political rights, economic and social rights, and so-called third generation rights as the right to development, clean environment, etc.), especially, if, as is often done, their origin is traced, respectively, to Western, socialist and Third World countries. As we have seen, ideas of social rights originated certainly in Western societies, where they have so far found their fullest (which by no means can be called perfect) realization in practice.

The introduction of socialist ideas into Russia's social life – where not only was the economic basis for the acceptance of these ideas non-existent but where the ideological preconditions for the acceptance of the truly humanistic ideas of socialist thinkers were utterly lacking (people like Kistyakovsky were certainly in absolute minority) – created the basis for the distortion of socialist ideas; for their dogmat-ization; and for the perception of only those positions of Marxism's teaching that spoke, for example, of violence as the midwife of history and the dictatorship of the proletariat as being restricted by no laws whatsoever, etc.

The ideas of Western socialist theories (e.g., ideas of social justice and social and economic guarantees) which aimed at overcoming the one-sidedness of the individualistic outlook dominant in the Western world, were ineffective where authoritarian and communal ideas and practices flourished and where the individual was of no value at all. Socialist ideas which put emphasis on the interests of the collective, on social justice and equality over the individual's rights and freedoms overlapped in Russia with already existing local ideas and practices which subordinated the individual to a collective (state, nation, church, community).

In practice, because of the lack of material and spiritual foundations, those ideas which were erroneous or utopian came to be realized rather than that expressed in the slogan 'the free development of each is the condition for the free development of all'.

The very idea of the division of countries into capitalist and socialist ones was erroneous. Many of the so-called capitalist nations have introduced many ideas that are essentially socialist, while in many so-called socialist countries these ideas remained only slogans.

The bitter experience of these nations has discredited the truly humane ideas of socialist teachings, for above all these ideas related to the social and economic rights of man. However, the idea of man's social well-being has already found expression in the right to work, to relaxation, to worthy standards of living, to social security, to education, etc. The idea that at a definite stage of a society's development, the society and the state must not only abstain from the violation of inalienable civil and political rights and secure and defend these rights, but also take on, within certain limits, concern for the economic, social and cultural interests of its citizens, is undoubtedly a progressive idea. In many Western countries social and economic rights, have become almost as natural as civil and political rights and the International Covenant on Economic, Social and Cultural Rights has approximately the same number of parties as the International Covenant on Civil and Political Rights.

Though on the one hand, as some authors note, such rights as the right to employment, education and health-care, if claimed as rights in the strict sense of the word (i.e. if they could be legally formalized and enforced by courts), would conflict with the logic of freedom and of the market,[19] this is a conflict or rather a contradiction, resolution of which makes the market more perfect, more civilized.

There does exist, of course, the danger of state paternalism in which it is possible to see the seeds of totalitarianism – especially where there is an insufficient level of economic and social development. Too much care for the individual on the state's part has the tendency to turn into the petty regulation of his or her behaviour. Besides this, strong social programmes do not always beneficially affect the economic activity of both the individual and society as a whole. Therefore, a balance between societal concern for the individual and his own responsibility for himself, a balance between freedom and justice, is essential.

In some of the newly born countries of Eastern Europe and the former USSR there is a danger that social and economic rights will not be properly taken care of, not only because of the lack of economic resources but also because they will be neglected due to their perceived link with the 'real socialism'.

The work on different drafts of a new Russian Constitution confirms this conclusion. Those who once emphasized social and economic rights, which were at that time considered to have, in the socialist concept of human rights, priority over civil and political rights, now shy away from social and economic rights as they would from a sin of their youth of which they feel ashamed. So Yeltsin's draft Constitution, published in May 1993 did not contain any reference to social and economic rights.[20]

One of the authors of the draft, Sergei Alekseyev, a member of the Presidential Council and a well-known professor of law, who as recently as 1991 wrote that it was extremely important that human rights under socialism included not only 'the political and legal protection of the individual' but also 'comprehensive social protection,'[21] now writes that social and economic rights are not rights at all, but only express aims, ideas and intentions towards which the society is striving either in reality or often only in declarations.[22]

But the answer is not to shy away from one extreme position only to find oneself in another extreme position. Of course, the economic conditions prevailing at present are rather poor. This in itself puts limits on the full implementation of economic and social rights as these are economically and financially conditioned rights. Nevertheless, it is necessary that Eastern European countries, and countries which have emerged in place of the former USSR, implement economic and social rights to the maximum of their available resources with a view to progressively achieving the full realization of the rights recognized in the International Covenant on Economic, Social and Cultural Rights, as required by article 2 of that Covenant.[23]

COMMON HERITAGE AND SPECIFIC PROBLEMS

As a result of the dissolution of the USSR there are now fifteen recognized subjects of international law in the territory of the former Soviet Union with problems and difficulties, many of which are common to all or to most of them. Naturally all of them also have their own specific problems, stemming from historical or religious traditions, their demographic situation, the gravity of inter-ethnic tension, etc. Therefore, it is possible to speak of the current human rights situation in the former Soviet Union only in rather general terms. The specific problems of the different new states probably outweigh their common heritage (but even here we have an interesting question: why?).

Common problems originate from factors which were shared by all the republics of the erstwhile USSR. The current human rights record of all of them is conditioned – though, of course, each to a different extent – by their common totalitarian past, transition from a centrally planned economy to a market-oriented one and the birth or revival of nation-states after the collapse of the USSR. All these are developments in a positive direction and are necessary and even inevitable. But at the same time they create enormous difficulties. First, because the past has conveyed its birthmarks to the new entities. Notwithstanding democratic slogans, and even sincere aspirations, politicians very often prefer to use old and therefore much more familiar methods in furthering their aims. Second, the transitional period has created disorder if not chaos in social relations. In some instances it seems that anarchy is an inevitable path from totalitarianism to democracy. For example, frequently, instead of freedom of the press which presupposes legal guarantees of that freedom (and, of course, certain restrictions), those writing and publishing in Moscow, Kiev, Tallinn and other cities of the former USSR enjoy limitless possibilities to interfere in the private life of others and to spread information without any responsibility as to its accuracy. But at the same time, state officials often do not reveal important information, which is of public interest, and take different extra-legal (it is difficult to always say, 'illegal', because of the absence of proper legal regulation) punitive actions against the mass media.

The immediate effects of all economic reforms in all the republics of the former Soviet Union are usually economic hardships and social strains. Even if, in the domain of civil and political rights, progress is obvious in most newly born states (except, of course, in regions where armed conflicts are going on), the level of implementation of social and economic rights is even lower than under totalitarianism. And there is hardly any exception. Differences in the various republics are only those of degree.

These are difficulties facing all states born from the ashes of the erstwhile USSR. There are certainly some positive achievements in most republics, especially in the legislative field, though practice very often lags behind. It is impossible in the scope of this chapter to discuss all republics and all developments. It would probably anyway be a useless endeavour because of the rapid changes in the legislation of all states. In some republics constitutions are not yet adopted, which means that after their adoption new rounds of legislative processes will start. Therefore in my analysis of current developments I will concentrate upon trends and certainly will draw on the legislation and practices of some states more than others.

RUSSIA'S AND ITS SLAVONIC NEIGHBOURS' STRUGGLE FOR DEMOCRACY

As we saw in the previous chapters, Russia is not simply a successor state to the USSR but a continuation of the former Soviet Union.[24]

Among other things which Russia inherited from the USSR was a legal system, which Russia has been, of course, trying quickly to reform. Soviet laws were applied in so far as they did not contradict new realities. In the domain of human rights this means that Russia already had, by the time of the dissolution of the USSR, certain standards in the form of Soviet legislation passed during the Gorbachev era.

As a continuing state of the Soviet Union, Russia also became automatically bound by the Soviet Union's treaty obligations on human rights matters, *inter alia*, by both Covenants on human rights and the Optional protocol to the Covenant on Civil and Political Rights under which individuals can apply to the Human Rights Committee, if, after exhaustion of domestic remedies, they feel that their rights under the Covenant have been violated.

At the end of 1991 and in 1992 the Supreme Soviet of Russia adopted several laws which deal with important human rights issues. The Law on mass media[25] prohibits censorship of the mass media and, if the political will of leading political forces were there, would be able to guarantee the freedom of the press. But there were several attempts by the conservative Supreme Soviet under the chairmanship of Ruslan Khasbulatov to curb press freedoms (e.g., a proposal to create supervisory bodies for mass media, attempts to take over *Izvestia*, etc.).

Though there is no direct censorship of the mass media it is hardly possible to be content with the freedom of the press in Russia, especially if one is comparing the current situation in Russia, not with the distant Soviet past but with international standards.

J. Wishnevsky is quite right in saying that 'there has been remarkably little progress in the development of free speech in Russia since the fall of communism in August 1991'.[26] There are economic and law and order reasons for such a situation, but I agree with Wishnevsky that

> what may be causing the most harm is the fact that many journalists in the Russian Federation inherited from the Soviet Union the totalitarian concept of the role of the mass media as largely a propaganda tool for this or that political party rather than as a source of information for the public.[27]

Though there are various journals and newspapers in Russia, most of them are clearly partisan ones. It is very easy to discover the political or ideological line of this or that newspaper or journal. Even those of them which generally support economic reforms and democratization often understand democracy as democracy for democrats (i.e. for like-minded people). So after Yeltsin's dissolution of the Parliament in September 1993, state television, which remained firmly pro-Yeltsin, dropped any pretence of objectivity and a newsreader 'began her evening report by reminding viewers that she and her colleagues remain loyal to the Kremlin leader'.[28]

In July 1992 the Supreme Soviet of Russia adopted the Law on psychiatric assistance and guarantees of citizens' rights.[29] This Law is especially interesting since abuse of psychiatry for political purposes was one of the most abominable crimes of the Soviet regime against its own people, and also had wide international repercussions. The new Law is indicative of Russia's will to drastically change the situation and, it seems to me, publicly and solemnly to renounce the old practice. Therefore the Law in its preamble notes that the absence of adequate legal regulation of psychiatric assistance may have been one of reasons for the use of psychiatry for non-medical purposes, with damaging effect on the health, dignity and rights of citizens and also on the international reputation of the state. One of the purposes of the Law, as declared in the preamble, is the necessity to implement in the legislation of Russia the rights and freedoms of individuals recognized by the international community and by the Constitution of the Russian Federation. The Law also provides that in case of contradiction between the provisions of the international treaties of Russia and domestic legislation, treaty provisions shall prevail (article 2). It is interesting also that article 10 establishes that the diagnosis of psychiatric illness is framed in accordance with generally recognized international standards and cannot be based on the non-acceptance by a person of the moral, cultural, political or religious values accepted by the society.

The Law really contains legal guarantees against the abuse of psychiatry. The most important of them is the provision which stipulates that a person can be held in a psychiatric hospital against his or her will only according to the decision of a court (articles 13, 19, 32–36). A special state body, independent from the national health service, will be created to protect the rights of those in psychiatric hospitals (article 38) and all hospitals themselves are subordinated to the health service (article 13(2)) which means that there will not be any more special psychiatric hospitals of the Ministry of Interior.

The Law on psychiatric assistance is a big step forward even in comparison with the steps undertaken at the end of the 1980s under Gorbachev in this field, and it indicates that Russian authorities are taking human rights seriously. But the lack of material resources, overcrowding in hospitals and shortage of personnel (who are incredibly underpaid) are the main obstacles in the way of the implementation of this Law.

A positive role in the promotion of human rights in Russia is now played by some former dissidents, who hold key posts in state bodies in charge of human rights. Sergei Kovaljov, a co founder together with Andrei Sakharov of the Committee on Human Rights in the Soviet Union in 1970s, was chairman of the Human Rights Committee of the Supreme Soviet of Russia before it was dissolved by Yeltsin. The allegiance of a man who spent years in Soviet labour camps for the human rights cause is no doubt genuine. Kovaljov remains active in politics after the tragic events of autumn 1993.

The start made by the first Constitutional Court of Russia, was rather promising. One of its most noticeable decisions concerned Yeltsin's Decree on the establishment of the Ministry of Security and Internal Affairs of the RSFSR of 14 December 1991. The Decree, which purported to merge into one super-ministry what previously had been the KGB and the Ministry of Interior, was declared unconstitutional by the Court because it did not correspond to the division of powers in the Russian Federation between legislative, executive and judicial powers as established by the Constitution of the RSFSR.[30]

But the Constitutional Court could not become the highest impartial judicial body in Russia. This was already felt during the acute constitutional crisis and power struggle in spring 1993. Chairman of the Court, Valerii Zorkin, made political statements and took sides in the ongoing political battle even before the Court had an opportunity to consider the case. This led to the call for the resignation of Zorkin by his deputy Nikolai Vitruk who cited the fact that most other members of the Court also disapproved of Zorkin's political activities. Vitruk also voiced the fear that the Court might turn into 'a political instrument in the hands of one or other branch of power'.[31] In the autumn of the same year Zorkin once more became actively involved in the political power struggle.

The absence of a new constitution and the quality of the old one were, of course, the major impediments for the Constitutional Court. But there was also another problem. The Congress of People's Deputies and the Supreme Soviet of Russia, both legislative bodies with practically unlimited (or at least unclear) competence, were elected for a period of five years at a time when the country was in a completely different situation and was not an independent state at all, and thus became active opponents of democratic reforms. Many members of the Constitutional Court who were elected for life tenure by the Congress of People's

Deputies, and some of whom were nominated for the elections by hard-line communist organizations, were sympathetic with the conservative Parliament. Thus the Constitutional Court simply reflected the situation in the country, and in the changed circumstances couldn't fulfil its designated role as the impartial, supreme judicial body.

I have no serious doubts that most of current Russian leaders (although naturally, not all) are generally committed to human rights and democracy, though they may often have rather vague ideas of what these mean and how to achieve them in the circumstances. Certainly there is a trend towards greater care for human rights and fundamental freedoms in Russia. But difficulties are also immense. All the difficulties and factors which are common for all newly born states (the totalitarian past, transition from a centrally planned economy to a market-oriented one, and the resurrection of nationalism) apply to Russia to a great extent.

One of the dangers for democratic reforms in Russia, as in many parts of the former USSR and in Eastern Europe, comes from the resurrection of Russian nationalism. Economic hardships, the soaring crime rate, and especially the loss by Russia of its superpower status which for many in Russia is tantamount to a kind of national humiliation, create a fertile soil for nationalistic ideas. Therefore, there are certainly some reasons for the gloomy perspectives described by Walter Laqueur:

> It is easy to think of reasons that seem to favour the growth of some extreme nationalist movement – the feeling of humiliation following the breakup of the Soviet Union; the need to pursue an assertive policy vis-à-vis the former republics in defence of Russian interests and the presence of many millions of Russians abroad; the bad economic situation and the need to engage in unpopular reforms; the frequent impotence of the authorities in face of a breakdown of law and order; the fact that democratic institutions are not deeply rooted in Russia; the traditional psychological need for a strong hand; the old Weimar dilemma of how to run a democracy in the absence of a sufficient number of democrats; the deep division on the left.[32]

There are extreme Russian nationalist movements such as the one led by Shirinovsky, or groups specializing in anti-Semitism. The elections of December 1993 served to remind us that one should not underestimate these groups. The Russian authorities have closed down a number of virulently anti-Semitic newspapers and at least three editors of such newspapers (V. Fomichev of Moscow's *Puls Tushino*, A. Andreyev of St Petersburg's *Narodnoye Delo*, and A. Batogov of the overtly neo-Nazist *Russkoye Voskressenye*) have been prosecuted for incitement of inter-ethnic and racial hatred.[33] These forces may have an influence in matters concerning Russian minorities in the other former republics of the erstwhile Soviet Union by threatening to use, if necessary, military force to protect their rights, thereby contributing not only to the aggravation of the situation of those minorities but also instigating armed conflicts with Russia's neighbours. Here the irresponsible behaviour of nationalists in some of the smaller neighbours of Russia, combined with the striving of the Russian imperialists to restore an empire, be it Soviet or Russian, may become dangerous for peace and democracy.

Though nationalists are not in power in Russia as they are in some other territories of the former USSR, large nations very often do not understand the national feelings of their smaller neighbours or of the ethnic groups in their own country, and may even get angry when these neighbours or ethnic groups at home want to arrange their lives according to their own will. But at the same time big nations are as a rule less prone to petty nationalism. The Russian citizenship law is probably one example of Russia's broad-mindedness in questions of inter-ethnic relations.

This Law[34] is rather liberal with regard to the acquisition of Russian citizenship. The Law establishes that

> all citizens of the former USSR who are permanent residents of the RSFSR on the day of the entry into force of the Law on citizenship will be recognized as citizens of the RSFSR if during a year they do not declare their unwillingness to be citizens of the RSFSR (article 13).

The Law also provides that in the Russian Federation nobody can be deprived of his or her citizenship (article 1), and indicates that Russia encourages the acquisition of its citizenship by stateless persons (article 7).

On another positive note I would also like to mention Russia's handling of issues arising from the referendum on the independence of Tartarstan. On 21 March 1992 Tartarstan declared itself to be 'a sovereign state and subject of international law building its relations with Russia and other republics and states on the basis of equal treaties'.[35] Though the Constitutional Court of the Russian Federation declared the referendum unconstitutional,[36] the Russian authorities were wise enough not to take any coercive measures against the Tartars. This reserved approach of the leadership of Russia was in striking contrast with the Soviet Union's actions in Lithuana, Georgia or Baku.

The respect for human rights is conterminous with the respect for law and judiciary. But law has never been highly esteemed in Russia. Before the 1917 revolution law was seen by the majority of the population of Russia as a tool against them. In 1909 Kistjakovskii wrote:

> The lack of development of the legal consciousness of the Russian intelligentsia and the absence of interest in legal concepts is the result of an old evil – the absence of any rule of law in the day-to-day life of the Russian people . . . The total lack of equality before the courts has killed any respect for law. A Russian, by whatever name he goes, will get around or violate the law anywhere he can with impunity; and the government will do the same.[37]

The Bolsheviks used law and the judiciary as a part of the repressive state apparatus. Legal norms, even in theory, were considered not as measures of freedom or guarantees of rights but as instruments of the state policy. Members of the legal profession did not rank high in the eyes of the Communist Party. This tradition goes back to the founding-fathers of Marxism-Leninism who derided bourgeois law and lawyers and wrote of the 'withering away' of any law under communism. It will certainly take time to change such an attitude towards law and the legal profession.

Rather typical was a reaction of President Yeltsin's entourage to ex-president Gorbachev's criticism of the reforms of the Government of Russia in June 1992. A spokesman for Yeltsin declared that in his criticism the ex-president had gone beyond his competence (I really wonder what this could mean) and measures would be taken against him. Later it was reported that Mr Gorbachev had been deprived of his limousine. The same story repeated itself in 1993 when the Vice-President of Russia, Rutskoi was deprived of his limousine and some bodyguards. These punishments follow the old communist traditions in which, rather than taking legal action, the deprivation of privileges for bad behaviour and the granting of certain benefits for good behaviour were typical methods of the past.

Much has to be done to overcome the psychological reticence of most Russians to go to court to protect their rights. The first step should be a reform of the court system and the creation of a really independent judiciary. A step towards this end is the new Law on the Status of Judges of 26 June 1992[38] which, *inter alia*, prohibits any interference in the functioning of the judiciary and provides that judges are to be elected to life tenure.

Economic chaos and transition from the command economy to a market-oriented one have created a fertile climate for criminal be-haviour. The necessity to combat a soaring crime rate entails measures involving increased powers for the forces of law and order. In the circumstances, guarantees for suspects or detained persons are seen as something secondary or even detrimental to the effective combat against crime. At the end of the Gorbachev era in the USSR this false dilemma (though it is necessary to recognize that it is not yet completely overcome in much more developed democracies than Russia) – either to effectively combat the soaring crime rate or to introduce effective procedural guarantees such as habeas corpus, trial by jury, the right to have a counsel at early stages of criminal procedure, etc. – was at the heart of the discussions on criminal law and procedural reforms.

The former Procurator-General of Russia, Stepankov, who was dismissed in autumn 1993, was strongly against trial by jury and in his intervention before the Parliament Supreme Soviet even resorted to distortion of the facts in order to show that trial by jury has been deficient in countries which use it and pointed out that it was completely alien to Russia (even though there was trial by jury in pre-revolutionary Russia).[39]

Such an approach to the problems of law and order leads not only to innocent people being sentenced but also to criminals remaining unpunished. Nevertheless, in newly born countries, where people demand harsher and quicker measures to deal with violent crimes, politicians and even courts are often eager to please the public opinion at the expense of procedural guarantees. And, of course, this is a familiar and therefore easier approach to dealing with crimes. During the state of emergency imposed by Yeltsin after the dissolution of Parliament in September 1993, the police in Moscow used its powers in a discriminatory manner against people of Caucasian and Central Asian nationalities. Many Muscovites welcomed such measures, and Yuri Luzhkov, the mayor of Moscow, announced plans for a reinforced *'propiska'* (resident permit) system for Moscow.[40]

Though citizens of Russia now travel more freely than did Soviet citizens, neither Russia's laws nor practice in matters of foreign travelling correspond to international standards. Exit visas for foreign travelling, which are still governed by the USSR 1990 Law, have not been needed since 1 January 1993. But if under the Soviet authorities foreign passports or exit visas were refused mainly on political grounds, now bureaucrats often ask for bribes. Restrictions may still be imposed also in the ground of secrecy. The notorious *'propiska* system' (internal resident permits), under which the freedom to choose one's place of residence was violated by Soviet authorities, is still in place, though already the Committee on Constitutional Supervision of the former USSR has found that this system was contrary to the Constitution of the USSR and the Soviet Union's international obligations.[41]

It is important to note that though Yeltsin has already several times (in 1991 and 1993) outlawed various communist parties in Russia, the Soviet Communist Party's faithful repressive arm – the KGB – has remained virtually intact. The Ministry of Security of Russia having lost its foreign intelligence directorate, which now exists separately, is practically the same old KGB. This is in striking contrast with the practice of Eastern European countries and many former Soviet republics (e.g. the Baltic states). One may, of course, agree that Russia needs intelligence and counter-intelligence services, and it is not easy to create new ones quickly, but such a complacency towards the KGB – a body which from the very beginning of its existence until the dissolution of the USSR was actively human-rights hostile – is not, to put it mildly, very encouraging.[42]

Human rights issues in two other Slavonic republics of the former Soviet Union, Ukraine and Belorussia, are much the same as they stand in Russia, though it seems that Russia, leading in the speed of its economic reforms, also has a slight edge in the field of human rights reforms – at least at the legislative level. Ukraine and Belorus, are like Russia, preparing their new Constitutions, and first drafts have been published and discussed. Both states have adopted their respective citizenship laws.

The Ukrainian Law on citizenship provides that all persons who are permanent residents of Ukraine at the moment of the Law enters into force, notwithstanding their origin, social or property status, education, language, political opinion, religious views or the character of their occupation, and who are not citizens of other states and do not object to acquisition of the Ukrainian citizenship, are Ukrainian citizens.[43] The Law on citizenship in Belorus provides that all permanent residents of the Republic at the moment of the entry into force of the Law on citizenship are citizens of Belorus.[44] The Belorussian Law seems to impose its citizenship to all permanent residents, leaving no choice for them.

The Ukrainian Parliament has adopted a Law on Information (October 1992) and a Law on the Printed Mass Media (November 1992) that conform with respective international standards.[45] Censorship is banned and the right to receive and disseminate information is guaranteed. There is a variety of printed mass media and even the state-run television, while generally supporting the 'official' line, allows representatives of various political forces to voice their views.[46]

It is difficult to predict the speed as well as all the directions of reforms in the field of human rights in Russia, Belorus or Ukraine. Much depends on the outcome of the struggle between different political forces. Generally speaking one may conclude, I think, that Russia has managed relatively well on its road from totalitarianism, via semi-anarchy, to democracy, though it is far, of course, from its declared goals. It seems that because of its historical traditions, immense economic and social problems, even the vastness of its territory, Russia is predestined, at least during the stage of coming out of a semi-anarchical situation, to choose a relatively authoritarian political regime. This presupposes a strong executive arm of the government, which in itself does not predetermine the level of implementation of the rights and freedoms of individuals. At the same time, however, strong executive powers, especially in the absence of democratic traditions, have a tendency to encroach upon these rights and freedoms.

SOME REFLECTIONS ON HUMAN RIGHTS IN OTHER FORMER SOVIET REPUBLICS

The Baltic republics (Estonia, Latvia, Lithuania) were at the forefront of the processes of democratization in the Soviet Union. At the end of the 1980s it frequently happened that what was still impossible in Moscow or elsewhere in the USSR, was already possible in the Baltics. For example, the first independent draft of the Soviet law on mass media, prepared by jurists from Moscow, was published in Estonia and thus became known to the larger audience in Moscow and elsewhere in the Soviet Union.

The introduction of elements of a market economy earlier than in other republics of the USSR brought about economic liberalization, which is a necessary basis for human rights and freedoms. In October 1991 Estonia adhered to most important UN instruments on human rights, including both Covenants and the Optional Protocol to the Covenant on Civil and Political Rights, thereby recognizing the jurisdiction of the Human Rights Committee to consider individual communications.[47]

In June of 1992, by means of a referendum, Estonia adopted the new Constitution.[48] Chapter 2 of the Constitution is devoted to human rights and fundamental freedoms. It corresponds to basic international standards on human rights and enshrines such inalienable rights as the right to life, the prohibition of torture and other forms of inhuman treatment, the right to liberty and security of person, the right to fair trial, etc.

The Constitution of Estonia also provides that in cases where Estonian laws or other acts are in conflict with international treaties which are ratified by the Estonian Parliament, the articles of the international treaty shall prevail (article 123). It is important and encouraging that the Constitution provides for guarantees of the independence of the courts, though much remains to be done to have a really competent and impartial judiciary.

In April 1993 Estonia and Lithuania were admitted to membership of the Council of Europe, which means on the one hand that the situation with regard to human rights in these countries is not as tragic as it is sometimes depicted by Russian diplomacy (though this does not mean that there are no serious problems, especially concerning the rights of minorities), but on the other hand implies that now these Baltic states are under the scrutiny of European human rights bodies, which certainly will be very important safeguard for human rights in countries embarking on the road towards democratization.

Issues arising from the legislation concerning citizenship issues and the status of aliens, which have created most serious difficulties, concern the rights of the so-called Russian-speaking minority in Estonia and Latvia. These were dealt with in some detail in Chapter 3, where minority issues were analysed, and in Chapter 5, which covered problems of state succession, because the position of these states on citizenship issues was to a great extent determined by their approach to questions of state succession. This exempts me from the necessity of dealing with this important human rights problem here in any detail.

But citizenship issues, language requirements for the acquisition of citizenship, and inter-ethnic problems generally remain concerns for the governments of these states as well as for the world community. In spring 1993 Mr van der Stoel, the CSCE High Commissioner for minorities, made a series of recommendations to the governments of Estonia and Latvia concerning changes in the legislation and practices of these states on minority issues.[49]

The new Estonian Law on elections for local authorities provides that non-citizens who are permanent residents of Estonia can participate in elections. But they cannot be elected.[50] This is, certainly, not the best option, especially for areas where non-citizens are in an absolute majority.

The Estonian Law on aliens, passed by the Parliament on 21 June 1993, not only poisoned relations between Estonia and Russia, but became the object of international scrutiny. The Council of Europe found 'a number of deficiencies in the law and inconsistencies with the norms of European law'.[51] A senior official of the CSCE recommended that Estonia amend the law.[52] As a result, the President of Estonia did not promulgate the Law and the Parliament had to reconsider the Act which it had just passed. After the changes had been made by the Estonian Parliament, the European Political Cooperation issued a Declaration in which it commended Estonia for its cooperation with the

European institutions and noted that '[th]is political act is a clear indication of the attachment of Estonia to democratic principles and its commitment to political dialogue and compromise and non-confrontation with its communities and its neighbouring countries'.[53]

This Law, which was a logical development of the citizenship legislation, contained very vague language and gave the authorities discretionary powers which were too wide. As Anatol Lieven rightly puts it: 'though it is entirely true that Estonian and Latvian policies towards the Russians have so far taken purely legal and non-violent forms, it still forms part of a pattern of exclusivist nationalism which risks tearing apart the entire fabric of Eastern Europe and the former Soviet Union'.[54] Though, as the EPC notes, the amendments represent 'a substantial improvement of this law'[55] they do not address all the concerns expressed by the experts.

Most serious human rights violations take place in areas of armed conflict. Of course, any such conflict in itself is a negation of the right to life. But many other gross and massive violations of elementary human rights and laws of armed conflict are being committed in the Caucasus, Moldova, and Tajikistan. Hostage-taking has been widespread and warring sides have boasted of the numbers of hostages taken.[56] In Nagorno-Karabakh both Armenians and Azeris have been at different times engaged in 'ethnic cleansing'.

In Central Asian states, the Turkmenistan and Uzbekistan opposition is under oppression and freedom of expression is severely restricted. For instance, Amnesty International reports the arrests of two prominent opponents of the Government, B. Shakirov and P. Akhunov in Uzbekistan.[57] Members of the opposition movement Birlik have been repeatedly harassed.

In Turkmenistan, Amnesty International representatives were detained by militia after less than 24 hours in the country and were forced to leave because of alleged visa irregularities. At the same time opposition leaders were placed under house arrest.[58] In this country it seems that the personality cult of President Nijazov has exceeded the level usually upheld in the former USSR. Newspapers report of the Decree of the Supreme Soviet of Turkmenistan on unlimited production and distribution of portraits of the 'Turkmen-pasha' (Leader of all Turkmens). There are a collective farm, a street, the Academy of Sciences and a steamship named after President Nijazov.[59]

As the head of a group of UN observers in Tajikistan, Livio Bota, said: 'The present government of Tajikistan has dealt harshly with its opponents, jailing and, according to some accounts, torturing those opposition leaders it has been able to capture.'[60]

PROSPECTS FOR DEMOCRACY IN POST-TOTALITARIAN SOCIETIES

The experience of all of the former Soviet republics in the field of human rights shows that the transition from totalitarianism to democracy is not an easy path. It has many pitfalls. Various factors of an economic, political, religious and cultural character and also of a psychological nature, which are not always taken account of in the analysis of democratization and the human rights situation in the Soviet successor states, often play a part in determining outcomes. This means, for example, that certain aspects of social psychology, culture, or historical traditions may lead to different outcomes though political and economic problems and difficulties may not differ so much. For instance, concepts of pride and honour are different in the Baltics and the Caucasus. Though the Baltic states are still far from resolving personal or intergroup conflicts ideally – through court procedures and compromises – for some peoples of the Caucasus it would be shameful and a sign of weakness to go to court to resolve conflicts with neighbours or to compromise themselves in politics or inter-ethnic relations. Compromises are seen as a sign of weakness. The winner has to take all. Power-sharing is usually not an option. Therefore conflicts which in different circumstances could be resolved through protracted negotiations, compromises and power-sharing often end in violent clashes.

In some Central Asian states, even under communism, which was supposed to be based on internationalism, republican leaders sought loyalty mainly amongst their tribesmen. The social system existing in these states, may be likened to a kind of feudal communism, where the bases of power for leaders are not political parties in the traditional Western perception but tribes, ethnicities, next of kin.

The events in the former USSR and in Eastern Europe do not in any way mark 'the end of history' and developments towards liberal democracy in some societies cannot be discerned even under a magnifying glass.

But even in those societies where democratic reforms have already borne some fruit, difficulties still remain immense. Robert Dahl writes that

> a country that has had little or no experience with the institutions of public contestation and political competition and lacks a tradition of toleration toward political opposition is most unlikely to turn into a stable polyarchy[61] in the space of the few years.[60]

One of the basic difficulties of the democratization process in countries which have emerged in the place of the erstwhile Soviet Union is the very nature of this process. Its order is reversed in comparison with the processes of democratization in Western countries; it is not gradual but very rapid; its roots do not always, and in some societies do not at all, lie in the internal developments of the society but are external ones.

Dahl speaks of three possible ways in which democratization can arise: (1) when liberalization precedes inclusiveness (i.e. when political contestation starts among a small elite and the population as a whole is included gradually into the political process); (2) when inclusiveness (i.e. inclusion of the population in the political life), precedes liberalization; (3) shortcut, which means that a closed hegemony is transformed into a polyarchy by a sudden grant of universal suffrage and right of public contestation.[63]

From Dahl's point of view, the first way is the easiest and the most natural, and the last one the most difficult and problematic. What happened in the former Soviet Union falls somewhere between the second and third ways. There was, of course, a universal suffrage in the USSR and the population was to a certain extent included in the political life of the country. But as public contestation was completely absent this inclusion was heavily distorted.

The first two paths outlined by Dahl, it seems, are closed in the contemporary world. The interdependence and transparency of the world and the closeness of different societies mean that traditional slow ways of democratization, being the outcomes of lengthy processes of social struggle and group conflict which themselves created conditions for the consolidation and persistence of democracy,[64] and having, most importantly, completely internal driving forces (England was probably the purest example of such a democracy), are hardly available any more.

It seems that in the case of the democratization of former socialist states we may have two major variations: the Soviet version, in which political reforms and liberalization precede economic reforms, and the Chinese version in which economic reforms have not yet led to any significant political liberalization. The Eastern European countries fit, at least partly, into the Soviet model because their democratization started with the sudden collapse of their totalitarian regimes. But as these regimes were imposed on them by the Soviet Union, and because at least some of these countries had certain more developed grounds for democratization than the former USSR (e.g., economic reforms in Hungary, Solidarity in Poland, a higher level of economic development in Czechoslovakia), their future seems brighter.

The second variant may be less painful. The political liberalization in the former USSR led to the disruption of economic relations and finally to the dissolution of the country. But I am convinced that in the Soviet case the Chinese version would have been impossible. The Soviet leadership was ideologically so rigid and numbed at all levels that a person who, like Chinese leaders, would have dared to say that it does not matter whether a cat is black or white, the important thing being whether it catches mice or not, would have been, at best, immediately declared to be opportunist and politically untrustworthy.

Therefore, political liberalization, which meant, *inter alia*, that Gorbachev had gradually to get rid of the most conservative elements in the party leadership, seeking at the same time the support of less conservative ones (and to kick them out during the next round of *perestroika* and *glasnost*), was a necessary precondition for any real economic reforms. At a certain moment Gorbachev needed the support of the population in order to further his reforms, and this meant that the genie was out of the lamp. And in contrast with Aladdin's genie this one would not go back in whatever the wishes of the master.

These difficult and even gloomy perspectives facing some of the former Soviet republics, especially in the domain of democratic reforms, inevitably raise the question of whether it is possible at all to export or impose democracy, which is certainly a product of Western development and which was gradually, through the method of trial and error, put into practice in these countries. Are those Russian national-ists, who insist that Russia does not belong to Europe and that therefore the reforms of both Gorbachev and Yeltsin are alien to the Russian spirit, right at the end of the day?

Kishore Mahbubani writes that '[e]arlier theorists of democracy would be surprised by the twentieth-century conceit that democracy can be applied to any society, regardless of its stage of development or its internal social divisions'.[65] And he suggests that for Third World states 'a period of strong and firm government, one that is committed to radical reform, may be necessary to break the vicious circle of poverty sustained by social structures that contain vested interests opposed to any real change'.[66]

The recent history of some rapidly developed countries (the 'small tigers' of East Asia, and of Chile under Pinochet) demonstrates that democracy is not indeed a *condition sine qua non* for economic growth.

Is an elected parliament and the presence of several political parties already a prima facie sign of democracy? There are a number of formally democratic countries where multi-party elections are held on a fairly regular basis but where at the same time human rights are grossly and manifestly violated.[67] For those who are killed or tortured and for their relatives and friends it does not matter whether this is done by, say, the Shining Path terrorists or governmental forces.

Governments of all of the newly born states have to make difficult, rapid and often unpopular decisions in order to cope with their deteriorating economic situation, soaring crime rate, social and often inter-ethnic unrest. This indeed presupposes strong and stable executive powers, and traditional parliamentary democracies may not do too well under such circumstances.

But at the same time we witness that though democracy is not a precondition for rapid economic growth most dictatorships do not do well even in the economic field. It is not clear whether limitations on democracy, for example in South Korea and Singapore, or massive repressions in Chile under Pinochet, contributed in any way to the economic growth of these countries. Moreover, a strong executive power is not at all tantamount to a repressive regime. And the examples of Mobutu, Idi Amin, Bokassa and a host of other dictators show rather convincingly that a strong government may become not a remedy but a disaster, not only for the human rights record of the country but for its economy as well. Gross human rights violations by authorities in some countries, like Sri Lanka, India or Peru play into the hands of Tamil and Kashmirian separatists or Shining Path terrorists, helping them to recruit new members.

Moreover, economic growth and social stability are not the only things which matter. In our world it has become really impossible to be indulgent to dictators, even if they do well in the domain of economic growth. The end of the Cold War has made it even more difficult to close ones eyes to gross violations of human rights and to retain normal diplomatic and trade relations with regimes which do not guarantee basic human rights.

At the same time, it seems, it would be unrealistic to request the full implementation of international standards of human rights from all countries, and, moreover, to always make this a precondition for the development of economic or other relations with all, and especially with newly born, countries.

The rapid introduction of elements of democracy into societies which have neither economic, social nor cultural prerequisites for accepting democratic institutions and processes may sometimes even be counter-productive. This is especially relevant to countries where economic backwardness is combined with cultural and religious traditions which are not conducive to democratic reforms. It would be unrealistic to expect, for example, that such European countries of the former USSR, such as the Baltic states, Ukraine, Belorussia or Russia, which themselves all face different problems and difficulties, on the one hand, and Central Asian states on the other, could move with the same speed in their democratic reforms.

As human rights and democracy are two sides of the same coin, and in a larger sense basic human rights may be considered as a part of democracy, it is too much to expect that in all the Soviet successor states there will be full freedom of the press or that all procedural guarantees for detained persons will be observed in the near future.

But tendencies and efforts are important even in countries where rapid democratization may even be counter-productive. If governments do not guarantee such basic rights as the right to life, liberty, and security of person, or if they torture those who are in opposition to them, then notwithstanding any elections and even the presence of several political parties, there will be neither human rights nor democracy.

Therefore, the world community should monitor the human rights situation in all countries in the light of the international standards of human rights but take into account underlying historical, social, economic, cultural and religious factors. What is important is constant progress and not rapid, unprepared reforms which do not take these underlying realities into consideration.

Such an approach to human rights, which calls for taking into account the historic, economic, cultural and religious environment in which human rights are implemented, does not mean that Musa Hitam, a leader of the Malaysian delegation to the Vienna 1993 World Human Rights Conference, is right in saying that '[e]ach country is entitled to its own perception of human rights and forcing developing countries to follow the western perception is unfair and unjust'.[68] Also, it is hardly possible to agree with his point that 'civil and political rights should come almost automatically after development has been achieved'.[69]

This type of approach is, from my point of view, an abuse of the problems and difficulties stemming from historical traditions and economic underdevelopment. When I call for taking into consideration the social environment in which international standards of human rights are to be implemented, I address the international community of states and special monitoring bodies and I am not preparing excuses for the governments of those states which like to hide behind difficulties, often created by themselves, in order to excuse their poor human rights records. Rhoda Howard is right saying that 'many human rights-abusive practices that do exist are not intrinsic to the culture; rather they are consequences of economic and political interest',[70] and that 'constant references to communal society can be, and are, used to mask systematic violations of human rights in the interests of ruling elites.'[71]

The UN Human Rights Committee, for example, always appreciates the genuine efforts of all states, and especially of Third World countries, which often face real difficulties in the implementation of the International Covenant on Civil and Political Rights, and understands quite well the governments which, notwithstanding their efforts, have not yet achieved full implementation of the Covenant. But those governments which usually hide behind the outdated non-interference concept and try to explain away their problems by referring to historical, cultural or religious traditions and economic underdevelopment often simply do not undertake any efforts even to gradually implement international human rights standards.

Sirous Naserri, the Iranian representative to the Geneva headquarters of the UN, for example, at the end of the consideration of the Iranian report on civil and political rights before the UN Human Rights Committee in October 1992, emphasized the need to take into account cultural criteria when interpreting international instruments.[72] But his remark missed the point because the observations and comments of members of the Human Rights Committee did not question the cultural values of the Iranian people or of Islam.[73] Is it really possible to explain discrimination against and even the persecution of Baha'is, the death penalty by stoning for adultery, mutilation as a punishment, and *fatwa* against Salman Rushdie as cultural requirements which should be taken into account while speaking of human rights in that country?

And do international human rights standards really reflect only Western values and does cultural relativism mean that these rights and freedoms, or at least a part of them, are alien to countries which do not belong to the Western civilization?

Certainly, Western countries and consequently Western concepts made the biggest contribution to the elaboration of the major human rights instruments after World War II. But by the adoption of the International Covenants on Human Rights as early as 1966 not only the Soviet Union and other so-called socialist countries but also most Third World states were able to influence the content of these documents which are now freely ratified or adhered to by considerably more than 100 states, of which the majority are non-Western countries. Therefore the World Conference on Human Rights of 1993 could emphasize that '[a]ll human rights are universal,[74] indivisible and interdependent and interrelated. The international community must treat human rights globally in a fair and equal manner, on the same footing, and with the same emphasis.'[75]

Even more important, in my opinion, is the fact that when one goes further, general assertions that the cultural, religious and historical traditions of a given country should be taken into account in assessing its human rights record, one can hardly say in concrete terms how generally accepted international standards conflict with the cultural or religious values of individual societies. It is interesting to note that while the Iranian delegation before the UN Human Rights Committee stressed the necessity to take into consideration the cultural criteria of any country while assessing its human rights record, the same delegation confirmed that the International Covenant on Civil and Political Rights and the Universal Declaration on Human Rights were compatible with Islam.[76]

Sometimes the arguments of those who deny the very possibility of the existence of universal human rights in the multi-cultural world simply miss the point.

I would agree, for example, with the Foreign Minister of Singapore Wong Kan Seng who in his statement at the World Conference on Human Rights in Vienna said that '[u]niversal recognition of the ideal of human rights can be harmful if universalism is used to deny or mask the reality of diversity'.[77] But later, as an example, he stated that 'Singaporeans, and people in many other parts of the world do not agree, for instance, that pornography is an acceptable manifestation of free expression or that a homosexual relationship is just a matter of lifestyle choice.'[78] Neither the freedom of distribution of pornography nor equality between homosexuals and heterosexuals are universal human rights norms. Indeed, there are many controversial areas such as euthanasia, abortion, pornography, homosexuality, etc. which touch upon deeply rooted moral and religious sentiments and which are considered differently in various societies.

Neither is it any excuse that development should be put before civil and political rights. They are not mutually exclusive. Quite the contrary.

When the Soviet Union's human rights record was criticized it was not because it put social and economic rights first and considered them higher than civil and political rights. The socialist concept of human rights as something different from and even higher than the so-called Western concept was used to conceal the real human rights situation. Human rights were considered not as a practical but as an ideological problem. The lack of civil and political rights was one of the reasons for the stagnation of the economy of the country and consequently of the poor situation regarding social and economic rights as well.

It is true that some fundamentalist religious concepts are really incompatible with international human rights instruments (especially regarding equality between men and women or tolerance towards other religions), but even here, I would dare to assert, we can hardly discover any imposition of specific Western values on culturally different societies. For example, Catholic fundamentalism is not so different from its Islamic counterpart as to their respective attitudes towards human rights. One may not be surprised with the findings, made by Adamantia Pollis, that in Orthodox theology 'woman is considered morally inferior' or that the 'inexorable conclusion . . . is that individual human rights cannot be derived from Orthodox theology'.[79] What may be surprising is the underlyning idea that human rights can be derived from any religion at all.

Though international human rights standards protect the freedom of religion, and different religions or individual clergymen have quite often contributed to the protection of human rights, no religion in its fundamentalist form (which in terms of fundamentalists means the only true or genuine religion) is conducive to human rights. Even in such a liberal church as the Church of England the decision to allow the ordination of women, which from the human rights point of view is quite natural, was only adopted in 1993, and then far from unanimously, and has alienated many followers of the Church.

The cultural traditions of many societies contain elements which do not facilitate the implementation of human rights norms. Rhoda Howard is right in saying that 'like the cultural underpinnings of most other societies, the cultural underpinnings of Western society do not all favour human rights'.[80] Obviously, the Western philosophical and cultural traditions include not only liberalism, but also communism, corporatism, racism, and fascism.[81] In Western European countries women were discriminated against (and in some of them still are), and in many European countries heretics were burnt. In Spain the Inquisition was abolished only in 1834,[82] and in 1925 a school teacher was condemned by a local court in Tennessee, USA, for teaching the theory of Darwin's *Origin of Species*.[83] As to the punishment of crimes, Western European countries have moved from cruel forms of execution such as hanging or guillotining to complete abolition of the death penalty. The main difference between these religious fundamentalisms is that while the Catholic one was powerful in the Middle Ages, the Islamic fundamentalism is a contemporary phenomenon.

This shows that contemporary human rights standards are not immutable values, inherent only to Western countries. These countries themselves, and others as well, came to the acceptance of these values through a long historical process. This also means that the receptiveness of different societies to international standards of human rights is less conditioned by the cultural peculiarities of a given society than by the stage of its social, economic and political development. How people are executed (hanged, stoned to death or guillotined) depends to a great extent on a specific culture, but whether people are executed at all depends more on the stage and level of societal development. One hundred years ago it was probable that those who hanged did not know much about those who used stoning, but today the world has become too small and interdependent to expect that it is only missile technology or computer hardware and software that transgress state boundaries. Human rights, likewise, have become universally recognized by different peoples.

Therefore, I can see no universal international human rights norm which would be culturally unacceptable for any society. It may be the case that some time would be needed in some societies to fully implement them, and that some quite deeply rooted traditions which are inexcusable from the point of view of these standards could not be immediately eradicated. India, for example, has not yet succeeded in completely eradicating such vestiges of the past as the 'dowry death' (where a wife is killed because of the insufficiency of her dowry) or *sati* (where a widow has to commit suicide or is encouraged to kill herself after the death of her husband), but the government is certainly trying to do its best to get rid of these crimes.[84]

There are no inherently Western international human rights standards. It may be true that for some countries certain rights may seem more important, and even if some countries, like Malaysia, view 'development as a basic human right' this does not mean that if development is guaranteed civil and political rights would automatically follow, or that the limitation of civil and political rights is necessary for securing development. 'While development facilitates the enjoyment of all human rights, the lack of development may not be invoked to justify the abridgement of internationally recognized human rights.'[85]

In my opinion human rights are conditioned by three categories or levels of factors: anthropological, societal and international. These factors are not immutable in time or space. While societal factors – that is, factors pertaining to the characteristics of a given society – have exercised the strongest influence on the content of the rights and freedoms of members of the society, international factors are of more recent origin, and their influence is rapidly growing. Some rights, like the right to life, freedom from torture and the right to found a family are of an anthropological nature, though they, as any other rights, can exist only in a society. Robinson Crusoe could have had no rights or obligations before the appearance of Man Friday.

The growing interdependence of the world as a whole and the transparency of most societies mean that international factors, through purposeful efforts as well as through inter-penetration of cultures, are influencing human rights concepts as well as practices in different societies. However, this does not and should not lead to the cultural uniformity of the world.

The Bangkok NGO Declaration on Human Rights adopted by 110 NGOs in the Asia and Pacific region on 27 March 1993[86] confirmed that it was not cultural differences in societies that gave rise to human rights violations, but rather that such violations take place as a result of the specific political interests of the ruling circules in some of these states. The Declaration, adopted just a few days before the regional conference of official representatives of the countries of Asia and the Pacific region, which emphasized cultural relativism in their approach to human rights, stressed that 'cultural practices which derogate from universally accepted human rights, including women's rights, must not be tolerated'.[87] It may be noted that this is not on this occasion voiced by western NGOs.

We may probably conclude now, returning to our main topic – human rights in post-totalitarian societies – that though in many of them democracy or even, using the term proposed by Dahl, 'polyarchy' is still quite far away, most newly born or re-born states have sufficient resources for democratization. Naturally, the efforts of governments and the assistance of other states and international inter-governmental bodies as well as NGOs, are necessary. Understanding difficulties and problems, and even the recognition of cultural diversity as a universal value, does not mean that one should or could be lenient towards the violation of fundamental human rights in countries which are facing objective difficulties.

Conclusion

I hope that the above analysis of some topical issues of the contemporary world confirms the point that today not only are more and more countries becoming open societies but the very international system has become more open than before to impulses from domestic societies. There is no clear-cut distinction between international and domestic affairs any more. Any comprehensive study of issues of an international character has to look deep into domestic matters and, vice versa, one often cannot comprehend what is going on within states if international issues are not taken account of.

Research of such problems as the self-determination of peoples, the protection of minorities, the recognition and succession of states, and questions of human rights in post-totalitarian societies has revealed also that it is impossible to abstract legal questions from those aspects of these issues which lawyers often left to specialists on international relations, political scientists or even ethnographers. Law and politics are inseparably intertwined in the international system. It is impossible today to recommend to leave to a lawyer what belongs to a lawyer and to an international relations theorist what should belong to the latter. Therefore inter-disciplinary and problem-oriented approaches have become a necessity in dealing with most big issues.

A watertight academic compartmentalization is especially unacceptable during revolutionary changes in the international system. One simply cannot comprehend what changes in law are needed if the overall picture of profound developments is not understood.

The world has become quite different from that of only a few years ago. The future will be less predictable, not only because we cannot extrapolate even our recent past into the decades ahead but also because, with the end of the Cold War, the bloc discipline and, the stability and predictability of the bipolar international system which was imposed by it have also disappeared. The current world disorder seems to be an inevitable result of the collapse of the old order, and even a necessary precondition for the emergence of any new order, because the latter could not originate directly from the previous frigidity. The future of the international system, like the future of the majority of new states born from the ashes of communism, will presumably be freer, looser and, consequently, less predictable than its past.

This in itself is neither good nor bad. It has already created new threats and aggravated some previously existing ones. But the new situation has also brought along unique opportunities for the resolution of many of the problems facing mankind. Democratic reforms in many countries, decrease of the threat of world-wide nuclear war, and the breakthrough in Arab–Israeli relations are only the most prominent recent developments.

In the current chaotic world it is especially important to distinguish between main trends and by-products, even if the latter may be more urgent and pressing than the former. The extinction of Leninism, the end of the Cold War, an increase in the number of democratic countries, and the possible emergence of a loose universal international system in which international law and its institutions will presumably play a much more active role than in previous international systems, are, it seems, the basic trends of the current changes in the world. Whether these trends prevail at the end of the day depends to a great extent, on how the world community will cope with by-products – that is, how it manages to contain civil wars, other forms of inter-ethnic conflicts, rising nationalism and racism, the threat of nuclear proliferation, and other evils which sprang to prominence once the big evil had disappeared.

The end of the division of the world into two equally powerful hostile blocs is certainly beneficial for the resolution of global problems such as the environmental crisis and the threat of global nuclear war.

Though in the new international system, law will presumably play a bigger part than before, its main function, it seems, will not be prescriptive. In the less predictable social environment law is even less able than before to prescribe concrete patterns of behaviour for states and other actors, especially in politically important and sensitive areas. International law has to rely much more upon pre-established or *ad hoc* legal procedures and mechanisms and its interpretation and application will presumably become more policy and value oriented and more contextual. 'Clever' or 'sophisticated' norms, which take account of all the complexities of the real world, will be needed to govern most sensitive areas of international relations. One of the main functions of international law will be to serve as a process for the avoidance, containment and resolution of disputes and conflicts on the basis of such agreed-upon values as peace, the self-determination of peoples, protection of the right of ethnic, religious and other minorities to their identity, and human rights generally.

Closely interrelated issues of the self-determination of peoples, the protection of minorities, of democracy and human rights will remain at the centre of the concerns of practitioners as well as of academics. This and some other developments analysed in the book mean that both international law and politics have to go far beyond the current state-centric approach to their discipline, not falling at the same time into the utopian rejection of the important role which the state will play at least in the foreseeable future.

Though the dissolution of the Soviet Union, Yugoslavia and even Czechoslovakia started under the slogan of the self-determination of peoples (understood by most participants of these processes as *their* right to secession), these events, and further 'successful' disintegrations (Bosnia-Herzegovina) and until now not so 'successful' secessionist claims in the Trans-Caucasus or Croatia, should have shown that the general trend of the post-colonial development of the principle of the self-determination of peoples, which the world community should support, is towards an entitlement to democracy rather than the right to secession.

Whether secession becomes an issue at all very often depends on the resolution of the problems of ethnic minorities. This means that democracy, which in a multi-ethnic society, means government by the majority, which takes into account the rights and interests of minorities, is one of remedies against secession. Another 'remedy' against it – outright repression – is not only legally and morally unacceptable but also politically less and less viable. The sad experience of the former USSR confirms that a repressive authority is not going to last forever in the contemporary world.

Notes

INTRODUCTION

1. R. Higgins, 'International Law and the Avoidance, Containment and Resolution of Disputes', 230 *RdC* 28 (1991-V).
2. Ibid.
3. See G. Kennan, *American Diplomacy* (expanded edn), Chicago, University of Chicago Press, 1984, p. 98.
4. See, for example, M. S. McDougal and W. M. Reisman, 'International Law in Policy-Oriented Perspective', in R. St. J. Macdonald and D. M. Johnston (eds), *The Structure and Process in International Law: Essays in Legal Philosophy, Doctrine and Theory*, Dordrecht, Martinus Nijhoff Publishers, 1983, p. 118; Lung-Chu Chen, *An Introduction to Contemporary International Law: A Policy-Oriented Perspective*, New Haven and London, Yale University Press, 1989, p. 16.
5. R. Falk, *Revitalizing International Law*, Ames, Iowa University Press, 1989, p. 39.
6. J. L. Gaddis, 'International Relations Theory and the End of the Cold War', 17(3) *International Security* 58 (1992/93).

1 THE END OF THE COLD WAR

1. L. Henkin, *How Nations Behave* (2nd edn), New York, Columbia University Press, 1979, p. 337.
2. L. Henkin, 'International Law: Politics, Values and Functions', 216 *RdC* 21 (1989-IV).
3. G. Tunkin, 'Politics, Law and Force in the Interstate System', 219 *RdC* 250 (1989-VII).
4. See, e.g. Falk, op. cit.
5. See, for example, R. Keohane and J. Nye, Jr (eds), *Transnational Relations and World Politics*, Cambridge, Harvard University Press, 1972.
6. A.-M. Slaughter Burley, 'International Law and International Relations Theory: A Dual Agenda', 87 *AJIL* 227 (1993).
7. R. Keohane, 'Compliance with International Commitments: Politics within a Framework of Law', *American Society of International Law Proceedings*, 1992, p. 180.

8. K. Waltz, *Theory of International Politics*, Reading, Addison Wesley Publishing Company, 1979, p. 99.
9. Ibid., p. 97.
10. Waltz, 'The New World Order', *Millennium: Journal of International Studies*, 1993, vol. 22, p.194.
11. B. Buzan, C. Jones and R. Little, *The Logic of Anarchy*, New York, Columbia University Press, 1993, p. 20.
12. F. Fukuyama, *The End of History and the Last Man*, London, Hamish Hamilton, 1992, p. 254.
13. K. Ohmae, 'The Rise of the Region State', 72(2) *Foreign Affairs* 78 (1993).
14. P. Kennedy, *Preparing for the Twenty-First Century*, London, Harper-Collins, 1993, p. 134.
15. See, e.g. P. Allott *et al.*, *Theory and International Law: An Introduction*, London, The British Institute of International and Comparative Law, 1991.
16. G. Fuller, *The Democracy Trap*, New York, Dutton, 1991, p. 92.
17. *The Economist*, 18 July 1992, pp. 35–7.
18. M. Shaw, 'Global Society and Global Responsibility: The Theoretical, Historical and Political Limits of "International Society"', 21 *Millennium: Journal of International Studies* 431 (1992).
19. See on these issues: O. Waever *et al. Identity, Migration and the New Security Agenda in Europe*, London, Pinter, 1993.
20. M. Walzer, 'Between Nation and World', *The Economist*, 1993, 11th–17th September, pp. 55–8.
21. M. Kaplan, *System and Process in International Politics*, New York, John Wiley, 1957, p. 21.
22. Ibid., p. 39.
23. J. Mueller, 'Quiet Cataclysm: Some Afterthoughts on World War III', in M. Hogan (ed.), *The End of the Cold War*, Cambridge, Cambridge University Press, 1992, p. 40.
24. R. Jervis, 'The Future of World Politics', 16(3) *International Security* 66 (1991/92).
25. A. Schlesinger, Jr, *A Thousand Days*, Boston, Houghton Mifflin, 1965, p. 769.
26. Fuller, op. cit., p. 244.
27. W. LaFeber, 'An End to Which Cold War?', in Hogan (ed.), op. cit., pp. 17–18.
28. Cited by A. Schlesinger, Jr, 'Some Lessons from the Cold War', in Hogan (ed.), op. cit., p. 57.
29. R. Gilpin, 'War and Change in World Politics', in G. A. Lopez and M. S. Stohl (eds), *International Relations: Contemporary Theory and Practice*, Washington, DC, CQ Press, 1989, p. 36.
30. Waltz, op. cit., p. 192.
31. Henkin, *How Nations Behave*, op. cit., p. 47.
32. H. Morgenthau, *In Defence of the National Interest*, New York, Knopf, 1951, p. 144.
33. Kaplan, op. cit., p. 23.
34. See on this issue, O. Schachter, *International Law in Theory and Practice*, Dordrecht, Martinus Nijhoff Publishers, 1991, pp. 8–9.
35. W. M. Reisman, 'Allocating Competences to Use Coercion in the Post-Cold War World: Practices, Conditions, and Prospects', in L. F. Damrosch

and D. J. Scheffer (eds), *Law and Force in the New International Order*, Boulder, Westview Press, 1991, p. 28.

36. K. Jowitt, *New World Disorder*, Berkeley, University of California Press, 1992, p. 277.

37. See M. Chege, 'Remembering Africa', 71(1) *Foreign Affairs* 148 (1992).

38. See M. R. Beschloss and S. Talbott, *At the Highest Levels*, London, Little, Brown & Company, 1993, p. 106.

39. B. Buzan, C Jones and R. Little, op. cit., p. 166.

40. Jowitt, op. cit., p. 304.

41. Ibid., p. 328.

42. Fukuyama, op. cit., p. 42.

43. Ibid., p. 279

44. V. Bunce, 'The Gorbachev Reforms in Historical Perspective', 47 *International Organization* 128 (1993).

45. Ibid.

46. Jowitt, op. cit., p. 46.

47. See, for example, M. W. Doyle, 'Kant, Liberal Legacies, and Foreign Affairs' (Parts 1 and 2), 12 *Philosophy & Public Affairs* 205, 323 (1983).

48. Thucydides, *The History of the Peloponnesian War*, London, Longmans, Green & Company, 1876, p. 397.

49. D. Artaud, 'The End of the Cold War: A Sceptical View', in Hogan (ed.), op. cit., p. 186.

50. Mueller in Hogan (ed.), op. cit., pp. 50–51.

51. See the table in Fukuyama, op. cit., pp. 49–50.

52. Fukuyama, it seems to me, correctly points out that 'part of the current, fundamentalist revival is the strength of the perceived threat from liberal, Western values to traditional Islamic societies' (Fukuyama, ibid., p. 46). If this is so, then the spread of liberal democracies should in the foreseeable future further consolidate Islamic fundamentalism.

53. S. Huntington, 'The Clash of Civilizations', 72(3) *Foreign Affairs* 39 (1993).

54. F. Fukuyama, 'The End of History?', 16 The National Interest 18 (1989).

55. *Hegel's Philosophy of Right* (translated by S. W. Dyde), London, George Bell & Sons, 1896, p. 33.

56. Fuller, op. cit., pp. 18–19.

57. C. Brown, '"Really Existing Liberalism" and International Order', 21 *Millennium: Journal of International Studies* 314 (1992).

58. Hindu fundamentalism, though confined basically to one country, may be as damaging as Islamic fundamentalism. It seems astonishing at the end of the twentieth century to read words like those uttered by Sardar Angre, an adviser to one of the founders of the extreme right-wing pro-Hindu Bharatiya Janata Party (BJP), Rajmata Vijayaraje Scindia: 'The Muslims must be made to understand that they must be proud of Hindustan . . . If the Muslims followed the Hindu ideology there would be no more trouble . . . They should accept our common culture and unite with us in the name of god' (*The Sunday Times Magazine*, 9 May 1993, p. 51).

59. Kennedy, op. cit., p. 208.

60. Some Security Council resolutions, though legally correct and even politically necessary (e.g. against Iraq or Libya), may be counter-productive in the long run, if approved only by Western countries plus Russia and seen by Third World states (or even only by Arab countries) as

directed only against these latter countries.

61. B. Buzan, *People, States and Fear*, London, Harvester Wheatsheaf, 1991, p. 156.
62. Jervis, op. cit., p. 57.
63. L. Freedman, 'Order and Disorder in the New World', 71(1) *Foreign Affairs* 33 (1992).
64. *The Times*, 5 April 1993, p. 1.
65. It remains to be seen how the Chinese will succeed in dismantling their socialism. I have no doubt that they have already started this process, though their leaders may not know or confess even to themselves that this is the case. Mikhail Gorbachev also started his reforms, not in order to get rid of socialism but to reform it, to make it more humane. Perhaps the Chinese way, though slower, is less painful. Nevertheless I am sure that it could not be applied in the Soviet Union (see the last chapter of this book).
66. W. Laqueur, 'Russian Nationalism', 71(5) *Foreign Affairs* 105 (1992).
67. W. G. Hyland, 'The Case for Pragmatism', 71(1) *Foreign Affairs* 48 (1992).
68. A. Migranjan, 'Opasnosti Sovremennogo Politicheskogo Protsessa v Rossii' [Dangers of the Current Political Process in Russia], *Nezavisimaya Gazeta*, 16 February 1993, p. 5.
69. *The Guardian*, 22 September, 1993, p.1.
70. *The Economist*, 25 September, 1993, p.15.
71. Ibid.
72. F. I. Tjutchev, *Stihi* [Verses], Ufa, Bashkirskoye Kniznoye Izdatelstvo, 1989, p. 174.
73. L. Kopelev, 'Russkaya Ideia – Ideia Spaseniya Tchelovetchestva', [The Russian Idea is an Idea of the Salvation of Mankind], *Izvestia*, 13 March 1993, p. 8.
74. A. Vladislavlev and S. Karaganov, 'Tjazhely Krest Rossii' [The Heavy Cross of Russia], *Nezavisimaya Gazeta*, 17 November 1992, p. 8.
75. S. Stankevich, 'Russia in Search of Itself', 28 *The National Interest* 47 (1992).
76. E. Pozdniakov, 'Rossiya – Velikaya Derzhava' [Russia – a Great Power], *Mezhdunarodnaya Zhizn*, 1993, No. 1, p. 8.
77. *Mezhdunarodnaya Zhinzn*, 1993, No. 1, pp. 18–20.
78. *Nezavisimaya Gazeta*, 29 April 1993, pp. 1, 3.
79. Ibid., p. 1.
80. Ibid., p. 3.
81. *RFE/RL Research Report*, 14 May 1993, vol. 2, No. 20, p. 58.
82. *RFE/RL Research Report*, 9 April 1993, vol. 2, No. 15, p. 28.
83. Laqueur, op. cit., pp. 107–8.
84. E. Pozdniakov, 'Rossiya Segodnia i Zavtra' [Russia Today and Tomorrow], *Mezhdunarodnaya Zhizn*, 1993, No. 2, p. 23.
85. E. Pozdniakov, 'Rossiya–Velikaya Derzhava' [Russia – a Great Power], *Mezhdunarodnaya Zhizn*, 1993, No. 1, p. 13.
86. E. Pozdniakov, 'Rossiya Segodnia i Zavtra' [Russia Today and Tomorrow], *Mezdunarodnaya Zhizn*, 1993, No. 2, p. 24.
87. Huntington, op. cit., pp. 29–30.
88. J. Dunlop, 'Russia: Confronting a Loss of Empire', in I. Bremmer and R. Taras (eds), *Nations and Politics in the Soviet Successor States*, Cambridge, Cambridge University Press, 1993, p. 43.

89. *Foreign Affairs*, 1993, vol. 72, No. 4, pp. 22–23.
90. Speech by H.E. Andrei Kozyrev, Minister for Foreign Affairs of the Russian Federation at the Royal Institute of International Affairs, Chatham House, 27 October 1993, London.
91. Ibid.
92. *The Economist*, 30 October 1993, p. 23.
93. Kaplan, op. cit., pp. 45–8.
94. Ibid., p. 46.
95. J. Nye, Jr, 'Soft Power', 80 *Foreign Policy* 154 (1990).
96. Ibid., pp. 155–6.
97. Jervis, op. cit., pp. 41–2.
98. Kennedy, op. cit., p. 336.
99. Freedman, op. cit., pp. 26–7.
100. H. Bull, *The Anarchical Society*, London, Macmillan, 1977, p. 287.
101. B. Buzan, C. Jones and R. Little, op. cit., p. 13.
102. Bull, op. cit., p. 13.
103. Ibid., p. 49.
104. Nguyen Quoc Dinh, P. Daillier and A. Pellet, *Droit international public* (3éme edn), Paris, LGDJ, 1987, p. 30.
105. Schachter, op. cit., p. 1.
106. H. D. Lasswell and M. S. McDougal, *Jurisprudence for a Free Society*, New Haven, New Haven Press, 1992, p. 183.
107. M. Reisman, 'The Arafat Visa Affair: Exceeding the Bounds of Host State Discretion', 83 *AJIL* 522 (1989).
108. Ibid., p. 527.
109. 7 ILM 1323 (1968).
110. An article in *Pravda* entitled 'Sovereignty and International Duties of Socialist Countries' claimed that accusations that five socialist countries had violated international law by intervening in Czechoslovakia were false as they were 'based on an abstract, nonclass approach to the question of sovereignty and the rights of nations to self-determination' and that 'formally juridical reasoning must not overshadow a class approach to the matter. One who does it, thus losing the only correct criterion in assessing legal norms, begins to measure events with a yardstick of bourgeois law"(7 *ILM* 1323 (1968)).
111. See S. Pounzin, 'Vedenie Sovietskih Voisk v Afganistan: Mezdunarodno – pravovie Aspekti' [The Soviet Intervention in Afghanistan – International Law Aspects], *Sovietskoye Gosudarstvo i Pravo*, 1990, No. 5, pp. 123–30.
112. See W. C. Gilmore, *The Grenada Intervention: Analysis and Documentation*, London, Mansell, 1984, pp. 65–7; R. Higgins, 'The Attitude of Western States Towards Legal Aspects of the Use of Force', in A. Cassese (ed.), *The Current Legal Regulation of the Use of Force*, Dordrecht, Martinus Nijhoff Publishers, 1986, p. 440.
113. Address Before a Joint Session of the Congress on the State of the Union, 6 February 1985, 1 *Pub. Papers of the Presidents of the United States: Ronald Reagan* 135 (1988).
114. E. Korovin, *Mezdunarodnoye Pravo Perechodnogo Vremeni* [International Law of the Transitional Period], Moscow, 1924, p. 59.
115. J. Kirkpatrick and A. Gerson, 'The Reagan Doctrine, Human Rights, and International Law', in *Right v. Might: International Law and the Use of*

Force, New York, Council of Foreign Relations Press, 1989, p. 23.

116. See, for example, E. Skakunov, *Samooborona v Miezdunarodnom Prave* [Self-Defence in International Law], Moscow, International Relations, 1973, p. 94.

117. See, for example, J. N. Moore, 'The Nicaragua Case and the Deterioration of World Order', 81 *AJIL* 151 (1987).

118. R. Higgins, 'International Law and the Avoidance, Containment and Resolution of Disputes', 230 *RdC* 29 (1993).

119. See, for example, 'Appraisals of the ICJ's Decision: Nicaragua v. United States (Merits)', 81 *AJIL* 77 (1987). There sixteen prominent American international lawyers expressed their views on the case.

120. See, for example, the positions of different Western governments on the American invasion of Grenada in 1983. Higgins writes that 'the United Kingdom government clearly regarded the United States action as legally unwarranted' and that there has in our opinion been a deep disquiet running through the Western European nations over such hegemony based uses of force as, e.g., the United States involvement in the Dominican Republic in 1965, and in El Salvador (on behalf of the government) and in Nicaragua (on behalf of the rightist opposition) today' (R. Higgins, 'The Attitude of Western States Towards Legal Aspects of the Use of Force', in Cassese (ed.), op. cit., pp. 439–40).

121. J. Weiler, 'Armed Intervention in a Dichotomized World: The Case of Grenada', in Cassese (ed.), op. cit., p. 243.

122. *UN Doc.* S/PV.3009, 1991, p. 59.

123. *The Financial Times*, 28 June 1993, p. 15.

124. *The Guardian*, 28 June 1993, p. 8.

125. *The New York Times*, 16 April 1986, p. 1.

126. The fact that at that time, in foreign affairs, Russia spoke with different voices was reflected in the Declaration of the Russian Parliament which protested against the raid as being an act of international violence (*Nezavisimaya Gazeta*, 30 June 1993, p. 1).

127. Ibid.

128. See, for example, A. Cassese, 'The International Community's "Legal" Response to International Terrorism', 38 *ICLQ* 598 (1989).

129. Ibid., p. 596.

130. See comprehensive analyses of these and other cases in D. J. Scheffer, 'Toward a Modern Doctrine of Humanitarian Intervention, 23 *University of Toledo Law Review* 253–93 (1992).

131. G. Klintworth, *Vietnam's Intervention in Cambodia in International Law*, Canberra, AGPS Press, 1989, p. 59.

132. Scheffer, op. cit., p. 265.

133. A. Roberts, 'Humanitarian War: Military Intervention and Human Rights', *International Affairs*, 1993, vol. 69, p. 446.

134. *UN Doc.* S/Res/794 (1992), 3 December 1992.

135. In his address to the Security Council, Chinese Prime Minister Li Pang said: 'In our view, such basic principles as sovereign equality of member-states and non-interference in their internal affairs as enshrined in the Charter of the United Nations should be observed by all its members, without exception ... In essence, the issue of human rights falls within the sovereignty of each country. A country's human rights situation should not be judged in total

disregard of its history and national conditions . . . China is opposed to interference in internal affairs of other countries using the human rights issue as an excuse (*United Nations Security Council Summit Opening Addresses by Members, Fed. News Serv.*, 31 January 1992, VP-5–1, 3–4).

India's Prime Minister P. V. Narashima Rao warned that 'uniformed international norms for human rights' should not be unilaterally defined and set up 'as absolute preconditions for interaction between states and societies in the political and economic spheres' (ibid.).

136. Nye, Jr, op. cit., p. 93.
137. L. Freedman, op. cit., p. 37.
139. R. Falk, 'The Role of Law in World Society', in W. M. Reisman and B. H. Weston (eds), *Toward World Order and Human Dignity. Essays in Honour of Myres S. McDougal*, New York, The Free Press, 1976, p. 149.
139. T. Franck, *The Power of Legitimacy among Nations*, Oxford, Oxford University Press, 1990, pp. 74–9.
140. Ibid., p. 80.
141. M. Virally, 'Panorama du droit international contemporain', 183 *RdC* 31 (1983-V).
142. R. Higgins, 'International Law and the Avoidance, Containment and Resolution of Disputes', 230 *RdC* 302–3 (1993–000).
143. Reisman is right in saying that 'the reason we do not have peacemaking in Somalia, in Bosnia, in the Sudan, or in Haiti has little to do with defects in the normative arrangements of the Charter. Much could be done within the existing regime. The real obstacles lie in features of international politics, and they must be overcome politically, whatever the changes in the U.N. system, (W. M. Reisman, 'Peacemaking', 18 *Yale JIL* 422 (1993).
144. Tunkin wrote at the beginning of the 1980s that 'the present stage of social development is marked by a clash between two basic conceptual models of the international system, namely, the socialist and the capitalist'. (See, G. Tunkin, *Law and Force in the International System*, Moscow, Progress Publishes, 1985, p. 156.) Both conceptual models, according to Tunkin, reflected different ideologies and saw the future of mankind quite differently. The Soviet Union at the end of 1980s jettisoned 'the socialist conceptual model of the international system' as contrary to the interest of the USSR as well as to international law. But it is impossible to deny that such a different perception of the world was not conducive to the effectiveness of international law and organizations.
145. Advisory Council on Peace and Security. *What is Peace Worth to Us? The United Nations after the Cold War*, The Hague, 1992.
146. *UN Doc.* A/47/ 277, S/24111, 17 June 1992.
147. 'Ins Allerheiligste der UNO', *Der Spiegel*, 10 February 1992.
148. *The Financial Times*, 2 July 1993, p. 5.
149. W. M. Reisman, 'The Constitutional Crisis in the United Nations', 87 *AJIL* 99 (1993).

2 SELF-DETERMINATION

1. I. Brownlie, 'The Rights of Peoples in Modern International Law', in J. Crawford (ed.), *The Rights of Peoples*, Oxford, Clarendon Press, 1988, p. 5.

2. *Documenty Vneshnei politiki SSSR* [*Documents on the Foreign Policy of the USSR*], vol. I, Moscow, Gospolitizdat, 1957, p. 11.
3. Quoted in C. L. Mee, Jr, *The End of Order*, New York, Elsevier Dutton, 1980, pp. 53–4.
4. R. Lansing, *The Peace Negotiations. A Personal Narrative*, London, Constable & Company, 1921, p. 87.
5. D. P. Moynihan, *Pandaemonium. Ethnicity in International Politics*, Oxford, Oxford University Press, 1993, p. 85.
6. See, V. Lenin, 'Theses on the Socialist Revolution and the Right of Nations to Self-Determination (March 1916)', in V. Lenin, *Selected Works*, London, Lawrence & Wishart, 1969, p. 37.
7. H. Hannum, *Autonomy, Sovereignty, and Self-Determination. The Accommodation of Conflicting Rights*, Philadelphia, University of Pennsylvania Press, 1990, p. 28.
8. Ibid p. 27.
9. See I. Brownlie, *Principles of Public International Law* (4th edn), Oxford, Clarendon Press, 1990, p. 513, H. Gross Espiell, 'Self-determination and Jus Cogens'; A. Cassese,' Political Self-determination – Old Concepts and New Developments', in A. Cassese (ed.), *United Nations – Fundamental Rights: Two Topics in International Law*, Alphen aan der Rijn, Sijthoff and Noordhoff, 1979; A. Cassese, *International Law in a Divided World*, Oxford, Clarendon Press, 1986, p. 136; Hannum, op. cit., p. 45.
10. *UN Doc.* A/Conf.157/23, 12 July 1993, para. 2.
11. See, for example, *The Right to Self-Determination. Historical and Current Developments on the Basis of United Nations Instruments*. Study prepared by Aureliu Cristescu, Special Rapporteur of the Sub-Commission on Prevention of Discrimination and Protection of Minorities, United Nations, New York, 1981, pp. 4–5.
12. *UN GA Res.* 2625 (XXV), reprinted at 9 *ILM* 1292 (1970).
13. Reprinted at 14 *ILM* 1293 (1975).
14. For example, free elections, a form of government that is representative in character, a clear separation between the State and political parties, etc. [29 *ILM* 1308 (1990)].
15. Ibid.
16. 4 *EJIL* 72 (1993).
17. *UN Doc.* A/47/277, S/24111, 17 June 1992, p. 5.
18. M. Kampelman, 'Secession and the Right to Self-Determination: An Urgent Need to Harmonize Principle with Pragmatism', *The Washington Quarterly*, 1993, vol.16, No. 3, p.10.
19. India made the following reservation to article 1 of the Covenant on Civil and Political Rights: 'With reference to article 1 of the International Covenant on Civil and Political Rights, the Government of the Republic of India declares that the words "the right of self-determination" appearing in [that article] apply only to the peoples under foreign domination and that these words do not apply to sovereign independent States or to a section of a people or nation – which is the essence of national integrity' (*UN Doc.* CCPR/C/2/Rev.3, 12 May 1992, p. 18). France, Germany and the Netherlands strongly objected to this reservation by India (ibid., pp. 39–40).
20. H. Gross Espiell, op. cit., p. 10.

21. See, for example, *The Right of Self-Determination. Implementation of the United Nations Resolutions.* Study prepared by Hector Gross Espiell, Special Rapporteur of the Sub-Commission on Prevention of Discrimination and Protection of Minorities, United Nations, New York, 1980.

22. For example, the German objection to the Indian reservation to article 1 of the Covenant on Civil and Political Rights states: 'The right of self-determination as enshrined in the Charter of the United Nations and as embodied in the Covenants applies to all peoples and not only to those under foreign domination' (*UN Doc.* CCPR/C/2/Rev.3, p. 39).

23. For example, the United Nations Human Rights Committee, during its consideration of reports of states parties to the International Covenant on Civil and Political Rights, always emphasizes the ongoing character of the principle of the self determination of peoples.

24. Lenin wrote: 'In the same way as mankind can arrive at the abolition of classes only through a transition period of the dictatorship of the oppressed classes, it can arrive at the inevitable integration of nations only through a transition period of the complete emancipation of all oppressed nations, i.e. their freedom to secede.' (V. Lenin, 'Theses on the Socialist Revolution and the Right of Nations to Self-Determination (March 1916)', in Lenin, op. cit., p. 160).

25. Quoted in M. Beschloss and S. Talbott, *At the Highest Levels*, London, Little, Brown & Company, 1993, p. 346.

26. B. Magas, *The Destruction of Yugoslavia*, London, Verso, 1993, p. xiv.

27. IILM 1292 (1970).

28. T. Franck, *The Power of Legitimacy Among Nations*, Oxford, Oxford University Press, 1990, p. 168.

29. Ibid.

30. Ibid.

31. In this connection it is interesting to note that while the majority of Russian dissidents suffered for their struggle for human rights and democracy generally (A. Sakharov, S. Kovaljov, L. Bogoraz and others); dissidents from other Soviet republics were usually sentenced, if not exclusively then at least primarily, because of their struggle for the independence of their countries (V. Chornovil in Ukraine, L. Parek and E. Tarto in Estonia etc.)

32. There have been some peaceful separations: the union between Norway and Sweden was amicably dissolved in 1905 but this was a union of two separate and equal kingdoms under one sovereign. In 1960 Senegal seceded from Mali Federation and in 1965 Singapore from the Malaysian Federation. In 1961 a short-lived United Arab Republic came to an end. But here it is difficult to assert that these were all separations from democratic countries, and, most importantly, these were rather special cases because even before the dissolution of these states, the separating parts were considered sovereign states. (See, e.g., L. Buchheit, *Secession*, New Haven and London, Yale University Press, 1978, pp. 98–9.)

33. Hannum, op. cit., p. 276.

34. P. Brogan, *World Conflicts*, London, Bloomsbury, 1992, p. 574.

35. Ibid.

36. Nguyen Quoc Dinh, P. Daillier and A. Pellet, *Droit international public* (3éme edn), Paris, LGDJ 1987, p. 467.

37. 54 *BYIL* 409 (1983).

38. There are several reasons why the term 'peoples' and not 'nations' was finally accepted in most international instruments. The first, at least in time, was that when in the 1960s most African colonies of European empires became independent it was not ethnic but pre-colonial boundaries that were accepted for new states that is – the *uti possidetis* principle was applied as it has been in Latin America more than a century earlier. But an even more important reason is that in the contemporary world there is practically no place for national (ethnic) self-determination, except maybe in Iceland. There are no ethnically pure states or even their sub-divisions. National (ethnic) self-determination, especially, if understood as the right of ethnicities to independence, could be achieved in the contemporary world only through 'ethnic cleansing'.

39. Stalin wrote in 1913: 'The right to self-determination means that a nation can arrange its life according to its own will. It has the right to arrange its life on the basis of autonomy. It has the right to complete secession. Nations are sovereign and all nations are equal (J. Stalin, 'Marxism and the National Question (1913)' in J. Stalin, *Marxism and the National and Colonial Questions. A Collection of Articles and Speeches*, London, Lawrence & Wishart, 1941, p. 19). But as Lenin himself indicated, the right of nations to self-determination was not only a stage in and condition of their final merger, but it was subordinated to interests of socialism (Lenin, op. cit., p. 37). It is interesting to note that the same argument was used by the Soviet leadership of 1968 during the invasion in Czechoslovakia and was called the 'Brezhnev doctrine' (see previous chapter).

40. For example, J. Murray Brown writes that 'no Western power, Turkey least of all, wants to see an independent Kurdish state in North Iraq for fear of Iranian exploitation' (J. Murray Brown, 'Kurds Seek Access to Turkish Lira', *The Financial Times*, 28 May 1993).

41. 6 *ILM* 368 (1967).

42. *UN GA Res.* 2625 (XXV), reprinted at 9 *ILM* 1292 (1979).

43. T. Franck, 'The Emerging Right to Democratic Governance', 86 *AJIL* 59 (1992).

44. *UN Doc.* CCPR/C/42/Add.12, p. 2.

45. *Self-Determination*, Report of the Martin Ennals Memorial Symposium on Self-Determination, Saskatoon, Canada, 1993, p.3.

46. J. Brossard, *L'accession a la souveraineté et le cas du Québec*, Montreal, Press de l'Université de Montreal, 1976, p. 191.

47. W. F. Shaw and L. Albert, *Partition: The Price of Quebec's Independence*, Montreal, Thorhill Publishing, 1980, p. 29.

48. This is, naturally, a conclusion from the point of view of contemporary international law and not ethnography. It is common knowledge that often the terminology of different sciences does not coincide. There is nothing tragic in it if representatives of different sciences nevertheless understand each other.

49. J. Dunlop, 'Russia: Confronting a Loss of Empire', in I. Bremmer and R. Taras (eds), *Nations & Politics in the Soviet Successor States*, Cambridge, Cambridge University Press, 1993, p. 48.

50. *Vedomosti Siezda Narodnih Deputatov SSSR i Verhovnogo Sovieta SSSR*, 11 April 1990, No. 15.

51. S. Jones, 'Georgia: A Failed Democratic Transition', in Bremmer and Taras (eds) op. cit., p. 295.
52. Ibid.
53. Ibid., p. 307.
54. G. Fuller, 'The Fate of the Kurds', 72(2) *Foreign Affairs* 109.
55. Ibid.
56. *UN Doc.* A/Conf.157/23, 12 July 1993, para. 2.
57. See, I. Bremmer, 'Reassessing Soviet Nationalities Theory', in Bremmer and Taras, op. cit., p. 6.
58. On recognition, see Chapter 4 of this book.
59. Beschloss and Talbott, op. cit., p. 164.
60. Buchheit, op. cit., p. 236.
61. See, for example, Peter and Leni Gillman, 'Tibet: The Land the World Forgot', *The Sunday Times Magazine*, 28 March 1993.
62. A. Buchanan, *Secession. The Morality of Political Divorce from Fort Sumter to Lithuania and Quebec*, Boulder, Westview Press, 1991, p. 88.
63. 8 *Australian JIL* 279 (1983).
64. *Department of State Bulletin*, 5 September 1977, p. 326.
65. J. Mayall, *Nationalism and International Society*, Cambridge, Cambridge University Press, 1990, p. 70.
66. E. Gellner, *Nations and Nationalism*, Oxford, Basil Blackwell, 1983, p. 44.
67. M. H. Halperin and D. J. Scheffer with P. L. Small, *Self-Determination in the New World Order*, Washington, Carnegie Endowment, 1992, pp. 9, 120.
68. Ibid.
69. *Self-Determination,* Report . . ., p. 7.
70. Ibid., p. 2.
71. Lung-Chu Chen, *An Introduction to Contemporary International Law*, New Haven, Yale University Press, 1989, p. 36.
72. Halperin, Scheffer and Small, op. cit., p. 120.
73. Just a few weeks before the *coup d'état* attempt in the USSR President Bush warned the Ukrainian Parliament in Kiev that the 'Americans will not support those who seek independence in order to replace a far-off tyranny with a local despotism. They will not aid those who promote a suicidal nationalism based upon ethnic hatred' (quoted from Moynihan, op. cit., p. 166).
74. Issues relating to nationalism are relevant to the problem of the self-determination of peoples as well as to that of the protection of minorities. But as my conclusion is that it is the right of peoples, and not nations or other ethnicities, to self-determination, and that in Eastern Europe and in the former USSR nationalism is seriously affecting minority issues, this phenomenon will receive more attention in the next chapter devoted to the protection of minorities.
75. Gellner, op. cit., p. 2.
76. F. Fukuyama, *The End of History and the Last Man*, London, Hamish Hamilton, 1992, p. 215.
77. Ibid., p. 119.
78. Gellner, op. cit., p. 1.
79. M. Kampelman, op. cit., p.11.
80. Moynihan, op. cit., p. 70.
81. Ibid.
82. Jones, op. cit., pp. 296–7.

3 MINORITIES IN EASTERN EUROPE AND THE FORMER USSR

1. A. de Balogh, *La protection internationale des minorités*, Paris, Les editions internationales, 1930, p. 23.
2. F. L. Israel, *Major Peace Treaties of Modern History 1648–1967*, New York, 1967, vol. 1, pp. 7–49.
3. See P. Thornberry, *International Law and the Rights of Minorities*, Clarendon Press, Oxford, 1991, p. 27.
4. See F. Capotorti, *Study on the Rights of Persons Belonging to Ethnic, Religious and Linguistic Minorities*, New York, United Nations, 1991, p. 3.
5. See, for example, ibid., pp. 16–26.
6. Ibid., p. 18.
7. Ibid., p. 19.
8. T. H. Bagley, *General Principles and Problems in the Protection of Minorities*, Geneva, 1950, p. 126.
9. J. Mayall, *Nationalism and International Society*, Cambridge, Cambridge University Press, 1990, p. 55.
10. 6 ILM 368 (1967).
11. *UN Doc.* A/47/678/Add.2, reprinted at 32 *ILM* 911 (1993).
12. *UN Doc.* E/CN.4/1993/2 and *UN Doc.* E/CN.4/Sub.2/1992/58 respectively.
13. 29 *ILM* 1305 (1990).
14. 6 *ILM* 1385 (1992).
15. See *Revue Générale de Droit International Public*, 1992, tome 96, No. 4, page 1094.
16. See, for example, *The Independent*, 13 July 1993, p. 12.
17. *World Directory of Minorities* (edited by the Minority Rights Group), Harlow, Longman, 1990, p. 124.
18. Ibid., p. 139.
19. Ibid., p. 126.
20. Ibid., p. 117.
21. France made a declaration which in substance was a reservation to article 27 of the CCPR stating that this article is not applicable to France (*UN Doc.* CCPR/C/2/Rev.3). France referred to article 2 of its Constitution which establishes that 'La France est une République indivisible, laique, democratique et social. Elle assure l'egalite devant la loi de tous les citoyens sans distinction d'origine, de race ou de religion. Elle respecte toutes les croyances.' (Constitution. Lois organiques et ordonnances relatives aux pouvoir public. *Journal officiel de la République Francaise*, Mai 1986, No. 1119.) The rational for the French declaration (reservation) was given in France's initial and second periodic reports to the UN Human Rights Committee: 'Since the basic principles of public law prohibit distinctions between citizens' origin, race or religion, France is a country in which there are no minorities.' (*UN Doc.* CCPR/C/22/Add.2; UN DOC. CCPR/C/46/Add.2.) There is obvious contradiction between the French reservation and article 2 of the Constitution. The fact that France is indivisible and respects all religions and beliefs does not mean at all that there are no minorities in France.
22. Though even then, as we saw, when political maps were redrawn religious minorities were to a certain extent taken care of.

23. *Argumenty i Facty [Arguments and Facts]*, October 1992, Nos 38–9, p. 7.
24. *World Directory of Minorities*, op. cit., p. 161.
25. *Nezavisimaya Gazeta*, 21 January 1993, p. 5
26. Ibid.
27. I. Bremmer and R. Taras (eds), *Nations & Politics in the Soviet Successor States*, Cambridge, Cambridge University Press, 1993, p. 558.
28. Ibid., p. 557.
29. E. Gellner, *Nations and Nationalism*, Oxford, Basil Blackwell, 1983, p. 1.
30. A. D. Smith, *The Ethnic Revival*, Cambridge, Cambridge University Press, 1981, p. 18.
31. L. L. Snyder uses the term 'mini-nationalism'. 'Under political control of larger nationalisms, mini-nationalisms are supported by those dissatisfied peoples who want either more autonomy inside the structure of the national state or demand independence' (L. L. Snyder, *Encyclopedia of Nationalism*, New York, Paragon House, 1990, p. 212).
32. J. Breuilly, *Nationalism and State*, New York, St. Martin's Press, 1982, p. 11.
33. Ibid., p. 19.
34. Constitution of the Republic of Hungary (as amended by Act No. XXXI of 1989), in G. Kilenyi and V. Lamm (eds) *Democratic Changes in Hungary (Basic Legislations on a Peaceful Transition from Bolshevism to Democracy)*, Budapest, 1990, p. 35.
35. *Constitution of the Republic of Macedonia*, Skopje, 1991, p. 17.
36. F. A. Hayek, *The Road to Serfdom*, London, George Routledge & Sons Limited, 1944, p. 11.
37. *Nezavisimaya Gazeta*, 13 April 1993, p. 5.
38. Ibid.
39. J. Goetz, 'Something Nazi Stirs', *The Guardian*, 12 February 1993.
40. *Megapolis-Express*, 1992, No. 48.
41. Goetz, op. cit.
42. *The Times*, 4 May 1992, p. 7.
43. Though one cannot, of course, equate nationalism and xenophobia, there is a direct link between them. As L. L. Snyder observes: 'The combination of xenophobia and nationalism was responsible for much of the discontent and dangerous confrontations rampant in the world in the closing decades of the twentieth century'. (Snyder, op. cit., pp. 427–8).
44. A. Eide differentiates ethno-nationalism and citizens' nationalism. The first has as its basis of primary allegiance a nation in the sense of an ethnicity, while the second has a state as such a basis. For the latter, the interests of its own state have primacy over the interests and values of larger communities, such as, for example, the United Nations or the European Community.
45. A. Eide, 'In Search of Constructive Alternatives to Secession', A paper presented in December 1992 at the Conference organized by International Alert in London, para. 23.
46. See H. Hannum, *Autonomy, Sovereignty, and Self-Determination: The Accommodation of Conflicting Rights*, Philadelphia, University of Pennsylvania Press, 1990, p. 281.
47. Snyder, op. cit., p. xvi.
48. United Nations Security Council Summit, *Fed. News Serv.*, 31 January 1992, VM-5-2, 3–4; VM-5-3, 1.
49. Smith, op. cit., p. 1.

50. Ibid., p. 3.
51. Mayall, op. cit., p. 42.
52. 6 *ILM* 368 (1967).
53. 429 *UNTS* 93.
54. 328 *UNTS* 249.
55. 6 *ILM* 1385 (1992).
56. *UN Doc.* A/47/678/Add.2, reprinted at 32 *ILM* 911 (1993).
57. See *UN Doc.* HRI/Gen/1, 4 September 1992.
58. See *Revue Générale*, op. cit., p. 1094.
59. I. Davidson, 'Interest Grows in Stability Pact Plan', *The Financial Times*, 22 June 1993.
60. *UN Doc.* HRI/Gen/1, 4 September 1992, p. 25.
61. G. Alfredsson and A. de Zayas, 'Minority Rights: Protection by the United Nations', 14(1–2) *Human Rights Law Journal* 2 (1993).
62. 29 *ILM* 1318 (1990).
63. See, for example, Thornberry, op. cit.
64. The Human Rights Committee, always paying much attention to issues of self-determination during its consideration of state reports, has in several instances observed that an individual cannot claim under the Optional Protocol to be a victim of a violation of the right to self-determination enshrined in article 1 of the Covenant, because this article deals with rights conferred upon peoples as such (*UN Doc.* A/42/40, p. 106).
65. See the Views of the Committee on the case in *Canadian Human Rights Yearbook* 1991–1992, pp. 221–58. I am making a reference to this Canadian publication purposely in order to show the proper publicity given to international human rights decisions, even if they are not the most favourable for the Government of the State.
66. Capotorti, op. cit., p. 96.
67. 30 *ILM* 1692 (1991).
68. Ibid.
69. For example, the Report of the United Nations High Commissioner for Refugees concludes that the term 'minorities' would not necessarily encompass aliens, refugees and migrant workers, who are normally protected under other international instruments, and that 'the inclusion of migrant workers in the category of minorities is still a controversial matter' (*Report of the Ad Hoc Working Group on UNHCR and Minorities*, Geneva, November 1992, p. 3).
70. Usually such minorities do not consist exclusively of foreigners. There is often a mixture of citizens and foreigners. In such a case it would be natural that they all enjoy minority rights in equal terms while only citizens participate in elections or could hold certain posts.
71. See 'The Citizenship Law of the Republic of Estonia of 11 April 1938', *Riigi Teataja* [The State Herald], 1992, No. 7, item 109; Resolution of the Supreme Council of the Republic of Latvia 'On the Renewal of Republic of Latvia Citizens' Rights and Fundamental Principles of Naturalization', in: *Citizenship and Language Laws in the Newly Independent States of Europe (Seminar held in Copenhagen, 9–10 January 1993)*, The Danish Centre for Human Rights, 1993.
72. *Izvestia*, 5 June, 1992, p. 1.

73. 'Strategiya dlja Rossii' [A Strategy for Russia], *Nezavisimaya Gazeta*, 19 August 1992, p.4.
74. Edited transcript of a speech given by the Foreign Secretary, Mr Douglas Hurd, to Atlantic College, at Fishmongers' Hall, London, on 15 February 1993.
75. A. Lijphart, *Democracy in Plural Societies. A Comparative Exploration*, New Haven and London, Yale University Press, 1977.
76. Ibid., p. 42.
77. Ibid., pp. 44–5.
78. Snyder, op. cit., p. xxii.
79. *UN Doc*. A/47/678/Add.2.
80. Ibid., p. 25.
81. See further in R. Dahl, *Democracy and its Critics*, New Haven, Yale University Press, 1989, p. 258.
82. Ibid., p. 257.

4 LAW AND POLITICS IN THE RECOGNITION OF NEW STATES

1. *Oppenheim's International Law. Vol. 1: Peace*. 'Introduction' and Part I (9th edn, Sir Robert Jennings and Sir Arthur Watts eds), Harlow, Longman, 1992, p. 130.
2. *Parliamentary Debates (Commons)* (written answers, 29 February 1984), Vol. 55, col. 226.
3. *US Digest* (1976) pp. 19–20.
4. 4 *EJIL* 72 (1993).
5. *Restoration of the Independence of the Republic of Estonia. Selection of Legal Acts (1988–91)*, Tallinn, Ministry of Foreign Affairs of the Republic of Estonia, 1991, p. 101.
6. *Rahva Haal*, 15 January 1991; *Paevaleht*, 13 January 1991.
7. *Vedomosti Siezda Narodnih Deputatov RSFSR i Verhivnogo Sovieta RSFSR*, 1991, No. 35, item 1155.
8. Ibid., item 1158.
9. *RFE/RL Research Institute. Report on the USSR*, 9 August 1991, vol. 3, No. 32, p. 28.
10. The statement of the Dutch Presidency said: 'The Community and its member States warmly welcome the restoration of the sovereignty and independence of the Baltic States, which they lost in 1940' (quoted from C. Warbrick, 'Recognition of States: Recent European Practice', 41 *ICLQ* 474 (1992)).
11. See, for example, *RFE/RL Research Institute. Report on the USSR*, 6 September 1991, vol. 3, No. 36, p. 53.
12. Ibid., p. 86.
13. *RFE/RL Research Institute, Report on the USSR*, 27 September 1991, vol. 3, No. 39, p. 27.
14. Ibid.
15. M. Beschloss and S. Talbott, *At the Highest Levels*, London, Little, Brown & Company, 1993, p. 443.
16. *RFE/RL Research Institute. Report on the USSR*, 6 September 1991, vol. 3, No. 36, p. 85.

17. J. Crawford, *The Creation of States in International Law*, Oxford, Clarendon Press, 1979, p. 262.

18. On 11 February, the Parliament of Iceland, Althing, passed a resolution recognizing Lithuania as an independent state and instructed the government to establish diplomatic ties as soon as possible (*RFE/RL Research Institute. Report on the USSR*, 22 February 1991, vol. 3, No. 8, p. 28). Diplomatic ties were established only after the August coup. As the recognition and establishment of diplomatic relations takes time (just how much depends on the competence of executive powers), it is difficult to tell whether Iceland really recognized Lithuania in February 1991 or not.

19. H. Lauterpacht, *Recognition in International Law*, Cambridge, Cambridge University Press, 1948, p. 430.

20. K. Marek, *Identity and Continuity of States in Public International Law*, Geneva, Droz, 1968, p. 562.

21. *RFE/RL Research Report*, 17 January 1992, vol. 1, No. 3.

22. Ibid., p. 66.

23. *Oppenheim's International Law*, op. cit, p. 133.

24. Q. Wright, 'Some Thoughts about Recognition', 44 *AJIL* 548 (1950).

25. Lauterpacht, op. cit., p. 67.

26. See ibid., p. 69.

27. Ibid.

28. Tanner, 'Slovenia and Croatia Secede', *The Independent*, 26 June 1991, p. 1.

29. J. Zametika, 'The Yugoslav Conflict', *ADELPHI Paper* 270, London, 1992, p. 36.

30. 4 *EJIL* 74 (1993).

31. For instance, on 4 October 1991, Minister van den Broek, on behalf of the EPC, read a statement in which the participants of the meeting in the Hague, attended also by the Presidents of Croatia and Serbia and the Federal Secretary for National Defence, agreed that recognition would be granted in the framework of the general settlement and would include *inter alia* 'a loose association or alliance of sovereign or independent republics' (M. Weller, 'The International Response to the Dissolution of the Socialist Federal Republic of Yugoslavia', 86 *AJIL* 581 (1992)). On 25 October Lord Carrington presented his arrangement for the general settlement which also included a point on 'a free association of the republics with an international personality' (ibid., p. 582). The President of Serbia did not accept these proposals (ibid.).

32. In its 'platform' adopted on 14 October 1991 the Assembly of BiH declared that the Socialist Republic of Bosnia-Herzegovina was prepared to become a member of a new Yugoslav Community if the new Community included at least Serbia and Croatia. ('Opinion No. 4 of the Arbitration Commission of the International Conference on Yugoslavia', 4 *EJIL* 75 (1993)). Misha Glenny writes that 'the Bosnian President Alija Izetbegovic – a Moslim, tried exceptionally hard to counter the bold secessionism of Tudman on the one hand and the merciless unitarism of Milosevic on the other' (M. Glenny, *The Fall of Yugoslavia*, London, Penguin Books, 1992, p. 144).

33. Glenny, op. cit., pp. 121, 123.

34. See, for example, J. Zametika, op. cit., p. 21.

35. See N. Stone, 'The Eagle's Curse', *The Sunday Times*, 9 August 1992.

36. Glenny, op. cit., p. 32.
37. See Beschloss and Talbott, op. cit. p. 199.
38. Lauterpacht, op. cit., p. 26.
39. Marek, op. cit., p. 162.
40. Lauterpacht, op. cit., p. 26.
41. Lauterpacht, op. cit., p. 28.
42. In 1949 when, because of the Soviet veto in the UN Security Council, South Korea was denied admission to the UN, Canada informed the Republic of Korea that its vote cast in the Security Council in favour of Korea's admission to the UN was 'to be regarded as full recognition by the Government of Canada of the Republic of Korea as an independent sovereign state' (J. Dugard, *Recognition and the United Nations*, Cambridge, Grotius Publications Limited, 1987, p. 59). The ambassador of Guinea Bissau to the USSR, during our talks in Moscow in September 1991 on bilateral Estonian-Guinean issues, stated that the Republic of Guinea-Bissau had recognized Estonia by voting in the UN General Assembly for its admission to the UN. Sweden considered that having participated in the unanimous decision of the UN General Assembly to accept Bosnia-Herzegovina as a member of the UN, 'this according to Swedish practice means that Sweden has recognized the Republic of Bosnia and Herzegovina' (quoting from R. Rich, 'Recognition of States: The Collapse of Yugoslavia and the Soviet Union', 4 *EJIL* 36, 64 (1993)).
43. R. Rich writes that there has been 'widespread recognition of a state which has no control over one third of its territory [Croatia]' (op. cit., p. 56).
44. Opinion No. 5 of the Arbitration Commission of the International Conference on Yugoslavia, 4 *EJIL* 76 (1993).
45. *The Constitution of the Republic of Croatia* (prepared by Dr Ljubomir Valkovic), Zagreb, 1991, p. 31.
46. Ibid.
47. *UN Doc.* CCPR/C/79/Add.15, p. 3.
48. M. Weller writes that 'only Germany appeared to argue that speedy recognition would result in "internationalizing" the crisis and thus entitle an EC force to enter individual former Yugoslav republics without the consent of the former central authorities' (Weller, op. cit., p. 575).
49. *Security Council Resolution* 713 (1991), 25 September 1991.
50. Glenny, op. cit., p. 92.
51. Ibid., pp. 150-1.
52. Opinion No. 4 of the Arbitration Commission of the International Conference on Yugoslavia, 4 *EJIL* 74 (1993).
53. Ibid.
54. Weller, op. cit., p. 593.
55. *RFE/RL Research Report*, 24 January 1992, vol. 1, No. 4.
56. *The Independent*, 30 December 1992.
57. 'Opinion No. 6 of the Arbitration Commission of the International Conference on Yugoslavia', 4 *EJIL* 77, 80 (1993).
58. See, for example, F. Capotorti, *Study on the Rights of Persons belonging to Ethnic, Religious and Linguistic Minorities*, New York, United Nations, 1991, pp. 2-3.
59. See Dugard, op. cit., p. 25.
60. See Weller, op. cit., pp. 586-7.

61. See, for example, V. Gowland-Debbas, *Collective Responses to Illegal Acts in International Law: United Nations Actions in the Question of Southern Rhodesia*, Dordrecht, Martinus Nijhoff, 1990.
62. It is interesting to note that not only Turkey but also Tartarstan, probably itself seeking some kind of international recognition, has recognized the Turkish Republic of Northern Cyprus (see *Nezavisimaya Gazeta*, 18 November 1992).
63. See Dugard, op. cit., pp. 100–108.
64. *RFE/RL Research Report*, 10 January 1992, vol. 1, No. 2, p. 70.
65. *RFE/RL Research Report*, 17 April 1992, vol. 1, No. 16, p. 72.

5 ISSUES OF CONTINUITY AND THE SUCCESSION OF STATES

1. Vienna Convention on Succession of States in Respect of Treaties, 23 August 1978, *UN Doc.* A/Conf. 80/31, reprinted at 72 *AJIL* 971 (1978); Vienna Convention on Succession of States in Respect of State Property, Archives and Debts, 8 April 1983, *UN Doc.* A/Conf. 117/14, reprinted at 22 *ILM* 306 (1987).
2. Sir Francis Vallat, 'First Report on Succession of States in Respect of Treaties, [1974] 2 *YBILC* 22; *UN Doc* A/CN.4/278.Add.1–6.
3. Vienna Convention on Succession of States in Respect of Treaties, op. cit., article 2(1)(b).
4. D. P. O'Connell, *The Law of State Succession*, Cambridge, Cambridge University Press, 1956, p. 7.
5. Ibid., p. 8.
6. New states are defined here as states which emerge as the result of a merger of two or more states, a dissolution of existing states or secession.
7. A special case not addressed here is that of devolution treaties concluded between a predecessor state and a successor state.
8. J. Crawford, *The Creation of States in International Law*, Oxford, Clarendon Press, 1979, p. 400.
9. Ibid., p. 406.
10. A. Kozyrev, 'Russia: A Chance for Survival', 71(2) *Foreign Affairs* 11 (1992).
11. Agreement Establishing the Commonwealth of Independent States, 31 *ILM* 138 (1992) (*ILM* Background/Content Summary, quoting a letter from the President of the Russian Federation to the Secretary-General of the United Nations).
12. Decision by the Council of Heads of State of the Commonwealth of Independent States, 21 December 1991, 31 *ILM* 151 (1991).
13. *UN Press Release* PM/473, 12 August 1947; *UN Doc.* A/CN./149 reprinted at 11 *YBILC* 101 (1962).
14. Ibid.
15. Crawford, op. cit., p. 404.
16. These materials have not yet been published, and I therefore use copies from my personal archive.
17. Treaty on Succession to the USSR's State Debt and Assets, 4 December 1991 (on file with the author).

18. Agreement between Heads of States of the Commonwealth of Independent States on Property of the Former USSR Abroad, 30 December 1991 (on file with the author).
19. Decision of the Council of Heads of States of the Commonwealth of Independent States, 20 March 1992 (on file with the author).
20. Protocol Concerning the Work of the Commission on State Succession Concerning Treaties, State Property, State Archives, Debts and Assets of the Former USSR, 15 May 1992 (on file with the author).
21. Decision on the Activities of the Commission on Consideration of Issues Related to State Succession concerning Treaties, State Property, Archives, Debts and Assets of the Former USSR, 9 October 1992 (on file with the author).
22. Memorandum on Mutual Understanding on Issues of Succession to Treaties of the Former USSR having Mutual Interest, 6 July 1992 (on file with the author).
23. Decision on the Establishment of the Commission for the Preparation of an Agreement on Division of Non-Military Maritime Vessels of the Former USSR, 16 June 1992 (on file with the author).
24. Decision on the Work of the Commission on the Division of Non-Military Maritime Vessels of the Former USSR, 9 October 1992 (on file with the author).
25. Treaty on Succession to the USSR's State Debt and Assets, 4 December 1991, op. cit., article IV.
26. Ibid.
27. Agreement on Division of All Property of the Former USSR Abroad, 6 July 1992 (on file with the author).
28. John Lloyd, 'Ukraine Renounces Debt Deal', *The Financial Times*, 6 January 1993.
29. *Nezavisimaya Gazeta*, 26 June 1993.
30. Treaty on Fundamentals of Interstate Relations Between Estonia and Russia, 12 January 1991, *Rahva Haal*, 15 January 1991.
31. 'Zayavlenie Prezidiuma Verkhovnogo Sovieta RSFSR v svyazi s situatsiej, slozhivshejsya v respublikakh Pribaltiki' [Declaration of the Presidium of the Supreme Soviet of the RSFSR in connection with the situation that has developed in the Baltic republics] 2 *Vedomosti RSFSR*, 1991, item 11.
32. Ibid., p. 28.
33. Ibid., p. 29.
34. *Riigi Teataja* [*The State Herald*], 1991, No. 25, item 312.
35. C. N. Alexandrowicz, 'New and Original States: The Issue of Reversion to Sovereignty', 45 *International Affairs* 474 (1969).
36. Crawford, op. cit., p. 407.
37. K. Marek, *Identity and Continuity of States in Public International Law*, Geneva, Droz, 1968, pp. 581–2.
38. There was no exchange of notes between the United Kingdom and Estonia concerning visa-free travelling between the two countries. They simply resumed the regime which had not applied for more than 50 years.
39. Exchange of Notes between the Ambassador of the Republic of Finland to Estonia and the Deputy Foreign Minister of Estonia, 5 February 1992 (on file with the author).
40. Exchange of Notes between the Ambassador of the Republic of Finland to

Estonia and the Deputy Foreign Minister of Estonia, 16 January 1992 (on file with the author).

41. Marek, op. cit., p. 583.
42. *Riigi Teataja*, 1992, pp. 7, 109.
43. Ibid.
44. On 23 March 1993 the State Assembly changed the clause in the 1938 Citizenship Law which discriminated against women and provided that any child whose father or mother were Estonian citizens are Estonian citizens by birth (*Riigi Teataja*, 1993, 17, 272).
45. *Riigi Teataja*, 1992, 26, 349.
46. This approach led to the deprivation of the political rights of almost 40 per cent of the population of the Republic, many of whom were born in Estonia or had lived there for decades. It seems to me that such a division of the permanent residents of Estonia into two categories (those who were citizens of the Estonian Republic of 1940 and their direct descendants on their fathers' side, on the one hand, and those who were not, on the other hand) is not based on objective and reasonable criteria and therefore constitutes discrimination. It clearly is in contradiction with the Estonian–Russian Treaty of 12 January 1991, which in article 3 provides that all citizens of the former Soviet Union who are permanent residents of Estonia or Russia respectively shall have the right to choose freely the citizenship of the country of their residence. (See, for example, *RFE/RL Research Institute. Report on the USSR*, 1 February 1991, vol. 3, No. 5, p. 15.)
47. *Estonian Constitution*, article 122.
48. Estonia–Russia, Treaty of Peace, 2 February 1920, 11 LNTS 30.
49. Vienna Convention on Succession of States in Respect of Treaties, 23 August 1978, op. cit., article 11.
50. Frontier Dispute (*Burkina Faso* v. *Republic of Mali*) 1986 *ICJ Reports* 565 (22 Dec.).
51. Opinion No. 3 of the Arbitration Commission of the International Conference on Yugoslavia, 3 *EJIL* 184 (1992).
52. Ibid.
53. Russia, for example, has voiced claims to the Crimean peninsula belonging to the Ukraine, which is one of the causes of tension in the relations between these countries.
54. Vienna Convention on Succession of States in Respect of Treaties, 23 August 1978, op. cit., article 34(1).
55. Ibid., article 17(1).
56. M. Nash (Leich), 'Contemporary Practice of the United States Relating to International Law: Arms Control and Disarmament', 86 *AJIL* 799–801 (1992).
57. 729 *UNTS* 161.
58. 23 *UST* 3425; *TIAS* 7503.
59. Vienna Convention on Succession of States in Respect of Treaties, 23 August 1978, op. cit., article 34(2).
60. S. Oeter, 'German Unification and State Succession', 51 *Zeitschrift fur auslandisches offentliches Recht und Volkerrecht* 359 (1991).
61. 4 *EJIL* 72 (1993).
62. For example, *Ivacevic* v. *Artucovic*, 211 F. 2d 565 (9th Cir. 1954), holding that an extradition treaty between the US and the Kingdom of Serbia had

survived the establishment of the Federal Republic of Yugoslavia; *R.v. Commission of Correctional Service (Ex parte Fitz Henry)*, 72 *ILR* 63.
63. *Restatement of the Law. The Foreign Relations Law of the United States*, 14 May 1986, The American Law Institute, vol. 1, 1087, pp. 110, 113.
64. See J. Malenovsky, 'La succession au Conceil de l'Europe'. A paper presented in the conference 'Dissolution, continuation et succession en Europe de l'Est', 7–8 Octobre 1993, Paris, CEDIN.
65. Ibid.
66. Ibid.
67. Ibid.
68. Telegram from the Chief of the Treaty Section of the UN Secretariat in New York to the UN Headquarters in Geneva, 10 July 1992.
69. As above, 19 October 1992.
70. As above, 13 August 1992.
71. See, for example, O. Udokang, *Succession of New States to International Treaties*, New York, Oceana Publishing Incorporated, 1972, p. 200.
72. Ibid.
73. Advisory Opinion No. 6, Settlers of German origin in the territory ceded by Germany to Poland, 1923 *PCIJ (ser. B)* No. 6, p. 36.
74. O'Connell, op. cit., p. 81.
75. 4 *EJIL* 72 (1993).
76. Opinion No. 7 of the Arbitration Commission of the International Conference on Yugoslavia, 4 *EJIL* 83–4 (1993).
77. O. Schachter, 'State Succession: The Once and Future Law', *Virginia Journal of International Law*, 1993, vol. 33, p. 258.
78. Conférénce International sur l'Ex-Yugoslavia. Commission d'Arbitrage. Avis No 13, Paris 16 July 1993.

6 HUMAN RIGHTS AND DEMOCRACY IN POST-TOTALITARIAN SOCIETIES

1. M. Gorbachev, *Perestroika i Novoye Myshlenie dlja Nashei Strany i dlja vsego Mira* [*Perestroika and New Thinking for our Country and for the Whole World*], Moscow, Politizdat, 1987, p. 149.
2. Of course, there was use of force in clear violation of international human rights standards in Tbilisi (1989), Baku (1990) and Vilnius (1991), and Gorbachev bears his share of responsibility for that. But as a whole Gorbachev's policy of a gradual introduction of reforms and balancing between different political forces, which may have been seen as demonstrating a lack of decisiveness (and to a certain extent clearly was) prepared Soviet society for the support of democratic reforms, helped to change the balance of political forces in Soviet society, awakened the population from social hibernation and was necessary for the rejection of the coup in August 1991.
3. *Vedomosti Siezda Narodnih Deputatov SSSR i Verhovnogo Sovieta SSSR*, 27 June 1990, No. 26; 10 October 1990, No. 41; 17 October 1990, No. 42; 12 June 1991, No. 24.
4. *Vedomosti Siezda Narodnih Deputatov SSSR i Verhovnogo Sovieta SSSR*, 17 July 1991, No. 29.

5. *Pravda*, 11 April 1989, p. 1; *Vedomosti Verhovnogo Sovieta RSFSR*, 1989, No. 37.
6. K. Marx, F. Engels, *Sobraniye Sochinenij [Selected Works]*, Moscow, Politizdat, vol. 3, p. 33.
7. V. Lenin, *Polnoye Sobraniye Sochinenij [Complete Works]*, Moscow, Politizdat, vol. 41, pp. 47–8.
8. *Novy Mir*, 1988, No. 10, p. 207.
9. N. I. Berdyayev, 'Istoki i Smysl Russkogo Kommunisma' [The Sources and Meaning of Russian Communism], *Yunost*, 1989, No. 11, p. 87.
10. *Krasny Terror*, 1 November 1918.
11. D. Feldman, 'Krestyanskaya Voyna' [Peasants' War], *Rodina*, 1989, No. 10, p. 57.
12. *Pravda*, 3 October 1988.
13. M. Djilas, *The New Class. An Analysis of the Communist System*, New York, Praeger, 1965, p. 2.
14. B. A. Kistyakovsky, 'Gosudarstvo Pravovoye i Sotsalisticheskoye' [The Rule of Law State and The Socialist State], *Voprosy Filosofii*, 1990, No. 6, p. 156.
15. Ibid., p. 146.
16. Bhikhu Parekh, 'The Cultural Particularity of Liberal Democracy', in D. Held (ed.), *Prospects for Democracy*, Cambridge, Polity Press, 1993, p. 157.
17. F. A. Hayek, *The Road to Serfdom*, London, George Routledge & Sons Limited, 1944, p. 44.
18. R. Howard, 'Cultural Absolutism and Nostalgia for Community', *Human Rights Quarterly*, 1993, vol. 15, p. 333.
19. See D. Zoo, 'Democratic Citizenship in a Post-Communist Era', in Held (ed.), op. cit., p. 264; J. M. Barbalet, *Citizenship*, Milton Keynes, Open University Press, 1988, pp. 59–79.
20. *Rossiiskie Vesti*, 1993, No. 83 (252).
21. S. Alekseyev, *Law and Legal Culture in Soviet Society*, Moscow, Progress Publishers, 1991, pp. 142–3.
22. S. Alekseyev, 'Ostrye Grani Svobody' [Sharp Edges of Freedom], *Rossiiski Vestnik*, 2 June 1993, p. 2.
23. 6 ILM 360 (1967).
24. See Chapter 4 of this book.
25. *Vedomosti Siezda Narodnih Deputatov Rossiiskoi Federatsii i Verhovnogo Sovieta Rossiiskoi Federatsii*, 13 February 1992, No. 7.
26. *RFE/RL Research Report*, 14 May 1993, vol. 2, No. 20, p. 86.
27. Ibid.
28. *The Times*, 24 September, 1993, p. 15.
29. *Vedomosti Siezda Narodnih Deputatov Rossiiskoi Federatsii i Verhovnogo Sovieta Rossiiskoi Federatsii*, 20 August 1992, No. 33.
30. *Vedomosti Siezda Narodnih Deputatov i Verhovnogo Sovieta Rossiiskoi Federatsii*, 6 February 1992, No. 6.
31. *RFE/RL Research Report*, 23 July 1993, vol. 2, No. 26, p. 1.
32. W. Laqueur, 'Russian Nationalism', 71(5) *Foreign Affairs* 114.
33. See *Sovietskaya Rossiya*, 25 February 1993; *Moskovskiye Novosti*, 1993, No. 17, p. 4A; *Nezavisimaya Gazeta*, 26 February 1993.
34. *Vedomosti Siezda Narodnih Deputatov i Verhovnogo Sovieta Rossiiskoi Federatsii*, 6 February 1991, No. 6.

35. *Report on the Tartarstan Referendum on Sovereignty, 21 March 1992.* Prepared by the Staff of the US Commission on Security and Cooperation in Europe, 14 April 1992, p. 1.
36. *Vedomosti Siezda Narodnih Deputatov i Verhovnogo Sovieta Rossiiskoi Federatsii*, 26 March 1992, No. 13.
37. B. Kistjakovskii, 'V Zastsitu Prav: Intelligentsiya i Pravovoe Soznanie' [In Defence of Rights: Intelligentsia and Legal Consciousness], *Vekhi*, 1909, reprinted Moscow, 1991, pp. 126–7.
38. *Vedomosti Siesda Narodnih Deputatov i Verhovnogo Sovieta Rossiiskoi Federatsii*, 30 July 1992, No. 30.
39. A. Larin, 'Procuror Protiv Suda Prisjazhnyh' [The Procurator is Against Trial by Jury], *Izvestija*, 12 May 1993, p. 5.
40. See, for example, *The Times*, 20 October 1993, p. 12.
41. *Vedomosti Siezda Narodnih Deputatov SSSR i Verhovnogo Sovieta SSSR*, 21 November 1990, No. 47.
42. On 21 December 1993, after the manuscript for this book had been submitted to the publisher, Yeltsin abolished the Security Ministry as 'incapable of being reformed'. But, as the former minister stayed at the head of the new structures, there are still doubts as to whether the old KGB is really gone.
43. *Vedomosti Verhivnogo Sovieta Ukraini*, 1991, No. 50.
44. *Zvjazda*, 2 November 1991.
45. *RFE/RL Research Report*, 30 July 1993, vol. 2, No. 27, p. 5.
46. Ibid.
47. *UN Doc.* CCPR/C/2/Rev.3, pp. 3, 96.
48. 'Eesti Vabariigi Pohiseadus' [The Basic Law of the Republic of Estonia], *Riigi Teataja [The State Herald]*, 1992, No. 26, item 349.
49. Letters of the CSCE High Commissioner on National Minorities to the Estonian and Latvian Foreign Ministers of 6 April 1993. Reference Nos 206/93/L/Rev. and 238/93/L/Rev.
50. *Riigi Teataja*, 1993, No. 29, item 505.
51. *The Guardian*, 7 July 1993, p. 8.
52. Ibid.
53. EPC Press Release, P.66/93, Brussels, 9 July 1993.
54. A. Lieven, *The Baltic Revolution*, New Haven and London, Yale University Press, 1993, p. 380.
55. EPC Press Release, op. cit.
56. See, for example, Amnesty International. *Concerns in Europe*, London, May–October 1992.
57. Ibid., p. 95.
58. Ibid., p. 85.
59. *Megapolis-Express*, 1992, No. 48, p. 21.
60. *RFE/RL Daily Report*, 19 May 1993, No. 95, p. 3.
61. R. Dahl reserves the term 'democracy' for a political system, one characteristic of which is the quality of being completely responsive to all its citizens. Closest to such an ideal are polyarchies. (R. Dahl, *Polyarchy. Participation and Opposition*, New Haven and London, Yale University Press, 1971, pp. 2, 8).
62. Ibid., p. 208.
63. Ibid., p. 34.

64. P. Lewis, 'Democracy and its Future in Eastern Europe', in Held (ed.), op. cit., p. 300.
65. K. Mahbubani, 'The West and the Rest', 28 *The National Interest* 8 (1992).
66. Ibid.
67. The Dutch *PIOOM Reports* (Projects for the International Study of Root Causes of Human Rights Violations) include a table measuring violations of the integrity of the individual in different Asian countries. In this table India, 'the biggest democracy in the world' has a poorer human rights rating than, for example, China (D. Potter, 'Democratization in Asia', in Held (ed.), op. cit., p. 368).
68. K. Cooke, 'Asians Challenge West on Human Rights', *The Financial Times*, 11 June 1993.
98. Ibid.
70. R. Howard, op. cit., p. 337.
71. R. Howard, Evaluating Human Rights in Africa: Some Problems of Implicit Comparisons, *Human Rights Quarterly*, 1984, vol. 6, p.175.
72. *UN Press Release* HR/3215, 30 October 1992 (afternoon), p. 5.
73. See ibid.
74. Not all human rights are, in my view, universal. There are certainly rights which are national or regional. The fundamental, or basic, human rights are universal or, though it may sound like a tautology, we may say that all universal human rights are universal.
75. *UN Doc*. A/Conf. 157/23, para. 5.
76. *UN Press Release* HR/3215, 30 October 1992 (afternoon), p. 1.
77. 'The Real World of Human Rights', Statement by Foreign Minister Wong Kan Seng of Singapore at the World Conference on Human Rights, Vienna, 16 June 1993, p. 2.
78. Ibid., p. 4.
79. A. Pollis, Eastern Orthodoxy and Human Rights, *Human Rights Quarterly*, 1993, vol. 15, pp. 344, 353.
80. R. Howard, op.cit., p. 335.
81. Ibid.
82. *Longman Illustrated Encyclopedia of World History*, London, Ivy Leaf, 1991, p. 463.
83. Ibid., p. 410.
84. A new offence of 'dowry death' was included in the Indian Penal Code and there is the Commission of Sati (Prevention) Act of 1987 (*Second Periodic Report of India to the UN Human Rights Committee*, 12 July 1989, *UN Doc*. CCPR/C/137/Add.13, paras 117, 119).
85. *UN Doc*. A/Conf.157/23, 12 July 1993, para. 5.
86. Bangkok NGO Decloration on Human Rights, 27 March 1993.
87. Ibid., p.1.

Index